Emerson Bennett

Forest and prairie: Life on the frontier

Emerson Bennett

Forest and prairie: Life on the frontier

ISBN/EAN: 9783337143121

Printed in Europe, USA, Canada, Australia, Japan

Cover: Foto ©Andreas Hilbeck / pixelio.de

More available books at **www.hansebooks.com**

"Good night, my fair Rose, and happy dreams to you." See page 373.

LIFE ON THE FRONTIER.

BY

EMERSON BENNETT,

AUTHOR OF "THE PRAIRIE FLOWER," "THE BANDITS OF THE OSAGE,"
"MYSTERIOUS MARKSMAN," "THE TRAITOR," ETC., ETC.

PHILADELPHIA:
THE KEYSTONE PUBLISHING CO.
1890.

COPYRIGHT
BY THE KEYSTONE PUBLISHING CO.

TO

WILLIAM W. HARDING, ESQ.,

OF THE

𝔓ennsylvania 𝔍nquirer,

PHILADELPHIA,

AS A TOKEN OF FRIENDSHIP AND ESTEEM,

THIS WORK

IS INSCRIBED,

BY THE AUTHOR

CONTENTS.

	PAGE
THE MINGO CHIEF．．．．．	15
THE KENTUCKY HERO．．．．．	27
THE MAID OF FORT HENRY．．．．．	39
WRECKED ON THE LAKE．．．．．	56
A LEAP FOR LIFE．．．．．	80
A DESPERATE ENCOUNTER．．．．．	69
LOVE TRIUMPHANT．．．．．	90
MAD ANN．．．．．	103
THE DARING SCOUTS．．．．．	115
THE GAMBLERS OUTWITTED．．．．．	125
A FIGHT ON THE PRAIRIE．．．．．	135
AN ARKANSAS DUEL．．．．．	146
THE POISONED BRIDE．．．．．	158
ATTACKED BY INDIANS．．．．．	169
THE TRAPPER'S STORY．．．．．	180
A MIRACULOUS ESCAPE．．．．．	189
A MOTHER'S COURAGE．．．．．	201
A DARING EXPLOIT．．．．．	215
ROCKY MOUNTAIN PERILS．．．．．	232
THE DEAD ALIVE．．．．．	245
FIGHT WITH A BEAR．．．．．	259

CONTENTS.

	PAGE
THE HAUNTED HOUSE	269
BILL LUKEN'S RUN	285
THE FAITHFUL NEGRO	298
THE GUERRILLA QUEEN	310
THE LAST STAKE	320
ADVENTURE OF A COLPORTEUR	333
A NIGHT WITH THE WOLVES	344
COLONEL BOWIE OF ARKANSAS	355
THE BACKWOODSMAN'S FIRST LOVE	372
A WOLF IN SHEEP'S CLOTHING	387
ON THE SCOUT	400

The Mingo Chief.

We talk of the ferocity, the vindictiveness, the treachery and the cruelty of the native savage; and, painting him in the darkest colors, tell how, when his hunting grounds covered the sites of our now proudest cities, he was wont to steal down upon a few harmless whites, our forefathers, and butcher them in cold blood, sparing neither sex nor age, except for a painful captivity, to end perhaps in the most demoniac tortures; and we dwell upon the theme, till our little innocent children shudder and creep close to our sides, and look fearfully around them, and perhaps wonder how the good God, of whom they have also heard us speak, could ever have permitted such human monsters to encumber His fair and beautiful earth. But do we reverse the medal and show the picture which impartial Truth has stamped upon the other side—and which, in a great measure, stands as a *cause* to the opposite *effect*—stands as a cause for savage ferocity, vindictiveness, treachery and cruelty? Do we tell our young and eager listeners that the poor Indian, living up to the light he had, and not unfrequently beyond it, knew no better than to turn, like the worm when trampled upon, and bite the foot that crushed him? That we had taken the land of his father's graves and driven him from his birthright hunting grounds? That we had stolen his cattle, robbed him of his food, destroyed his growing fields, burned his wigwams, and murdered his brothers, fathers, wives and little ones, besides instigating tribe to war against tribe—and that, knowing nothing of the Christian code, to return good for evil, he fulfilled the law of his nature and education in taking his "great revenge" upon any of the pale-faced race he should chance to meet? No! we seldom show this side of the medal—for the natural inquiry of the innocent listener might contain an unpleasant rebuke:

"Father, were we all savages together then?"

But I have a story to tell. Listen!

More than eighty years ago, when the great West was a howling wilderness, and mighty, unbroken forests stretched away for hundreds of miles, and covered the broad, fertile lands of Western Virginia, Pennsylvania, Ohio and Kentucky, and so onward to the vast prairies beyond the Father of Rivers, the unrivalled Mississippi—forests that threw twilight over the gliding, purling, or rushing streams, and gave wild freedom to the bear, the buffalo, the panther, catamount, and deer—more than eighty years ago, I say, on a fine, pleasant spring day, a party of border hunters were encamped upon the left bank of the Ohio, above the present site of Wheeling, which then boasted only a single trading fort, and was considered the extreme frontier.

This party numbered more than a dozen strong, hardy bronze-visaged men, dressed in true border fashion, with green hunting frocks, caps, buckskin trowsers, leggings and moccasins, and they were armed with rifles, tomahawks, and knives. They had built themselves a temporary cabin, and had fished and hunted in the vicinity for several days; and furs, and game, and articles of traffic were strewn carelessly about their cabin, which had been erected rather for the purpose of protecting their goods and weapons from the weather than for sheltering themselves, for your true borderer likes to sleep in the open air. The party was about to break up camp and return to the eastward; and some were packing their furs and skins, and some were cleaning their rifles, and some were mending their torn garments, and some were lounging idly about, smoking and drinking, and stretching their huge limbs, and wishing for some keen excitement to rouse their sluggish natures.

The leader of this party—a man of fair proportions, but with low brow, bushy hair, a snaky eye, and a red, rough, ferocious-looking countenance—was standing apart from the others, leaning upon his rifle, thinking wicked thoughts and planning wicked deeds. Suddenly he wheeled about, and drawing near his men, said, in a hard, harsh voice:

"Boy's, this here's a —— bad business, going back without nary scalp. What'll the people think of us? I tel you, boys, we must raise some red-nigger top-knots, or our reputation 'll spile, by ——!"

"Thar's Injuns 'tother side the river," replied a big, double-fisted, coarse-featured fellow, who was smoking his pipe, with his back braced against a huge sycamore; "'spose you jest go over, Cap, and take what you want!"

"It moughten't be so easy gitting back," replied the first speaker; "and I hain't no incline to take a scalp at the risk of mine. If we could only get a few of the —— heathen over here!"

"Why, so you can, Cap, if you'll only keep quiet, for there comes a few now," answered the other, taking his corn-cob pipe from his mouth, and pointing with the stem across the river to a canoe filled with Indians.

"By —— ! Sam!" cried the first speaker, using an oath that we will not repeat, "I hope they'll come across. If they do, we'll have fun. I'll go down and beckon 'em over."

And hastening down to the water's edge, the leader of the whites made friendly signs to the Indians in the canoe, inviting them to cross the river to his camp.

And the Indians came across, without apparent fear or hesitation—five men, and one woman with an infant in her arms. Two of the men, one quite advanced in years, were fine, athletic, noble looking specimens of humanity; and the woman, the daughter of one and the sister of the other, was more than usually comely, and had a soft, dark eye, a mild, pleasant-looking countenance, and a sweet, musical voice. All landed and shook hands with the leader of the whites, who seemed greatly pleased to meet with them, and invited them up to his cabin to take a drink. Three of the Indians readily accepted the invitation; but the three we have mentioned declined—the venerable head of the party observing, with a smile:

"Rum no good for Injun—make drunk come. Me buy tobac—tobac good for smoke."

And while three of the party entered the cabin and drank the liquor proffered them, the other three, including the woman with the infant, remained outside, and opened a trade with the leader of the whites, for tobacco and powder, paying for the same in the current coin of the frontier, pelts and furs, of which they had on hand a goodly stock.

An hour passed away in friendly barter, and then the old man signified his intention of recrossing the river. He stepped into the cabin, and found three of his party ying on the ground, and so much intoxicated as not to be conscious of any thing going on around them.

"Ah! me said rum bad for poor Injun!" observed the old warrior; "him take Injun sense, and make him worse as beast."

He called his son to him, said something in his native tongue, and the two were about to begin to remove their helpless comrades, when the leader of the whites, who had been holding a short consultation with his men, came in and said:

"Afore you go, my boys, I want to see you shoot at a mark. I hear you're some at a shot."

"Me hit dollar," returned the old man, with gratified vanity.

"Come on—we've put up the mark—and if you hit it, I'll give you a pound of tobacco; and if you don't, you're to give me a deer skin."

The old warrior and his son went out and looked at the mark, and the former said:

"Me bet."

"And will you try, too?" said the leader of the whites to the son of the Indian sage.

"Me bet," was the quiet answer.

"Fire away, then—you shoot first."

The son said something to his father, the old warrior

nodded, and the young man, drawing himself up and taking deliberate aim, fired.

"Hit, by ——!" said the white leader, as the white mark, the size of a dollar, showed a hole near its centre. "A —— good shot! Come, old man, let's see what you can do!"

"Me beat him," said the father, with a smile.

He raised his rifle slowly, brought it to a level, fired, and drove the pin through the centre.

"Now, boys," said the white ruffian, "all right, give 'em h—ll!"

And at the word he raised his own rifle and shot the old man through the brain, who fell back dead; and the next instant his son fell upon him, a ghastly corpse, pierced by four bullets from as many rifles in the hands of the whites. The poor woman with the infant in her arms, who was standing apart from the crowd, looking quietly on, uttered a shriek of horror on seeing her father and brother thus inhumanly butchered, and, clasping her offspring to her bosom, ran swiftly toward the river. But crack went some half a dozen rifles, and she fell to the earth, mortally wounded, but not dead. The first who reached her was the leader of the whites, who, grasping her infant roughly, raised his tomahawk to give the poor innocent mother the finishing blow.

"Spare child!" shrieked the dying mother, with a look of affectionate, pleading anguish, that would have melted the heart of a stone. "Child got white fader—child one of you—spare poor child!"

She said no more, for the hatchet of the white fiend at that instant crashed through her brain and set her spirit free, to roam the hunting-grounds of her faith with the spirits of her father and brother.

"Give me the child, Dan," said the brother of the white leader, who reached his side just as he was about to dash out its brains. "I reckon I know its father, and we'll make it pay."

The bloody ruffian gave him the infant, accompanied with a savage oath; and whipping out his knife, he bent over the dead mother and tore off her scalp. The whole work of butchery was now complete; for while these events were taking place outside the cabin, another fiend within had chopped to pieces the drunken Indians, and now came swaggering forth, shaking three gory scalps in triumph.

"Now, boys," said the white leader, "we've got a good show, and let's make clean tracks afore some other red-niggers get arter our hair."

And hastily they stripped the dead of every thing of value, broke up their camp, and departed for the interior settlements taking the poor motherless infant with them

Meantime, the Indians on the other side of the river, being witnesses of the horrible massacre, hurried into their only remaining canoe, and rowed swiftly down the Ohio. On passing the fort at Wheeling they were espied, and chase was given by a party of whites. Far below they were overtaken, a short fight ensued, and another of their party was killed—the others making their escape through the deep dark forests

---

While the bloody events we have recorded were taking place on the Ohio, a Grand Council of chiefs and warriors was convened at the Indian town in the interior of what is now the State of Ohio. They were deliberating upon the propriety of digging up the hatchet and going to war against the whites, who were fast encroaching upon their homes and hunting-grounds, and, judging from precedents, would soon require them to leave again for the still Far West. Most of the chiefs were for war; but there was one brave and eloquent man among them, who spoke for peace, and spoke with such reason, power and pathos, that he carried his point over strong opposition, and the pipe of peace was smoked in the Council House of the assembled nations.

This brave and eloquent chief had ever raised his voice for peace between the white man and the red, because, as he said, the same Great Spirit had made them all, and designed them to be brothers; and the earth was large enough, and rich enough, in forest, streams, and game, to give them all shelter, food, and happy homes.

His earnest eloquence conquered the fiery war spirit of his fierce comrades, and he was rejoicing in his peaceful triumph, when lo! a poor Indian, half dead with hunger and fatigue, appeared before him, and told him how his father, brother and sister had been brutally butchered by his pale-faced friends. Instantly the dark eye of this Chief of Peace gathered a storm of fire and shot forth lightning glances of anger, and his mighty voice, before the reassembled chiefs and warriors of many nations, was soon heard thundering:

"War! war! war!—war upon the pale-faces!—war upon the Long Knives—death to all of either sex and every age!"

And the cry of "War! war! war!—death to the pale-faces!—death to the Long Knives!" was echoed and re-echoed, with wild, savage shouts, by many hundreds of fiercely painted, half-naked, savage men.

And down upon the unprotected frontiers poured a fierce, dusky horde of human beings, whose rallying war-cry was,

"Revenge! Revenge!"

And old men and infants, and young men and maidens,

and men in the prime of life, and wives and mothers, were roused at the midnight hour by those yells of vengeance, and were butchered in their cabins, scalped on their hearthstones, and burned with their burning homes.

"I will have ten scalps for every kin of mine slain!" said that Chief of Blood, so lately a Chief of Peace.

And ere the war, so terribly and suddenly begun, was closed by a treaty of peace, thirty human scalps, thirty pale-fale scalps, hung dangling at his gory belt.

This war is known in history as LORD DUNMORE'S WAR.

That man of peace, roused to such bloody deeds by the aggressions of his white brothers, was the world-renowned LOGAN, THE MINGO CHIEF!

The leader of the party who butchered his relatives, was DANIEL GREATHOUSE.

The leader of the party who sallied from the fort at Wheeling, and followed and slew one of the flying fugitives, was CAPTAIN CRESAP.

Logan always supposed it was Cresap who murdered his relatives; and in his celebrated speech, sent to Lord Dunmore at the treaty of peace—for he proudly refused to appear in person—he mentions him as the cause of the war. We quote this speech, delivered at old Chillicothe town, and sent to Governor Dunmore at Camp Charlotte, as one of the finest specimens of eloquence extant.

"I appeal to any white man to say if ever he entered

Logan's cabin hungry and I gave him not meat—if ever he came cold or naked and I gave him not clothing!

"During the course of the last long and bloody war, Logan remained in his tent, an advocate for peace. Nay, such was my love for the whites, that those of my own country pointed at me as they passed, and said, 'Logan is the friend of white men.' I had even thought to live with you, but for the injuries of one man. Colonel Cresap, the last spring, in cool blood, and unprovoked, cut off all the relatives of Logan, not sparing even my women and children. There runs not a drop of my blood in the veins of any human creature. This called on me for revenge. I have sought it. I have killed many. I have fully glutted my vengeance. For my country, I rejoice at the beams of peace. Yet do not harbor the thought that mine is the joy of fear! Logan never felt fear. He will not turn on his heel to save his life. Who is there to mourn for Logan? Not one."

Reader, you who are now sitting in judgment upon the deeds of the past, I challenge you to say that the white man was always the Christian and the red man always the fiend!

A Kentucky Hero.

It was a wild, fearful scene—a scene of carnage and destruction. Loud shrieks of pain, and yells of rage, defiance, and triumph, commingled with reports of musketry, and here and there the clashing of steel, resounded on every hand.

A small, but gallant, band of Kentuckians, were completely surrounded by an overpowering horde of dusky savages, and were fighting desperately while falling victims to superior numbers—fighting for the hope of retreat, but with none of victory.

The scene was partly in an open glade, and partly in a surrounding forest, not far from the banks of the Ohio, in what is now the State of Indiana, but which was then an unapportioned and unsettled wilderness.

Over this open glade were hurrying hundreds of human beings—some mounted and some on foot—some white, and dressed in the rough costume of the borders—but more of the dusky hue, half naked and hideously painted—and all with passions excited to the fierce, ungovernable fury of fighting wild beasts.

Many a riderless horse went snorting and bounding away; while the ground was strewed with the dead and dying—the latter soon ceasing from the agonies of life, as the knife or tomahawk of either foe made his work sure. There were old men and youths, and men in the prime of manhood, all doing their duty bravely, and bearing down the foe in close encounter, or being themselves borne down to a bloody end.

Foremost among the Kentuckians, in the very hottest of the fight, more desperate even than the oldest veterans, rode a tall, fine-looking youth, who charged upon the foe without regard to numbers or peril—and fast they fell beneath the almost superhuman strength of his single arm. Several times his horse was seized by the bit, and borne back almost upon its haunches, while the uplifted tomahawk was aimed at the head of the rider; but with the quickness of thought, and the strength of a Hercules, the blows were parried right and left, and returned with a precision that laid his opposers bleeding beneath the feet of the fiery animal, which literally trampled them into the dust, as the undaunted youth still urged him on to new scenes of peril and victory.

"On, comrades!" he shouted—and his loud, shrill voice was heard above the din of battle. "On, for the honor of old Kentucky! Though surrounded by four times our number, we are not yet defeated; and will not be while there is an arm left to strike!"

Almost as he spoke, a shower of balls was poured in upon him, some cutting his clothes, some wounding him seriously, while his gallant steed sunk under him. Springing from the back of the falling beast, into the very midst of his dusky foes, this noble youth, wounded and bleeding though he was, still laid about him with desperation, the balls whistling around him fearfully and a dozen arms raised for his destruction.

Recklessly and desperately, however, alone and unaided, he continued to fight his way through his savage foes, back to the main body of his friends, where he arrived just as the order came for retreat.

As several, who were mounted, wheeled their horses to obey this welcome command, our hero dashed suddenly in among them, and, seizing the bits of two animals, one in either hand, he fairly brought them round, and so quickly as almost to throw their riders, at the same time shouting:

"For shame! for shame! who dares retreat—by any order—by any command—and leave our wounded comrades to the vengeance of our foes! Bear back, men—if you be men—and let us bring off our companions with honor, or perish with them!"

But his valiant call was unheeded by those who thought only of saving their own lives; and the moment the youth released his hold of their bridles, they dashed swiftly away.

"My curses go with you, for pusillanimous cowards!" he shouted after them; and then discovering another party on foot, as eagerly retreating also, he threw himself in before them, and exclaimed:

"Hold! I command you, by every feeling of honor, to turn back and save the lives of our wounded friends!"

"Out of my way, boy!" said a tall, strapping fellow, as he pushed eagerly forward to pass the youth: "you're not our captain! Haven't you heard the order for retreat? and don't you know, if you stand here a minute, you'll be butchered and scalped by the bloody varmints around, who've hemmed us in?"

"Yes! yes!" cried most of the rest; "Joe Hinkins says right!"

"We'll all be killed if we stop here!" said one.

"Turn back, Bill, and don't make a fool of yourself!" cried another.

"If we'd attempt to save the wounded, we'd purty soon want somebody to save us!" put in a third.

"There, boys—the red devils are a-coming like mad!" shouted a fourth.

With this they all set up cries of alarm, and plunged

into the nearest thicket, where they met the very doom they were seeking to avoid—for there a considerable body of Indians fell upon them, and, gaining an advantage through their surprise and terror, tomahawked and scalped them to a man.

With a cheek red with shame, our young hero now darted forward and intercepted still another party, who had likewise begun their flight—and this time his appeal was listened to. Turning back, they stopped a small mounted party; and getting them to dismount, they began to pick up the wounded wherever they could find them, and place them upon the horses—which, as fast as loaded, they dispatched with a small escort toward the Ohio, nearly half a mile distant—the youth still exerting himself to cheer all parties.

While thus engaged in their work of mercy, a body of Indians, about twice their number, came rushing down upon them; and another terrible encounter took place; during which the youth was struck by some four or five more balls—one shattering his left arm, three inflicting flesh-wounds upon different parts of his body, but none of them, fortunately, touching a vital part.

Finding the victory not so easy as they expected, several of their number having either been killed or wounded in this new encounter, the assailing Indians suddenly drew back from our dauntless little band, and set off in pursuit of those who, judging from the eagerness of their flight, would not be likely to make so desperate a stand.

"Three cheers for us, comrades!" cried the youth.

Three cheers were accordingly given, with hearty good will; and then they recommenced gathering up their wounded friends, there being now several of their own immediate party to be assisted likewise.

In his different encounters thus far, our young hero had broken every weapon—his rifle, knife, and tomahawk— and he now proceeded to re-arm himself. Having found and thrust two weapons into his belt, he picked up a rifle, and, holding it between his knees, his left arm hanging useless by his side, he coolly proceeded to load it with his right, all the while speaking encouragingly to those around him. By the time this was completed, his companions were ready to set out for the river; but just as they were about to depart, a voice from another quarter of the field cried out:

"Save me! save me! For the love of God, save me!"

"I know that voice," said the youth; "it is a brave fellow who calls on us; and we must save him at all hazards!"

"I fear it's more than we can do to save ourselves," returned one; "the cursed Indians are at work all around us; and if we escape as it is, it'll be a miracle.

"Save me!" called out the voice again; "in human-name, don't let the savages butcher and scalp me! If I've got to die, I want to die in Old Kentucky, among my friends."

This was an appeal hard to be resisted by brave men with feeling hearts; but it might have been resisted, nevertheless, and the poor fellow been left to his fate, had it not been for the gallant youth, who declared he would die on the field sooner than leave a companion in such a strait.

On reaching the spot where the poor fellow lay, they found him with one leg and one arm broken, and a serious wound in his breast. Lifting him up carefully, they hastily bore him to the only horse which was not yet laden; and carefully placing him upon the back of the beast, they were just in the act of setting forward, when the youth, who had been quickly darting over the field and examining the fallen, called out to them that there were two more yet with life, who must on no account be deserted. As two of the party ran back to pick them up, another small body of Indians—who for the last few minutes had been busy in a different quarter, and had now returned to the main field of slaughter—poured in upon them a close volley, and literally cut them down over the wounded they were assisting, at the same time rushing in upon them with brandished tomahawks and furious yells.

Finding there was no hope of saving any more, our

young hero now ran back to the main party, shouting, "Let us give them a farewell volley!" which was immediate.y done—several of the savages in turn falling beneath the fatal aim of the Kentuckians.

"Now, then, for a retreat!" pursued the youth, who, though himself a mere private in the ranks, was listened to and obeyed with the deference due to an officer in full command. "Load up, men, and guard the wounded with your lives! In Heaven's name, do not desert them, whatever may be your fate! I will run forward and give notice of your approach, that those who set out ahead of us may not push off the last boat before you reach them."

"We'll all come in together, William, or you'll never see us again!" replied one of his comrades; and as they began to urge their horses forward, the youth darted into a thicket and disappeared in advance of them.

As he ran through the wood toward the river, his rifle thrown across his shoulder, his eye constantly on the alert for the foe, he passed over the gory corpse of many a companion, who had been overtaken, slain, scalped, and even stripped of his clothing—and which, in fact, at different intervals, marked the course of the retreat from that disastrous field of battle.

At last, faint and almost exhausted, our brave youth reached the bank of the river, just as the only boat at that point, heavily laden with the escaping fugitives, was in the act of being pushed from the shore. Here at the moment were, fortunately, none of the enemy—but above and below were sounds of conflict—and an attack was every instant expected.

"Hold, comrades!" he shouted, presenting his weak and bloody figure to their view. "I am just in advance of a few more of our friends, who are hurrying up with the wounded!"

"Get aboard yourself, if you want to," replied one; "but don't ask us to wait for any more—for another party would sink us—to say nothing of the savages, who may attack us here at any moment."

"Yes, jump aboard," said another; "and quick, too— or we'll have to leave you as well as them."

"Never!" returned the youth, with a mingled flush of pride and shame; "never will I desert my friends in such a cowardly manner! Until the others arrive, I will not put my foot aboard your boat, whatever may be the consequences."

"Then we'll have to leave you among the rest," called out a third; "for it's better a few should perish than all; and all will, if we stay here a minute longer."

He seized an oar as he spoke, and was about to push off the boat, regardless of all lives save his own, when the youth, throwing his rifle across the root of a fallen tree, pointed the muzzle at his breast, and exclaimed:

"Beware! the first man that sends that boat one inch from the shore until our comrades are aboard, I will shoot so help me God!"

The man, knowing the youth, and knowing him to be one who would keep his word, at once threw down the oar, muttering some bitter curses upon his folly; but a few of the others, moved to feelings of shame and admiration by his heroic self-sacrifice, took part with our hero, and declared that all should escape, or all perish together. This at once raised an altercation; and hot and angry words had begun to pass between the different parties, when, fortunately for all, the last escort arrived, and were immediately hurried on board—the boat, by this additional weight, being sunk to her very gunwale, so that it was feared another pound might swamp her.

The youth, who had meantime stood back, giving directions, and refusing to enter till the very last, on seeing the condition of things, told his comrades to push off at once, and he would find a way to save himself; and without waiting for a reply, he hurried up the stream a few yards, to where some horses stood panting, which had escaped from the field of battle; and selecting one of these he, by great exertion, considering his weak and wounded condition, got upon his back, and forced him into the stream, and toward the opposite shore.

The moment the men in the boat perceived that the

youth had fairly made his escape, they pushed off from the bank; but not a moment too soon; for they had scarcely got a dozen yards out, when a large body of Indians, who had been attacking the boats below, came hurrying up along the bank, and at once poured in upon them a heavy volley. Only one or two of them were wounded, however—most of the enemy's balls going wide of the mark—and with loud yells of defiance, the Kentuckians returned the fire, and then pulled eagerly for the opposite shore.

The wounded youth urged his horse toward the boat; but just before he reached it, another ball of the enemy struck him, and shattered his right arm; when, bending over, he seized the mane of the horse with his teeth, and so clung to him, till, overcome by pain and the loss of blood, he fainted and rolled from his back into the water, from whence he was rescued by his companions at great peril to themselves.

This heroic youth, who so self-sacrificingly saved his friends, and was himself most providentially preserved through many a perilous encounter besides these enumerated, subsequently rose to enviable distinction, and became one of the prominent men of the West. In 1810 he removed to Cincinnati, where he passed the remainder of his days. During the war of 1812 he was appointed Major General of the Ohio Militia; and, in 1829, Surveyor General of the public lands of Ohio, Indiana, and

Michigan. He proved to be as noble in heart as he was brave in deed, and was ever noted for his public spirit and benevolence. He died in 1831; and the public were then called to mourn the loss, and do honor to the memory, of a distinguished fellow-citizen—the subject of our present notice—GENERAL WILLIAM LYTLE.

The Maid of Fort Henry.

READER! come with me, and together let us enter a wilderness-fort, at a period when our now great Republic was in its infancy—at a period when the heroes of the American Revolution were in the very heat of strife, doing those brave and noble deeds which have brought their names down to us covered with immortal renown.

There! we now stand within the walls of a Western fortress; and on all sides we are enclosed by strong palisades, about eight feet in height, which mark out the ground, some three-quarters of an acre, in the form of a parallelogram. At each of the four corners is a blockhouse made of logs, which rises above and projects beyond the stout pickets or palisades; and in each of these blockhouses are loop-holes, which enable us to look out upon the surrounding country, and also along the outside of the pickets, without being ourselves exposed to the view of whatever enemy may be lurking about.

And what do we see? On one side the Ohio river; on another a straggling wood, stretching back into a mighty forest; on the third a large cornfield, enclosed by a Virginia fence; on the fourth a small village of log-houses; and on all sides hideously painted and half-naked savages.

Yes! we are surrounded by Indians—a large body of vindictive red men—who are thirsting for the blood of those who are in the fort with us, for we are not the only occupants of this stronghold. It is now past one o'clock of a warm, clear, bright, autumnal day; and since the golden rising of the sun, there have been some terrible scenes enacted, and many human beings have passed from time to eternity by the most violent and bloody of deaths.

Last night—soon after the tenants of yonder log-houses, which we have pointed out to you, had retired to rest—the whole village was roused by the alarming intelligence, brought by an Indian hunter, that a great body of savages were prowling about the vicinity; and men, women and children, catching up their most valuable articles, rushed into the fort, and spent the night here in peace and safety. This morning the garrison numbered forty-two fighting males, including several youths, some quite young, but all brave, and all sharp-shooters.

About daylight this morning, there being no signs of the enemy, the commandant of the fortress dispatched a white man and a negro back into the country on an errand—but the white man never will return. As he was passing through yonder cornfield, a hideous-looking savage suddenly rose up before him, knocked him down with his musket, and then killed and scalped him. The negro saw the bloody deed performed, and, with a yell of horror, fled back to the fort, where he communicated to anxious listeners the startling fact.

"We must dislodge the enemy, which doubtless is small," said Colonel Shepherd, the commandant of the fort. "Captain Mason, take fourteen picked men, and let the red devils have a taste of your bravery and skill."

And Captain Mason marched out with his fourteen brave followers, through that large gate which you see in the centre of the eastern line of pickets, and hurried down to the cornfield, which he thoroughly searched for his savage foe, but without finding him; and he was on the point of retracing his steps, when suddenly there came the crack of a hundred muskets; a hundred balls came whizzing among his little force, killing several and wounding nearly all; and then up-rose, on every side—front, flank and rear—many hundreds of vindictive red men, who, with shrill whoops and yells, rushed upon the gallant few still living and began to hew them down. They made a brave resistance—but what could such a handfull do against such a host? One by one they fell, and were tomahawked and scalped. Captain Mason fought desperately; and cutting his way through the ranks of the enemy, succeeded in reaching some fallen timber, where, though badly wounded, he is now concealed, though all his friends in the fort think him dead.

Twelve more men, under Captain Ogle, rushed from the fort to cover the retreat of their gallant comrades; but they too were drawn into an ambuscade, and were all cut off from rejoining their friends in the fortress—only some two or three of the party being now alive, secreted in the underbrush of yonder wood. And still three more of the little garrison sallied forth to the support of Captain Ogle; but they were forced to make a hasty retreat, and were pursued to the very gate of the fort, and fired upon as they entered, and had one of their number mortally wounded.

And now the siege commenced in earnest. With whoops and yells of triumph, some five hundred savages surrounded the fortress, and began to fire upon it. And now the little garrison—numbering only twelve, all told—began to return their fire; and so sure was their aim, that some one of the besiegers bit the dust at every shot. Several times did the enemy make a rush, in large bodies, to effect a lodgment under the walls—but the unerring rifles of the heroic borderers, fired through the loop-holes of the different block-houses, drove them back in dismay, burdened with the weight of their fallen comrades.

Once only was there a pause in the conflict. A white flag was thrust out of a window of one of yonder cabins, and the head of a white man appeared, demanding, in

English, the surrender of the fort, in the name of His Britannic Majesty. He read the proclamation of a British Governor, and promised protection to all in the fort, if they would surrender at once, and swear allegiance to the British crown. He was answered with derision.

"If you want the fort, why don't you and your red howling devils come and take it?" replied the intrepid Colonel Shepherd.

"And if we do take it, by ——! we'll put to death all that are in it!" replied the white leader of the savages.

"You would do that even if we surrendered, you red-headed, white-livered renegade!" was the taunting rejoinder.

"No! You shall be protected; I swear it, by all I hold sacred!"

"And what do *you* hold sacred, you treacherous scoundrel!" cried the gallant Colonel. "Bah! Simon Girty, we know you; and this place shall never be surrendered to *you*, while there is an American soldier left to defend it."

Girty, the renegade—for the white chief was none other—was about to renew his treacherous proposition, when one of the men in the fort, becoming exasperated, lodged a bullet in the logs, just above his head, as a warning of what he might expect himself, unless he withdrew, which he did immediately.

Again were hostilities renewed, and continued up to the

moment when we have seen proper to enter the fort with the reader.

And now, for the second time since daylight this morning, have the Indians ceased their assault. It is one o'clock, and for eight long hours has there been almost incessant firing. Let us look through the loop-holes.

Away there against the wood, at the base of the hill, beyond rifle range, you see a body of savages collected, holding a council of war. Yonder, along the edge of the cornfield, partly hidden by the fence and partly concealed among the fallen timber, you may see many dusky forms, and may readily believe you see only a few of the number which there lie in wait, as a sort of *corps de reserve*. And up among the cabins, yonder, you see a few more savages—some sauntering about, some peering through the palings, and some gazing out of the windows. And look where you may, in every direction you behold Indians.

How is it within the fort? In the centre of the area which the palisades enclose, in front of yonder row of cabins—where many a brave father, husband, and son slept last night, whose mangled bodies now repose in yonder cornfield—in the centre of the area, I say, a group of men, women and children are collected. There stand gray-haired sires, and strippling youths—staid matrons, and maidens in bloom—and all look sad and anxious. Some of the men, with doleful faces, are leaning upon their rifles, and wiping the perspiration, blackened with powder, from their bronzed features; and some of the women are clasping little innocent infants to their hearts, and looking down upon them with fond eyes dimmed with tears.

"God help us!" says the gallant Colonel Shepherd—a fine, noble specimen of humanity, who is standing in the centre of the group—and as he speaks, he casts down his eyes and sighs. "If we could only die like soldiers, fighting to the last, selling our lives at a heavy price to our accursed foes, it would not seem so hard; but to be compelled to stand idle and helpless, and see the hideous monsters enter our stronghold, and butcher our mothers, wives, sisters, and children, while we ourselves are secured for future tortures—oh! it is terrible! terrible! And yet it must come to this soon, if the Indians renew their attack unless kind Providence saves us by a miracle. Men," he added, with a kindling eye, "you have done nobly—you have fought like heroes: boys, you are worthy of your sires—I see no cowards here; and oh! would to God we all had the means to continue our gallant defence! But what are rifles without powder? *and it is a startling fact that we have but three rounds left!*"

"What an oversight," says another, "that we did not fetch all our powder with us! There is a whole keg in my house; and if we had it now, it would be our salvation."

"It must be procured," returns a third.

"But how?" inquires the Colonel. "The Indians are all around us, and more than a hundred eyes are constantly on the fort, so that no movement can be made outside the walls that will not be discovered. And yet, my friends, that powder must be procured, or we are lost. It is a perilous undertaking—and, in all probability, whoever makes the attempt will lose his life, and so I will detail no one to the duty—but if there is any one here brave enough to volunteer, I will accept his services; and if he falls, and we escape, we will remember his name and do it honor; and if he saves us, and is saved with us, our blessings shall be upon him through life. Is there any one present who will volunteer to go into the very jaws of death?"

Four young men instantly spring forward, and, almost in the same breath, each exclaims:

"I will go."

"But we can spare but one of you, my noble lads!" says the Colonel, while his features flush, and his dark eye sparkles with pride, at the self-sacrificing bravery of his young comrades. "Which shall it be?"

"Me!" cries one; "I spoke first."

"No, no, John—I was ahead of you."

"No you wasn't, Abe—no such thing."

"I will leave it to the Colonel, if he didn't hear my voice first of any!" cries a third.

"I was before *you*, Joe; I call all here to witness!" exclaims the fourth.

"Ho! listen to Robert—I was first I tell you!"

"No, I was first!" cries John. "You know I was, Colonel!"

"But I tell you I am going—for I can run the fastest, and therefore will stand the best chance of getting back alive!" cries Abe.

"I can run as fast as the best, and I'm much stronger than either Abe, Joe, or Robert," says John, laying his hand on the Colonel's arm. "Let me go—do! And besides, I've got no mother or sister here to mourn for me, if I fall."

"There!" cries one of the others—"he talks as if he might fall! and I'm sure I could get back safely."

Look at their flushed faces, and eager, sparkling eyes, as thus they wrangle for the privilege of being permitted to go forth to almost certain death! for the chances are five hundred to one, that he who leaves the fort for the village will never return alive. And listen to the murmurs of approbation which come from the surrounding circle of females! A mother looks fondly on her son—a sister looks proudly on her brother—and a maiden's heart swells with emotions unspeakable, as she hears him who is the light and life of her world, boldly contend for the right of being allowed to go forth into a peril from which most men would shrink aghast.

"Come! come!" chides the Colonel, at length, speaking almost sternly to the now angry disputants; "you will ruin all, unless some of you yield—for the Indians may renew hostilities at any moment, and then we are lost indeed. You are all brave, noble fellows; and if I could spare four, you should all go; but as it is, three of you must give way to the fourth; and I pray you do so speedily, for time is precious."

"I will never yield!" cries one.

"Nor I!" exclaims a second.

"I will go, if I have to scale the walls to get out!" says a third.

"Colonel, I am the strongest and fleetest, and was the first to accept your offer; and I demand, therefore, that you settle the dispute by sending me!"

Look! In the circle of men, women and children that are now promiscuously gathered around these hot, eager, passionate youths, do you observe one human face that wears a very singular expression? that seems to be animated by some strange and powerful emotion? It is the face of a young and beautiful female, about whom there is a certain air of refinement—seen in the grace of attitude, dress, and general demeanor—which contrasts rather forcibly with many of her coarse-featured, rustic companions. But I wish you to observe that face particularly—not alone for its beauty—but to mark the expression of noble, lofty, heroic resolve which is settling upon it! Do you see the head gradually straightening back, as if with pride?—do you see those dark, bright eyes kindle with the almost fanatical enthusiasm of daring self-sacrifice?—do you see the warm blood spring upward to the temples, and broad, white forehead, and finally settle in a bright, red spot upon either soft, downy cheek, as if the passion-fires of a mighty soul were already burning within? —do you see the thin nostrils of a slightly aquiline nose gradually dilate? and the thin, determined lips gradually close over those white, even teeth?

There! she moves; and mark, I pray you, the proud step, as she advances into the center of the circle, and catches all eyes, and sweeps the whole group of curious and anxious spectators with a lightning glance! And now her thin lips part, and she speaks in clear, silver tones. There is no quivering, no tremulousness, in her voice— and every other voice is hushed. Listen!

"Hold!" she exclaims: "cease this wrangling! cease this contention for the privilege of being allowed to throw away a life that cannot be spared! You are all brave— almost too brave—since you so eagerly court death for the honor it will confer on the name of him who may die in the noble attempt to save the rest. But not another heroic defender of this fortress must be lost! Already thirty of the forty-two men we numbered this morning are gone; and shall we take another from the gallant twelve that remain? No, no—this must not be! The powder must be procured from my brother's dwelling—but let the first attempt to obtain it be made by one who cannot use a rifle. *I will go!*"

There is an almost simultaneous burst of "No! no! no!" from the astonished listeners to this heroic offer.

"I am resolved!" replies the noble heroine; "seek not to alter my determination!"

"But you will be killed!" cries one.

"Then I shall die with the consolation of knowing that, so far, this brave little garrison is not weakened."

"No, no—leave this adventure to us!" cries one of the late disputants: "we can run faster than you, and are therefore more likely to be successful. We cannot yield this peril to a lady, the fairest of her sex, and see her throw her life away—we should not be acting like men, and shame would ever rest upon us."

"The race is not always to the swift, nor the battle to the strong," proudly replies the noble girl. "What is my life compared to yours, who can skilfully use the rifle against our savage foe, and are required here for the protection of these helpless beings who stand around you? Look at these little, innocent children, each of whose lives is as valuable as mine; and remember their whole dependence is on you!"

"Lizzie! Lizzie!" now interposes one of her two brothers who are present—"this must not be! You must not go! We cannot suffer it and retain the name of men. You cannot comprehend what you ask—you do not consider the peril. Remember, you are just from Philadelphia, where you have lived in safety, in ease, in comparative refinement and luxury; and you cannot surely be aware of the risk, the danger, of trusting yourself alone with a savage, merciless foe, who spares neither sex nor age! Consider! there are numbers of Indians strolling about yonder village, to whom your scalp would be a prize of victory: consider every thing, and give over this mad folly!"

"Brother," replies the fair girl, "you have seen little of me of late, and you know little of my invincible will, or you would not attempt to thwart me in what I have resolved to perform. Come! come! we lose time. Open yon gate, before it is too late, and let me go! for go I must: something whispers me that the good God will sustain me!"

In vain they try, with reason, with remonstrance, with representations of the danger put in every conceivable form, with affectionate appeals, with downright pleading, to induce the brave girl to abandon her purpose; and at last, with the utmost reluctance, they yield assent to her heroic proposition. Instantly this assent is gained, she strips herself of every unnecessary article of clothing, and demands that the gate be opened to her

All crowd to the gate, speaking words of affection, encouragement and hope. Now it slowly opens, and attracts the attention of the savages in the village, who wonder if a sally or surrender is to follow. The fair girl now fixes her eyes steadily upon her brother's house; the distance is sixty yards; she measures it in her mind; she calculates the time that will be required to reach it; she draws a long breath; and now, like a ball from a cannon, she bounds from the fortress; and sincere, earnest prayers, from the hearts of every being she goes forth to save, ascend to Heaven for her protection and safe return.

See how she flies over the intervening space, with the basilisk-eyes of many swarthy savages fixed upon her! who stand amazed at the daring of a woman, and are lost in wonder at what can be the meaning of such a desperate act! and how the hearts of her white friends beat with hope and fear as they behold yard after yard of distance put between them and her! Will she succeed? Will those brutal savages stand idle and not molest her! who is thus, with a noble heroism almost unparalleled in the annals of history, thrusting herself into their very hands —putting herself into the power of beings that are unprepared to show mercy? God help her! God sustain her! How long the distance seems for a space that is so short!

There! she nears the house; she reaches it; she enters it; the eyes of the savages have followed her; and now they move toward the building; they do intend to capture her after all; God help her, poor girl! See! they draw nearer—nearer; they are almost at the door. Why stays she so long? Why does she not come back while there is an opportunity? One minute more and it will be too late!

There! there!—she comes! she comes! She holds some dark object tightly in her grasp; she has the powder; the fort will be saved! But no! no!—she is lost! she is lost! The Indians see her; they now comprehend her purpose; they bound after her, with terrific screams and yells; they raise their muskets; they fire; they throw their tomahawks. Still she comes on—on; nearer—nearer; the balls pass her; they lodge in the walls; she is still unharmed. One moment more! They gain upon her—God help her! One moment more! Nearer—nearer! And now—see! she bounds through the gate, and is caught in her brother's arms, almost fainting. But she has the keg of powder clasped to her breast; she is safe; the gate shuts behind her. And now the welkin rings—cheer on cheer—cheer on cheer—for now the fort and all it contains will be saved!

No longer any fear in that lonely fortress!—all is now hope, and animation, and joy. Soon again the Indians renew hostilities; but the brave little garrison is prepared for them; and as fast as they venture forth against its stout walls, so fast they fall back in the arms of death. The women cut patches and run bullets; and the men load and fire, with the utmost rapidity, all the day long; and as their rifles get heated, they change them for muskets; and still keep on firing—fearing nothing now—for they have plenty of ammunition, and as brave a girl to protect as ever the world saw.

The sun goes down and sees nearly one hundred of their enemies slain; but not a single life lost within the fort, and only one man slightly wounded.

And all night long the Indians prowl about, and keep up an irregular fire upon the fort, but do no harm.

And at break of day, after a siege of twenty-four hours—during which twelve brave, noble fellows have withstood five hundred savages—reinforcements arrive; the Indians become disheartened; they burn the village and kill the cattle; and at last, with loud yells of disappointment and rage, they raise the siege and depart.

Such was the siege of Fort Henry, on the present site

of Wheeling, Virginia, in the month of September, and the year 1777—and such the heroism of its gallant defenders

IMMORTAL BE THE NAME OF ELIZABETH ZANE, THE NOBLE HEROINE OF FORT HENRY.

Wrecked on the Lake.

In the fall of 1850, as I was passing down Lake Erie, from Sandusky City to Buffalo, I formed some acquaintance with an elderly gentleman, who was also a passenger. Mr. Warren, for so he gave me his name, had been one of the early adventurers in the western country, and especially along the lake shore; and finding me interested in matters pertaining to early times, he took not a little pains in pointing out to me, from the deck of the steamer, the different localities where important events had occurred connected with the early settlement of the country. With each locality he had a story to tell—either longer or shorter, as the case might be; but the most remarkable one of all, and which I am going to relate, occurred to himself and a small party of his dearest friends.

"Do you see that dark line, yonder?" he said, pointing to the distant shore.

"I see something," I replied, "that resembles a small cloud stretched along the horizon."

"Well, that, sir, is not literally a cloud, though it proved a cloud of sorrow to me."

As he said this, in a voice somewhat tremulous with emotion, I looked up, and observed a tear stealing down his aged cheek.

"Ah! my friend," he pursued, shaking his gray head solemnly, and passing his hand across his eyes, "the sight of that dark spot yonder brings up a dark memory, and makes me weep as a child rather than as a man. It was a great many years ago," he continued, "and I have since lived to experience a great many changes and reverses—have lived to see one friend after another taken down to his narrow home—but the events of that awful day are as vividly in my recollection now, looming above all others, as if they had occurred but yesterday. Excuse me a few minutes, and I will tell you the story," he added: and turning away, he seated himself, buried his face in his hands, and did not again alter his position till the dark line he referred to had faded from my view.

At length he looked up, as one starting from a dream; and having swept the horizon with his still keen, bright eye, he turned to me and requested me to take a seat beside him.

"That dark line I pointed out to you," he resumed— "and which, thank Heaven! is now gone from my sight— is an almost perpendicular bluff of rocks, of from sixty to eighty feet in height, upon the base of which the storm-raised waves dash with wild fury, throwing a fine white spray nigh into the air, and filling the listening ear with an almost deafening roar, not unlike the thunders of Niagara. I heard it once, as a dreadful requiem over the loved and lost, and Heaven grant that I may never hear it again!"

Here he paused, as if overpowed with the recollection, brushed another tear from his eye, and once more resumed:

"It was many years ago—I need not tell you how many, for time counts as nothing in those great events that rend the heart: it was many years ago, I say, that a small party of us—consisting of my mother, sister, a younger brother, and a young and lovely maiden to whom I was engaged—embarked in a Canadian bateau at a point far down the lake, with the intention of finishing the remainder of our long journey from the eastward by water, and joining a few friends who had gone before us and settled just below the rapids of the Maumee."

"For several days we had good sailing—the weather fair and the wind in our favor—in consequence of which our hearts became light and buoyant, for we felt that we were near our journey's end, and should soon be mingled with those we sought. But who knows aught of the future?—who has a right to say that joy and happiness are his?—for in a single moment all his brightest hopes may be dashed forever, and he be either overtaken by death, or by a calamity that shall make him a life-long mourner!

"One day, with the most gloomy apprehensions—with a presentiment that made me wretched—I saw a storm begin to gather, and I watched it with feelings of the most painful anxiety. It was not long in gathering, but loomed up quickly and fearfully, and, almost ere any one save me was aware of the danger, it burst upon us with fury.

"I had taken in sail, and prepared for it as well as I could, but the first dash nearly capsized us. The waves suddenly rose, and threw their spray completely over us, and we began to drift toward the dark bluff which I pointed out to you. All was now excitement and confusion on board, for all believed that we should soon go to the bottom. I pretended to have a stout heart, and to laugh at their fears, and so quieted them in some degree. But to tell you the truth, I was fearfully alarmed myself, for the boat at once became unmanageable, and set rapidly toward the rocky shore, upon which the surge was now beating frightfully, and I felt that nothing short of an interposition of Providence could save us from being dashed to pieces.

"I spoke not of my fears, however, till I saw it was vain to hope—till I beheld the rocks looming up, black and fearful, immediately before us, the waves lashing them terrifically, throwing up their white spray, and rolling back with a crash which could be heard amid the howlings of the storm—and then I told my friends, shouting the words above the roaring of the tempest, that it was time to commend our souls to God, for we were about to pass the dread portals of eternity and enter His awful presence.

"The scene that followed I may only describe as wild, fearful, terrible—each clinging to the other in the most agonized distress, and all appealing to God for mercy. The painful and horrible suspense of waiting for death, while staring it in the face, was of short duration; we seemed but as a bubble on the crest of the angry waters, which now bore us swifter and swifter to our doom; and suddenly, while we all stood locked as it were in each other's embrace, we struck. There was a fearful crash— loud shrieks that seemed blended into one despairing cry —and the hissing waves rolled over us.

"We all went down clinging to each other, knotted as it were together, and were whirled about in the seething waters, till at length, as we rose to the surface, we seemed to be caught by an unusually large wave, and were thrown violently upon a narrow shelf of the rock, where, the huge wave instantly retreating, we were left comparatively dry. From the time of going under till we were thrown upon the rock, I had not for a single moment lost my presence of mind; and though now half stunned and bruised by the concussion, I instantly comprehended all that had happened; and that, if I would save myself and friends, it must be done ere the return of such another wave as had placed us in our present position.

"Instantly I worked myself loose from my almost death-griping companions, dragged them back as far as I could, shouted in their ears the joyful news of their escape, and then got between them and the water, so that, in their bewildered state, they might not roll back to their destruction. I had scarcely succeeded in making them understand what had happened, and they were just beginning to gather themselves upon their feet—my brother with as little presence of mind as any—when I saw another huge wave returning; and, quick as thought, I threw them down, and fell prostrate across their bodies. The wave came, amid our shrieks of terror, and completely submerged us, but not to a sufficient depth to float us from the rock.

"This occurred at intervals of about a minute; and it took me several of these to make my friends comprehend that we were comparatively safe, though in a perilous position—to give them, in fact, a true understanding of the whole matter; and then the task of keeping them where they were became less laborious to me, because of their assistance.

"I now for the first had a little time to look about me, which I eagerly employed in ascertaining what might be our chances for escape. But, alas! I saw nothing to give me any hope. It was an awful scene—a scene to excite feelings of the blackest despair! The shelf upon which we had been thrown was narrow, some ten or fifteen fee. in length, and about five feet above the level of the boiling and seething surge; while behind us and over us, was a high, black, overhanging rock, the top of which our position did not permit us to see. There was no chance of escape except by the water; and there the wreck of our boat, in a hundred pieces, was whirling about on the foam-crested waves and frothing eddies—the storm the while still raging in wild fury—and the shrieking winds, the descending torrents, and the lashing waves, making a horrid concert for our affrighted senses.

"'My son,' shrieked my mother, in a voice of despair, 'there seems to be no hope for us. It would have been better had we perished at once, and so ended our misery.'

"'While there is life there is hope,' I replied, in the same shrill, shrieking tone—the only human sound that could be heard amid the howlings of the tempest.

"Let me not dwell upon that scene—the recollection of which, even now, after a long lapse of years, makes the blood run cold in my veins. But little was said by any— for, as I have remarked, the human voice could only be heard when pitched on its highest key—and each was too terribly impressed with the sense of our desolation, to **give** vent to the feelings of agony which stirred the depths of our inmost souls.

"We clung there together for hours—in almost silent waiting, watching, and trembling—and then, with unspeakable misery, we saw the night close in upon us—shutting out the horrid view, it is true—but leaving us as it were only the sense of feeling that each other was there. Oh, that long and terrible night! an age to me of horror—the storm still unabated—the shrieking winds driving coldly through our drenched garments, and ever and anon a large wave engulfing us! There was no chance for sleep—but only for thought—thought the wildest, most terrible, most agonizing! If we looked around, our gaze encountered nothing but the deepest blackness, or here and there the phosphorescent light of the foaming waters, which seem'd to our now distracted fancies only a sepulchral light to guide us to destruction.

"Somewhere about midnight, as near as I may judge—feeling weak, faint, cold and benumbed—through the painful position in which I had thus far clung to my friends, and my continual submersion beneath the rushing and retiring waves—I released my hold for a few moments, in order to chafe my limbs. But scarcely had I done so, when I was suddenly startled by a wild shriek; and, on feeling for my companions, I found to my horror that my mother and brother were gone! leaving only my dear sister, my beloved Mary, and myself upon the rock.

"I need not dwell upon that night. If your imagination cannot fill the picture of wo which I have so imperfectly sketched, you will never form an idea of my feelings, for language has no power to describe them.

"Morning broke at last—after that long, long night of horror—the storm still raging as furiously as ever—but only three of us alive to know the miseries of living. By the returning light we once more surveyed the awful scene around us; and there, upon the rocks below, but at some distance from where we were, we beheld the bodies of my mother and brother, locked in each other's arms, the lashing waves just sufficiently swaying them about to give an appearance of life. But they were dead—cold in death—and the sight so affected my poor sister, that she arose with a shriek, and, whether intentionally or accidentally, plunged over into the boiling surge.

"Almost beside myself with the accumulated horrors, I threw my arms around my only companion, my beloved Mary, and held her down by my side.

"And thus I sat for hours, in a state of comparative stupefaction, gazing off upon the storm-maddened lake, but with a kind of stony gaze that scarcely had speculation in it.

"When I again turned to Mary, I found she had fainted;

though how long she had been in that condition I did not know. This in some measure recalled me to myself; and I began to chafe her limbs, calling upon her dear name in the wildest tones of despair. She did not revive immediately, and I had just begun to think that she had perished in my arms, when I saw signs of returning life, and redoubled my exertions. At last I had the joy of seeing her open her eyes, and of knowing that her senses had returned. She now looked wildly around her, and, scarcely comprehending what had occurred, asked for her absent friends.

"'They are gone, dear Mary,' said I, with a bursting heart; 'they will return to us no more; you are all that is left to me now; and may God in his mercy either preserve you, or take us both together to the land of spirits!'

"'Yes,' she replied, faintly—so faintly that I had to put my ear close to catch the words—'and we must perish, too —but we will perish together. We must die—we cannot live—we cannot escape—and so let us die at once, and join those who have gone before us!'

"'In God's own good time!' I rejoined. 'We have no right to take our lives in our own hands. He gave and must take. It is our duty to be ready at His call.'

"'But I cannot survive this!' she said; 'death is a hundred times preferable to this agonizing suspense!'

"I encouraged her as well as one in my situation could;

I repeated, that while there was life there was hope; I used every argument and every term of endearment I could think of, to persuade her to cling to life; and at last she seemed to be more resigned to her fate—the fate of waiting and watching with me for the coming death.

"Why should I dwell upon that horrible scene? Why live over again in relating the agony I suffered in reality? No! rather let me hurry on to the awful close—for awful it was, and made these then black hairs turn white in the very prime of manhood.

"Mary gradually drooped—grew faint for the want of food—grew benumbed and torpid through repeated drenchings of the chilling waters; and at length, when another night began to close around us, with the storm still unabated, I feebly but painfully foresaw that, should I still live on, I must soon live alone—be the last survivor of that once happy group.

"My forebodings were awfully fulfilled! Another night set in—and proved, oh God! the last to the last being I then had in the wide world to love! I had gradually grown weak myself—so weak that I could scarcely keep my hold upon the rocks—to which I still clung with the instincts of life, and for the preservation of my poor Mary, who had long since given up the attempt of preserving herself.

"But the end came. A larger wave than ever burst

over us, loosed my feeble hold, dashed me against the rocks behind, and left me half-stunned and bleeding on the very verge of the abyss. I crawled up again, and felt for Mary. Great Heaven! she was not there! she was gone! With a shriek of despair, I threw myself flat upon my face, determined to make no further effort for life.

"But God, in his inscrutable Providence, saw fit to preserve me. The storm had now reached its height, and from that moment it began to abate. The morning found me alive, but alone; and the angry waves, which had snatched from me all I prized on earth, were gradually subsiding to quietude, as if satisfied with their work of destruction.

"More dead than alive, I kept my position upon the rocks through that day and another night; and then, being discovered by some Canadian fishermen, I was taken off, and conveyed to their home, on the other side of the lake. There, after a long and delirious illness, I finally recovered, and learned that the bodies of my friends had been found, taken from the water, and decently interred upon the American shore.

"I have many times since," concluded the aged narrator, in a tremulous voice, "visited the humble grave where they quietly repose together, and never but with a regret that I did not sleep beside them. It was there, over that lonely grave, I took a solemn oath to be true to my first love, and you now behold me a wifeless and childless old man, whose only abiding hope is, that I shall soon join them in **better world!"**

A Desperate Encounter.

ADAM WISTON, though even now unknown to fame, was one of the boldest and bravest of that hardy band of daring spirits who led the van of civilization into the great wilderness of the West. Born on the soil of Pennsylvania, nurtured among her wild and romantic hills, he early imbibed a love for bold and daring exploits, and even as a boy became the hero of some remarkable adventures.

In those days of peril, the frontier afforded no facilities for the training of youth in the knowledge of books; and staunch, robust, intellectual men entered upon the active duties of life without other education than that which fitted them for a victorious march into the very depths of the savage wilds, which still stretched before them for hundreds and thousands of miles. The learning gained from letters is a species of mental luxury, seldom indulged in by those who find it necessary to be constantly on the alert to provide the daily wants of physical life and guard themselves from a thousand surrounding perils.

Adam Wiston was, therefore, no scholar; but no man

of his day had a more practical and thorough knowledge of the forest, in which he wished to live and hoped to die, than he had at the time he bade his friends adieu, shouldered his rifle, and, afoot and alone, set off on a bold exploration toward the wilds of Kentucky. What he saw, what he enjoyed, what he encountered, and what he suffered, from that eventful period till the day of his death, will probably never be known to the world; but there are some traces of his daring and checkered career, which show that his was not a life to be envied by the man who considers personal ease and personal safety the paramount objects of his existence. Tradition, the mother of written history, the preserver of unrecorded deeds and facts, has handed down a few of the adventures and exploits of this hero of the wilderness, and which it is the purpose of this article to relate.

Adam was a large, powerfully built man, six feet in height, and well proportioned, with iron nerves and whipcord muscles, and, at five-and-twenty, regarded himself as the equal in physical strength and endurance of any human being on the frontier, whether foreign or native, white or Indian, and always stood ready to put the matter to the test in any manner which any adverse believer might think proper. He was, moreover, supple, active, long winded, and quick of foot; and had more than once, even when a mere boy, borne off the prize from older and renowned competitors, in such physical contests as wrestling, running, leaping, throwing weights, and the like; and when it is added that he was true of eye, steady of hand, and a dead shot, it will be perceived that he was a man whom no single antagonist might encounter with safety. Like nearly all of his class, Adam Wiston had come to regard his natural foe, the native savage, with an implacable hatred, and he never missed an opportunity of testifying to the fact in the most vindictive manner. It was an invariable rule with him, to kill an Indian whenever and wherever he could; and so noted had become his feats of daring in this respect, that the savages had named him *Papapanawe*, (Lightning,) and spoke of him with dread, and the few whites that knew him hailed him as the hero of heroes, the bravest of the brave.

Early one morning in the spring of the year, when the great forest had donned its new mantle, and looked delightfully green and gay, Adam crept stealthily and noiselessly over a steep ridge, which formed the left bank of a well-known stream, and, gliding silently down into a narrow ravine, ensconced himself in a dense thicket, within thirty yards of a famous deer-lick. Here, carefully stretching himself out at full length upon the earth, with his long rifle properly adjusted, and the clustering leaves before him just sufficiently parted to give him a sight of the spot which some timid deer might be expected to visit at any moment, he waited with the patience of an old, experienced hunter for the happy moment when he should be able to bring down his game, and thus provide himself with many a coveted meal.

Adam was not destined, on this occasion, to have his patience tried by any unusual delay; for he had scarcely watched the "lick" a quarter of an hour, when, in the direct line of his vision, appeared a sleek, fat buck. The rifle was already pointed, Adam was quick of sight, and the next instant there was a flash, a crack, and the unerring ball had sped on its fatal mission. The buck suddenly bounded into the air, and fell over on its side, where for a few moments it lay quivering in the last throes of death.

But, strange to relate, there was another report of another rifle, so exactly timed with Adam Wiston's, that the two sounds were blended into one, and two balls at the same moment struck the same animal at opposite sides. The quick ears of the old hunter barely caught the foreign sound, and he by no means felt certain it was not an auricular deception; but trained from his youth to prudence and caution, he was not the man to slight the faintest warning of danger when nothing was to be gained by bold and reckless daring. If it was indeed the report of another gun he had heard, it was, he thought, more likely to be that of an enemy than a friend; and situated as he was in the great wilderness, his very life depending in no slight degree upon his own vigilance and care, it stood him in hand to ascertain if he had aught o fear, before rashly venturing from his covert.

Gathering himself upon his knees, therefore, and slowly and cautiously pushing his head up through the interlacing bushes, he directed his glance to the opposite side of the stream, where there chanced to be a ravine similar to the one he occupied; and there, in direct confirmation of his suspicion, he beheld a thin wreath of smoke slowly ascending and dispersing itself in the clear morning air; while just below it, barely perceptible among the bushes, and so blending with them that no eye but a practiced woodman's might have detected it, he perceived the shaven crown and painted face of a hideous savage, with its black, basilisk eyes fairly gleaming, as it seemed, with fierce desire, and fixed steadily and searchingly upon himself.

Had there been in the mind of Adam Wiston the faintest shadow of a doubt of the Indian's simultaneous discovery of himself, he would have silently and cautiously withdrawn himself from exposure, reloaded his rifle, and awaited his opportunity of a fatal shot; and even as it was, he hurriedly debated with himself the propriety of boldly unmasking; but yielding the next moment to an almost uncontrolable impulse, he uttered a loud yell of defiance, and called out to his adversary in the most taunting manner:

"Hello! you greasy curmudgeon of a sneaking tribe! ef you want my hair, you'll have to come arter it, and it'll take a *man* to crop it; but ef I had a squaw here, I'd send her for yourn, and consider her time wasted when she'd got it. Come, you old painted brute! I dar' you to a fair stand-up fight, and no rifles atween us, and the best man gets a scalp and a buck! But, bah! what's the use o' talking? for it arn't in you to understand any thing like human language; and it 'ud be worse nor a seven-year agur for sich as me to break my jaws over gibberish that no sensible human ever did know any thing about."

While Adam was thus giving vent to his rage and contempt, he was not idle; but, with his person all concealed except his head, his hands were actively engaged in putting a new charge into his rifle. He had succeeded in getting in the powder, and was in the act of ramming home the ball, when the Indian, who had up to this time apparently remained immovable—and who, perhaps, from some slight but perceptible motion of his enemy's head, had conjectured what he was doing—suddenly uttered a short, shrill whoop, and disappeared.

"Only one minute more, Greasy, and thar'd been another dead carcass for the buzzards!" muttered Adam, as, aware of his own dangerous exposure, he suddenly ducked his head and crawled stealthily among the stems of the bushes, away from the spot he had occupied, for fear a venture-shot of the savage might chance to strike him. And then, as he re-primed his piece, keeping as wary a watch the while as his situation would permit, he added: "Now for it; it's eyther me or that red-skin afore night."

Thinking it the most prudent course to maintain his concealment for the present, in case the savage, whom he fancied would not leave the vicinity, should attempt to steal upon his retreat, Adam again stretched himself upon the ground, and for something like an hour listened keenly to every sound, and sharply watched the motion of every leaf around and above him, to be certain it was stirred by the breeze and not by his foe. Then finding his time was likely to be wasted, and fearing the savage might escape him after all, he resolved upon a venture of exploration into the retreat of his enemy, though not with that careless haste which might give the other the audantage he had himself hoped to gain.

With the greatest caution, therefore, and by a sinuous, snake-like motion, so that no movement of the bushes above him would indicate his course, he worked his body up the ravine and over the top of the ridge; and then gliding into the thick wood on the other side, he set off more boldly on a circuitous route, intending to cross the stream some distance above and come up carefully behind the point where he had espied the savage

Now it so chanced that there was a very si.gular and remarkable train of coincidences, formed by the same thoughts and desires actuating these two human beings at the same time; for both had stolen to their different concealments together, had together espied the deer, had fired together, had examined each other in a like manner, had both disappeared together, and waited and watched for each other, and each had actually set off to circumvent the other at the same moment, both going up the stream; while, as if to put a climax to the whole, both came out face to face on opposite sides of the narrow river, with a distance of less than thirty yards dividing them; when, quick as lightning, both pieces were simultaneously raised and fired, there being as before a blended report. Adam felt a sharp, burning twinge in his right arm, and saw the savage suddenly press his hand to his right breast; and the next moment these brave, undaunted men, with loud yells of rage and defiance, were springing toward each other for a mortal hand-to-hand combat.

Casting their pieces aside, they met in the middle of the stream, which was here shallow, and rushed foaming and gurgling over a stony bed; and had there been a spectator, conscious of all that had occurred, he would have considered their individual chances of life about equal—for the Indian was a large, athletic fellow, supple and active, strong and determined, and both were actuated with a mutual hate and a fierce desire for victory.

With their knives gleaming, they met as recorded, and for a few moments there was a flashing and crashing of steel, as both struck and parried with something of the skill of two masters of fence. But a fight like this, at such close quarters, and with such short weapons, could not long continue without some serious wounds on one side or both; and with a quick and sudden blow, Adam succeeded in giving his adversary a fearful gash across the breast, followed by another which nearly severed the tendons of the left arm. With a howl of rage and pain, the savage started back a pace, the blood flowing profusely; and then, measuring his already panting antagonist with a quick glance of his eagle eye, he suddenly bounded forward, and made a fearful lunge for his heart. The old hunter, though in a measure prepared for this, could not altogether avoid the thrust; but he so quickly turned as to receive the wound in his right side; at the same time plunging his own knife half way to the hilt in the back of his foe, barely missing the vertebra, which would have terminated the contest in his favor.

Too highly wrought up by a fierce and vengeful excitement, and too eager for the finishing stroke to give a proper heed to defence, both combatants, badly wounded, covered with blood, panting for breath, and with failing strength,

7*

but with glaring eyes and gnashing teeth, now struck fast and furiously, each blow telling with fearful effect upon the other. At length their knives met in such a manner that both dropped from their hands together; and then they clinched, swayed to and fro like intoxicated men, and fell, and rolled over and over in the water upon the protruding stones, locked in each other's embrace, knotted together, and each struggling to be uppermost and strangle or drown his antagonist.

It was still a fearful and desperate fight, and was continued in the manner described for some five minutes, during which no one could have told who would eventually be the victor.

At last Adam, in rolling under the Indian for the sixth or eighth time, perceived that chance or Providence had brought him back to the very spot where he had lost his knife; and bethinking him of this, he, by a desperate exertion, released one of his hands, and placed it partially beneath him, in the hope of getting hold of the weapon. To his unbounded delight, the attempt proved successful; and the next moment, with all his remaining strength, he was actively plunging it, with rapid thrusts, into the back and sides of his enemy.

This, and it may be this alone, gave him the victory; for the Indian, though still holding out with a wonderful tenacity of life, and exerting himself even against hope,

A DESPERATE ENCOUNTER. 79

gradually gave way in strength, till the hunter, with far less exertion thar formerly, was able to turn him again, when, plunging the knife into his throat, he ended the contest.

Adam, finding the savage was at last really dead, slowly gathered himself up, seated himself upon the body, wiped the blood and perspiration from his face, and, in a somewhat doleful, half ludicrous tone, complimented his late adversary by saying:

"You war the toughest old red nigger as ever Adam Wiston fou't."

He then, in a slow and deliberate manner, proceeded to scalp the dead Indian; which done, he took from his person all that he considered of any value, secured both rifles, and then sat down on the bank and dressed his own wounds in the best manner he could. Though seriously, he was not dangerously, wounded; and having rested himself for an hour, he set to work on the dead buck, cut off his breakfast, kindled a fire, cooked and ate it. Then cutting off another large piece of meat, to serve his necessities for the journey, he set off at a slow, feeble pace for the nearest station, where he arrived during the night, and narrated his desperate encounter to a crowd of eager and wondering listeners.

A Trap for Life.

During the early settlements in the western part of Pennsylvania and the northwestern portion of Virginia, the hardy adventurers into those then wilderness solitudes at times suffered severely from the incursions of the Indians. As early as 1780, quite a large body of warriors, from the vicinity of the Cuyahoga Falls, came suddenly down upon the unprotected frontier, and, before any check could be put to their ravages, succeeded in murdering and plundering quite a number of the whites, and effecting their retreat in safety.

At this time there was a well-known Indian hunter in that vicinity, one Captain Samuel Brady, whose many daring exploits and hair-breadth escapes had rendered him as famous throughout that region as his cotemporary, the celebrated Daniel Boone, was in Kentucky; and having under his leadership a goodly number of as brave and daring spirits as himself, he at once called them together, selected a certain number for the expedition, and set out on the trail of the savages, hoping to overtake them and inflict a severe chastisement before they should reach their villages.

In this respect, however, the captain and his friends were disappointed; for the Indians had gained a start which enabled them to reach their towns in advance of their pursuers; but as they belonged to different tribes, it was discovered that they had separated on the bank of the Cuyahoga—one part crossing it and going to the northward, and the other turning off to the westward, as it was supposed to the Falls, where it was known there was a village.

This division of the Indians rendered it necessary for the whites, if they would follow each trail, to divide their force also, which would weaken it materially, and render their further pursuit still more hazardous; and in view of this new danger, Captain Brady stated the whole matter fairly to his companions, and inquired of them what they were disposed to do under the circumstances.

Should they follow either one of the trails, he said, the other half of the Indians would escape; should they follow neither one, all would escape; and should they divide, each division would be comparatively small, and they might all be cut off in detail; therefore it was for them to choose whether they would go forward in one party or two, or return as they were without striking a blow.

The men were not long in deciding; they were unanimous in their desire to push forward and take vengeance upon the enemy; they also preferred a division of the party; and accordingly about one-half of them immediately crossed the river and set off to the northward, while the remainder, under Captain Brady, followed the westward trail to the Cuyahoga Falls.

It was the design and expectation of the gallant captain to take the Indians by surprise; but the latter, expecting to be pursued by the whites, were prepared to receive them; and it was only by a mere accident that the borderers were saved from falling into an ambuscade which would have proved fatal to all.

Seeing that the Indians were fully prepared for them—that there was no chance of taking them by surprise—that their numbers were at least four times as many as their own—our friends judiciously determined upon a retreat; but they had not gone far, when the Indians, uttering their wildest war-whoops, set after them in a body.

Knowing that if his men continued together, there would be no hope for any of them, Captain Brady, in order to save as many lives as possible, called out to them to disperse in every direction, and each man to look out for himself. By this means he expected to divide the Indians into small parties in their pursuit of single individuals; and this might have been the result, had they not, unfortunately for his own safety, discovered in him their most vindictive and troublesome foe, and at once resolved upon his capture.

Captain Brady was well known to the Indians; in former times he had hunted with them over these very grounds; but he had subsequently become their most implacable enemy, and had done them so much injury as to create in them a fiendish desire to take him alive and put him to the tortures—they well knowing that the accomplishment of this purpose would not only rid them of the man they both hated and feared, but would deprive the whites of their bravest and most daring leader, and would thus strike a more effective blow against the latter than would the destruction of a dozen or twenty men of lesser note. For this reason, therefore, the moment it was ascertained that he was one of the party, his capture was determined on by all; and turning from the pursuit of the others, the whole yelling crew set after him.

Captain Brady had something of the start, and was one of the fleetest runners on the border; that he could distance and escape from a few, he was sanguine enough to believe; but when he found himself recognized, and, looking behind him, saw the whole body in chase of himself, his very heart seemed to die within him. What chance had he of escape indeed - single-handed and alone —afar from the refuge of even a wilderness fort—and with fifty infuriated Indians in hot pursuit, urged on by a spirit of revenge, and resolved, above every other earthly consideration, upon taking him alive or dead?

But the captain was a brave man, and a brave man dies but once; he was a sanguine man, too, and would not consider his case hopeless while the freedom of his limbs remained; and though, as he afterward expressed it, "it was hardly one chance in fifty, yet he was determined to do his best, and have no fault to find with himself from a lack of effort."

Near the point where the race first started, the Cuyahoga makes a bend to the south, so as to nearly enclose an area of several square miles in the form of a peninsula; the direction taken by Brady soon brought him within this enclosure; and the Indians, by extending their line to the two banks of the stream, at the point where they most nearly approach each other, considered him as in a net, and announced their satisfaction by yells of triumph. There was now, in fact, no chance for him to escape except through their lines or across the Cuyahoga river; and considering that the foremost pursuers were not fifty yards behind him, either of these chances was regarded by the savages as an impossibility.

Still the hardy and gallant captain did not despair; he had many a time hunted over this very ground, and knew every inch of it, and all the windings, turnings, and peculiarities of the river as well as the Indians themselves; he knew, too, there was one point where the river, compressed within a few feet, rushed roaring and foaming through a rocky gorge; and it at once occurred to him to shape his course for this point, and make a bold, desperate leap for the other shore. He might fall short, and be dashed to pieces upon the rocks beneath, it was true; but this would only be a quick and sudden death; the awful tortures of the stake awaited him if taken alive; and to take him alive was unquestionably the design of his pursuers, since they had neglected to fire upon him from a distance which would have made their aim fatal

Casting away his rifle, as only an incumbrance which could not serve him in this strait, he bounded forward with renewed energy; and with a bare hope of life before him, he fled with a speed that few could equal—slightly gaining upon the fleetest of his foes—but not sufficiently, during the whole race, to take him beyond the easy reach of a rifle ball.

Nearer and nearer he came to the rushing and foaming stream; and as he heard the roar of the waters, and saw but a few seconds could intervene between the present and the awful leap which might save or destroy him, his heart beat wildly, and his whole frame seemed to tremble with the intense concentration of his mind upon the fearful venture.

Nearer and nearer he came; louder grew the roar of

the waters; the awful chasm gradually yawning before him, and the white spray of the fearful torrent rising to his view; the Indians yelling behind, and his only hope here; nd then, contracting his muscles, as his feet lightly pressed the precipitous rock, and throwing into them all the power of his concentrated will, he leaped into the air, like a bounding ball, and landed safely upon the other rocky verge of the abyss, striking a little below the height from which he sprung, but passing a clear distance of twenty-two feet between the mural shores.

Instantly grasping some bushes which fringed the verge of the awful chasm, to prevent himself from falling backward into the seething stream, the gallant captain stood for a few moments, panting from his exertions, and striving to recover his breath for still another flight.

In those few moments the Indians appeared upon the opposite bluff, expecting to find that he had been dashed to pieces upon the rocks below; but on discovering him safely on the opposite side, their astonishment was so great as involuntarily and simultaneously to draw from them some two or three short, approving whoops—forgetting in their first surprise that he was clearly beyond their reach, and not seeming to recollect it till he had begun to vigorously climb the ridge above him in his further efforts at escape. Then drawing up their rifles, with a quick aim, they poured in upon him something like a regular volley—

A LEAP FOR LIFE.

most of the balls whistling close around him, and one of them lodging in his hip and inflicting a severe and painful wound.

Notwithstanding this, the gallant fellow continued his ascent, and, on reaching the top of the ridge, gave a yell of defiance, and disappeared on the other side.

Captain Brady was now aware that the Indians would have to make a considerable circuit in order to reach him; and had he not been so severely wounded, he would have considered his escape as almost certain; but knowing he would still be followed, and finding his wound very painful, and the cords of his leg fast stiffening, he cast about him for some place to secrete himself from their search.

After running a short distance, he discovered a pond, and, near the shore, a large oak which had fallen into it; there might be nothing better than this; and hurrying forward with all his might, he boldly plunged in, swam under water to the tree, and came up beneath the trunk and among the branches, in such a manner as to be barely able to breathe without exposing any portion of his person to his enemies.

Here, in a state of mind which may be imagined but cannot be described, the gallant borderer remained for a long time, watching his enemies as they collected one by one along the shore at the point where his bloody trail had disappeared in the water.

Still resolved upon finding him, either living or dead, the savages were by no means disposed to give up the search; and after running along the shore for a considerable distance, on either side of his trail, to ascertain if possible where he had emerged from the water, several of the party plunged in, swam out to the oak, and actually seated themselves upon it, while they conversed in their own language, which he understood, concerning his wonderful escape.

At last, with such feelings of joy as no one not similarly circumstanced might comprehend, he heard them state their belief that he was drowned, and his body lost to them by being sunk in deep water; and soon after this, to his still greater joy, they quietly returned to the shore, and one by one all gradually disappeared.

Remaining in his uncomfortable position till he considered it safe to leave it, the wounded captain himself then swam back to the land; and weary, lame, and hungry as he was—alone, and without a weapon for his defence—he set off on his long, tedious journey through the wilderness for his own home; which he eventually reached more dead than alive; and where, to his great gratification, he found the companions of his perilous expedition already returned in safety.

This has truly been considered one of the most wonderful adventures of a region teeming with adventure; and to this day the pond in which the captain secreted himself bears his name; while the rocky chasm of the Cuyahoga, across which he made his desperate spring, is known far and near by the name of "Brady's Leap."

Love Triumphant.

If there is any one who needs the philosophy of this world's changes to make him wiser and better, by bringing hope to his despair, or humility to his pride, let him take a given number of individuals, and a given number of years—say twenty of each—and observe the condition of the different parties at the beginning and end of the time that is named. The result in all cases will be astonishing—in many it will be wonderful.

If old enough, reader, think back twenty years, and see where and how you stood in the world then, with nineteen others, selected at random from all you then knew. Take the names that first present themselves to your memory, and write them down, with the condition and prospects of each individual annexed; and then, underneath, write the condition and prospects of each at the present moment; and if you find not the result almost startling, and full of moral philosophy, then has time dealt gently with you and your friends, and you require not the lesson which would otherwise be taught.

Twenty names and twenty years! Ah! here they come—substance and shadow—the living and dead; but oh! how great, how startling, the change between that time and this—the past and the present!

Foremost of the group, I behold a bright, gay, fascinating and beautiful little being, who seemed born to love and be beloved. Her promise was a golden future of joy—her reality an early rest in the dark, cold grave. Nineteen years has her mortal form reposed in the quiet churchyard, and few now living remember the name she bore.

Next I recall an aspiring youth—proud, wealthy, and ambitious—bending his whole energies to academic honors and collegiate distinction. His promise was a brilliant career, with living applause and posthumous fame—his reality a loss of sight, mental disease, and a suicide's death.

The third comes up before me a poor, pale, blue-eyed cripple, whom one loved, a few pitied, and the rest despised. His promise was a short and miserable existence—his reality an honorable position, great wealth, and plenty of what the world calls friends.

And so I might go on, disposing of the number one by one; but there are two whose names rise together and blend in my memory, and who may more properly fill the limits of my space—for theirs is a history "to point a moral and adorn a tale."

Twenty years ago, then, a slender, pale young man, thinly but decently clad, was one cold, autumnal evening hurrying his steps over the ground that divided his own humble home from the large and somewhat aristocratic dwelling of a neighbor. As he drew near the mansion, which loomed up white, and seemingly cold and proud, in the frosty, star-lit air, the pale features of the young man flushed, and the hand that timidly knocked at the door trembled not a little. The door, however, was almost immediately opened, by a blooming, beautiful girl of eighteen, who said, in a rather quick and apparently excited tone:

"Ah! Walter—so it is you! Walk in!"

"I hope I see you well this evening, Mary!" returned the young man, in a slightly tremulous tone, that seemed to result from strong but partially suppressed emotions.

"Yes, I am well," replied the girl, hurriedly, as she closed the door and led the way to the sitting-room, where she motioned her guest to be seated, though without showing any inclination to sit herself. "You received my note, I suppose?" she interrogatively asserted, in a quick and flurried manner, hastily turning her flushing features from the keen scrutiny of him she addressed.

"Yes, Mary Ellsworth," replied the other, more slowly and distinctly, "I received a line or two from you, saying all the family would be absent to-night except yourself, and you desired to see me alone for a few minutes."

The young man paused, keeping his fine, hazel eyes steadily fixed upon the other, who now, with averted head, seemed much embarrassed and disconcerted. Stepping forward a few paces, she dropped into a chair, and, still without reply, appeared to busy herself in looking at the jeweled rings on her fair, soft, lady-like-fingers.

"Mary," spoke young Walter Harwood, after an impressive silence of more than a minute, "what is the meaning of this?"

She played nervously with her fingers, but still remained silent.

"Mary," continued Walter, placing a chair and seating himself in such a position that he could catch a partial view of her features, "let me remind you exactly how we stand in regard to each other; and then speak frankly, and say why you sent for me!"

He paused a moment, passing his hand rather quickly and nervously along his high, white forehead, and up through his dark, clustering hair, and then proceeded:

"I am four years your senior, Mary, and have loved you from infancy. It was my delight as a child, when you were a mere infant, to hold you in these arms; and even then, young as I was, and strange as it may seem, I often prayed that I might grow up a strong man, and be ever able to support you and protect you through the journey of life.

"We were playmates when little—we grew up companions—and there was never a period of your life that I did not love you, and daily pray to be loved in return. But your father was rich, and mine was poor; and as I grew older, I learned to feel the distinction which existed, and still exists, between the families of Ellsworth and Harwood; though I will do you the justice to say, that I do not believe you ever intentionally made me perceive the difference I allude to; but I did see, know and feel it; and though loving you almost to madness, I dared not venture to tell you so, lest my motive might either be thought mercenary, or myself too presumptuous, and thus all my brightest hopes and fondest dreams be in an evil moment blasted.

"But why dwell upon this which I have many times told you already? Rather let me come to the point at once.

"About one year ago then, Mary," the young man went on, with deep feeling, while his listener grew deadly pale and trembled violently, "such an opportunity presented itself for declaring my passion, that to delay it longer seemed flying in the very face of fortune; and carried away by an almost uncontrollable impulse, I poured out my very soul to your listening ear, and received in return such assurance of your affectionate regard, to call it by no stronger term, that I went home the happiest being in the wide, wide world. Ah! Mary—Mary—you may not love me now—you may never have loved me—but you will never be so loved by another as you are by the poor, miserable being who now addresses you.

"Well, I went home happy, as I have said—but how long did my happiness last? The very next time I met you, you seemed troubled and displeased; the second time you were dignified; the third reserved; the fourth cool; the fifth cold; the sixth you scarcely noticed me; and then we ceased speaking altogether, and I have been an unhappy being ever since. Now, after a long, painful lapse, your note has brought me to you, and I have come trembling with hope and fear. Oh! Mary—dear Mary, shall I venture to call you?—am I here to learn from your lips that the past is forgotten? and that henceforth I am to be again enraptured with your esteem, your regard, your——"

"Hold!" interrupted Mary, suddenly starting to her feet, and speaking in a tone that betrayed great agitation: "I have let you proceed too far, Mr. Harwood. In short," she hurriedly went on, "I find, on examining myself, I have not, do not, never can, esteem you as I could wish; and I sent for you to-night, for the purpose of telling you so, calmly, and asking your forgiveness for my unintentional deception; and to beg you will go and forget me—that you will go in a friendly spirit, and have no harsh and bitter feelings rankling in your heart. I would like your good opinion as a friend, and as a friend I shall always be pleased to meet you; but a warmer feeling it is not in my power to bestow."

"Can this be true? and am I thus suddenly made wretched forever!" groaned young Walter Harwood, as he buried his face in his hands, and rocked to and fro in an indescribable agony of mind.

For a few minutes there was not another word spoken—the young man swaying to and fro and breathing heavily—and the fair maiden watching him with features pale, anxious and troubled.

"Mary," said Walter at length, raising a face so altered and ghastly that his fair companion fairly started with surprise and alarm, "answer me two questions, truly, as God is your judge! First, has either of your parents ever brought to your view the difference between yourself as an heiress, and myself as a poor and humble young man?"

"I cannot deny, Walter," returned Mary, in great agitation, "that something has been said to me on the subject."

"Secondly, then," pursued the other, "is there any one you esteem, or love, more than you do me?"

"I - I—would rather not answer that question!" replied Mary, turning away her head in confusion.

"Enough!" rejoined Walter; "I am answered. I knew that Henry Wilder had been a somewhat regular visiter here for the last six months; but I did not allude to it sooner, because I feared you would think me captious or jealous. I understand all now!" he continued, rising and presenting his hand, which the maiden took almost mechanically. "Farewell!" he added, in a faltering voice, his trembling form and quivering lips betraying his deep and painful emotions. "Farewell, Mary Ellsworth! it is not likely we shall ever meet again. Yet one word of caution before we part! Beware of him I have named! He is a mere adventurer, seeking you for your wealth. He is not a true and honest man, and I speak from personal knowledge. Oh! give him not your hand and heart, as you value your peace and happiness! which will always be dear to him you now reject. God bless you, and prosper you, and guard you from the misery I now suffer, shall ever be the prayer of him who now bids you an eternal adieu!"

Saying this, he gave the hand he held a strong, nervous pressure, and rushed madly from the presence of the fair being he so wildly worshipped: who, for a few minutes, remained as one speechless with a strange surprise, and then gave way to her emotions in a flood of tears.

A week later it was known to all in the vicinity, that Walter Harwood had gone abroad, perhaps never to return. Three months later, a gay bridal party assembled at the mansion of 'Squire Ellsworth, to witness the beautiful heiress give her hand to him against whom she had been warned.

Nineteen years passed away—a short period or a long one, according as existence has proved bright or gloomy, happy or miserable—and in a Southern city, which shall be nameless, the Governor of the State sat reading in his library, when a servant in livery announced to his Excellency that a lady in black most urgently craved a few minutes audience.

"Conduct her hither," replied the Governor; and as she appeared, he rose, advanced a few paces, politely handed her a seat, and resumed his own.

The lady, who was dressed in deep mourning, with a black, heavy veil entirely concealing her features, trembled violently, as she hurriedly but silently reached forward a paper to his Excellency, which he quietly and courteously received.

"This," he said, after a few minutes of silence, during which he was engaged in unrolling and perusing a lengthy document, "is a petition—signed, among others, by quite a number of respectable and influential citizens—praying for the pardon of one Thomas Calcraft, lately convicted and sentenced to the penitentiary for the term of five years, for the crime of forgery. Madam, what is this man to you?"

"He is my husband, your Excellency," faltered the woman, trembling nervously.

I am sorry for it, madam—because it is hard for a man of feeling to deny the petition of a wife in behalf of him she has solemnly vowed to love and honor; but my sense of duty becomes paramount to feeling, and I must refuse your prayer. This man, though your husband, has no redeeming antecedents, and I am sorry to say I do not think he merits executive clemency!"

"Oh! say not so, your Excellency!" cried the poor woman, suddenly starting from her seat, and dropping down upon her knees before the Governor. "He always meant to do right; but he has been unfortunate; and in a moment of insanity—I can call it no less—insanity caused by want, and a husband's and father's desire to give bread to his starving wife and children—he wrote another man's name to a note, and got it cashed, intending to take it up before it came due; but was discovered, arrested, and is now groaning out his life within the dark, gloomy walls of a prison! Oh! pardon him, your Excellency! pardon him! as you hope God to pardon you; and I solemnly declare to you, **he** shall immediately leave the State, and never again offend against its righteous laws!"

While she was thus speaking, in a wild, impassioned

strain, she impulsively threw back her heavy veil, and revealed to the astonished gaze of her listener the pale, careworn, but still beautiful features of a woman fast verging upon forty. At the sight of this face, the Governor started back, clasped his hands, and, like one petrified with amazement, kept his eyes riveted upon hers, without further gesture or motion, and with even his breath suspended.

"Do my eyes deceive me! or do I behold in this kneeling figure the once happy Mary Ellsworth?" he exclaimed, the moment her musical voice ceased.

"Just Heaven! who speaks that name?" almost shrieked the kneeling petitioner, starting suddenly to her feet, clasping her temples with her hands, and fixing her eyes in wild amazement upon the ruler of a State.

"Mary," he groaned, "it is Walter Harwood you see before you—the once poor, penniless man, who always loved you better than his own life, but whose suit you rejected, and whose existence your rejection has ever since rendered miserable; for though the Governor of a State, Mary and blessed, as men call it, with honors, wealth and power, I am at heart a lonely, wretched being, who lives because it is a duty, and with only the hope of finding happiness in a better world. Would to God we had never met again!"

The interview between these two beings, after a lapse

of nineteen years, was, if any thing, more painful than the one already recorded. She freely told him of all her troubles and sorrows; how her parents, having been induced to sell their property to enable her husband to enter into some speculation, had soon been stripped of all, and had died in poverty; how her husband had since squandered all he could lay his hands on, and then, falling into habits of dissipation, had gradually sunk lower and lower, till crime had been added to his other faults and errors, and he was now, under the assumed name of Thomas Calcraft, suffering the penalty of broken laws; and, finally, how she herself, deserting him never, had, through good and evil report, in weal and woe, wealth and poverty, happiness and misery, clung to him as a guardian angel might cling to the wicked for his salvation.

"Oh! had you only so loved me, Mary!" groaned Governor Harwood, as he buried his face in his hands, and gave vent to his emotions in scalding tears. "It is well," he added, in a solemn tone, "that we can think God orders for the best! or else this life of trial and tribulation would not always be supportable."

When poor Mary Wilder left the presence of the Governor, it was with the assurance that her husband should soon receive a pardon, and the belief that herself and his Excellency would never meet again on earth

But "man proposes and God disposes." That night Thomas Calcraft, alias Henry Wilder, committed suicide, by hanging himself to the bars of his cell; and beside his dead body Mary Ellsworth and Walter Harwood met again.

The sequel may be told in a few words. One year later, the even round of twenty years, Governor Harwood was united, by the holy rite of marriage, to his first and only love; and it is the earnest prayer of all who know them, that their future may be blessed with a happiness that their past has never known.

Oh, what a strange world is this to him who sits down to note the changes of a few revolving years!

Mad Ann.

TOWARD the close of the last century, there lived in the interior of Virginia, in the very heart of the Allegheny mountains, a strange, eccentric woman, who bore the soubriquet of Mad Ann, but whose rightful name was Ann Bailey. She was a native of Liverpool, England, and in her younger, and perhaps better, days, had been the wife of a British soldier. How she found her way to this country, and why she chose to spend the remainder of her life in the backwoods of the frontiers, going on lonely journeys through the dark, heavy forests, and exposing herself to hardships and perils innumerable, was never probably known to many, perhaps to none beside herself.

During the wars of the early white settlers with their savage foes, Ann Bailey performed much efficient service for the frontier, in carrying messages between distant forts, over long and dangerous routes, as between Fort Young and Point Pleasant—a distance, as the way led, of some two hundred miles, up steep mountains and down dark valleys, through deep woods and dense thickets, and across rocky and dashing streams, and streams that could only be passed by swimming.

But Ann Bailey seldom went afoot and alone. She was the owner of a remarkable horse, an animal almost as sagacious as its singular rider. This beast she had named Liverpool, in honor of her birth-place, and she bestrode him in the fashion of a man.

She was a short, dumpy woman, with large, muscular limbs, and a full, bluff, coarse, masculine countenance; and her dress was such an odd mixture of the two sexes, that one would have been puzzled from her appearance, especially when mounted in the manner described, to say to which she belonged. She disdained a gown, as being altogether too feminine for her taste; but after putting on buckskin breeches, with leggins and moccasins, she effected a sort of compromise, by adding a linsey-woolsey petticoat; which was in turn again partially overlaid by the regular hunting-frock of the opposite sex; and her head, with its coarse, bushy hair, in that condition which nature must perforce display it when untouched by a comb, was surmounted by a raccoon cap.

Thus dressed, and armed with a rifle, tomahawk, and hunting knife—weapons which she could use with the skill and strength of the best woodsman of the day—Ann Bailey, though a woman, was no mean antagonist against either wild beasts or savages.

She likewise had a few other qualifications, which belong almost exclusively to the sterner sex. She could swear like a trooper, drink whiskey like a bar-room lounger, and box with the skill of a pugilist. She was withal rather intelligent, could read and write, and could narrate her wild adventures, trials and sufferings, with a power and pathos that alternately thrilled, charmed, and deeply affected her sympathizing listeners, the simple and single-minded settlers among whom she made her home.

Her strange appearance and eccentric ways led the mountaineers to bestow on her the appellation of Mad Ann—but they loved rather than feared her, and she was always a welcome guest beneath their sheltering roofs and at their humble boards.

One cold, autumnal night, when the frosty breeze swept sharp and keen over the high mountains and through the deep valleys around the almost isolated station of Fort Young, and while most of its inmates were sitting half dreamily before their blazing log fires, there came a series of loud, impatient knocks upon the gate of the pallisades. For the moment these sounds startled all, both old and young—for in that lonely region those were days of peril to the little band of pioneers who had boldly ventured thither—and the arrival of a stranger was an event to be followed by a feeling of peace and security, or by a general excitement and alarm, according to the report of the newcomer of good or evil tidings.

"Who's there?" challenged the sentry on duty.

"Mad Ann!" returned a loud, gruff voice.

All had listened eagerly for the response, and breathed freer when it was heard—though the news might still be either good or bad—and several of both sexes went forth into the area, to meet and welcome the messenger.

As the sentry threw open the gate, the heroine of a thousand perils, astride of her coal-black palfrey, and with her rifle over her shoulder and her knife and tomahawk in her belt, rode quietly into the station, and, without deigning a reply to the dozen eager questions concerning the news, dismounted deliberately, and strode silently into the largest cabin of the row which formed one side of the station.

As she came to the light of the fire, however, there arose several quick exclamations of surprise and alarm, from those who were there and those who followed her; for it was immediately discovered that her face (and much of her person) was covered with blood, which was even then slowly oozing and dropping down from a long, ugly gash that crossed the upper portion of the left temple and extended from her forehead to her ear.

"Good heavens! what's happened?" exclaimed one.

"There must be Injuns about!" cried a second

"Is there danger for us?" demanded a third.

"Speak!" almost shouted a chorus of excited voices.

Mad Ann gave no heed to any, however; but taking the best seat in front of the fire, she bent partly over it, and, with hands extended to the cheerful blaze, and eyes fixed steadily upon the glowing coals, proceeded to warm herself with the indifference of one who was not aware of being in the least degree an object of interest.

But those around her were too much excited to remain quiescent; and though fully aware that her eccentricity would keep her silent till the whim seized her to talk, they still continued to importune her to reveal what all were so anxious to know.

"See here, folks," exclaimed Mad Ann, at length, drawing the back of her large, rough hand across her face, to clear away some of the blood, and looking ghastly and hideous, as she turned her eyes glaringly around upon the group, who instinctively drew back a pace, as if fearful of a sudden assault: "See here, folks," she repeated, slowly and deliberately, but adding a wicked oath—"if you don't know me well enough to know that I won't tell you any thing till I get ready, you don't know me as well as you ought to, and I'll just keep my mouth shut for a month to l'arn you."

"Look you, Ann," replied a large, strong, robust man, the commander of the garrison, "if this here matter only consarned you, we'd give you two months, and say nothing; but if thar's Injuns about, we ought to know it at once, and be gitting ready to defend ourselves."

"Put up Liverpool, and fodder him well, and fetch me some whiskey,—quick!" rejoined the strange woman, turning again to the fire, and deigning no reply to the last speaker.

Knowing that the shortest way to her favor lay in obeying her instructions, two or three of the group bestirred themselves actively; and presently it was announced that Liverpool was in the best of quarters, and that Mrs. Ann Bailey would much honor her friends by drinking their healths, the speaker at the same time presenting her a pewter cup containing nearly half a pint of her favorite beverage.

Mad Ann seized the cup, looked steadily at its contents for a few moments, and then poured it down her throat as if it were so much water. She then turned her attention once more to the fire, but had not watched it many minutes, when she suddenly burst into a loud, hoarse laugh, and exclaimed:

"Cap'n Bolder says if there's Injuns about, he ought to know it. Why, there's Injuns about somewhere most always, as Mad Ann knows to her cost; but there's been a few mean, sneaking devils right nigh, as you can all tell from these here;" and thrusting her hand into the bosom of her hunting-frock, she drew forth, and displayed triumphantly to the astonished gaze of those around her, two Indian scalps, from which the fresh blood was yet dripping.

"Ha! ha! ha!" laughed Mad Ann; "did you ever see a cleverer sight than two such topknots, took by a woman's hand? Beat that if you can, you big, robust, blustering male fellows, who call yourselves the lords of creation! Do more'n that, and show it, any one of you, and I'll eyther beat you ag'in or stand treat. But it's your treat now, my masters, and so fetch on the whiskey."

Another drink, nearly equal to the first in quantity, put Mad Ann in a good humour and communicative mood; and bidding the anxious and excited parties around her get seats and listen, she waited till all had complied, and then began and told her story in her own peculiar way.

"You see, Cap'n Bolder," she commenced, addressing individually the commander of the station, "I left here to go to Point Pleasant, to carry a message from you to the Cap'n there somewhere about the last of August, or the first of September, and a right dreary time I had on't."

"And what news do you fetch from thar?" inquired the commander, thinking there might be something important for him to know.

"See here! am I telling this story, or you?" inquired Mad Ann, deliberately folding her arms and looking steadily at the other.

"You, in course."

"Then," rejoined Mad Ann, with another wicked oath, "just s'pose you keep quiet and listen."

She then proceeded, in a kind of wild, rambling, incoherent manner, to give an outline sketch of her long journey out and back—what she had seen, what she had heard, what she had felt, and what she had suffered—while her listeners, eager for the sequel, were obliged to wait, with what patience they could, till she came to it in her own time and way.

But once she had fairly launched herself upon the incident of deepest interest, her whole appearance and manner changed, and she drew the closing picture with that graphic power for which she was at times remarkable.

"It was about five miles back from here," she said "just as dark was setting in, that I first got warning of danger. I always have warning when there's danger about—not from man—not always from beast—not from winds, and trees, and earth—things I can hear, and feel, and see—but ——"

She stopped, looked around mysteriously, and then, lowering her voice, added, with a strange impressiveness that caused more than one of the superstitious listeners to shudder:

——"From the t'other world.

"Yes," she resumed, "something whispered me, 'There's

danger about;' and I whispered it into the ear of Liverpool who answered me by raising his head and snuffing the tainted air.

"I rode on further, with my eyes all about me; and then something come and touched me—something from t'other world—and I knew the danger was nigh and great—for when something from t'other world touches us mortals, it's always for a last warning before death.

"Then I got down ever so gentle and quiet off the back of Liverpool, and told him in a whisper he mustn't run away; and if his poor old mistress didn't ever come back to him, to go on to Fort Young—where the kind folks, who'd always been good to poor old Mad Ann, God bless you all for it—would see that he'd never want for attention and care; and the bonnie black beast (b'ess his noble heart!) answered me with a rub of his nose and a whinney, that said he understood me and good-bye as plain as any human could.

"Then I started on afoot before the beast, and kept looking sharp all about me, till I seen the twinkle of what might have been a dreadful demon's eye in the black wood before me—but which wasn't, that I knows on—but the light of a fire, about which was three painted Injuns, that fetched al. my blood to b'iling with rage and fury.

"'They musn't live to work mischief!' said I; and I went creeping, creeping, creeping, toward 'em, with my rifle leveled forward for a sudden aim, and my tomahawk and knife where my hands could grapple them for close work.

"Creeping, creeping, creeping, like a painter on to a deer—I come up, up, up—nigher, nigher, nigher—till I could see their eyes glisten as they talked, and their faces wrinkle as they smiled, and their teeth show white as they laughed—whilst they toasted their meat at the fire, and eat it like hungry men—and then something whispered to me and said:

"'Ann Bailey, them beasts of men are in the road to take your life, and you must eyther kill them or die yourself.'

"'Yea, Lord!' I answered the spirit voice: 'even so will I kill or die!'"

"And I raised my rifle, and looked along the barrel, and seen the sight, by the light of the ruddy fire, cover the eye of the middle one, just as he was raising a piece of meat to his opening mouth; and then I pulled the trigger, and sent the bullet whizzing through his brain. And then wildly mad with a kind of fiendish joy, I bounded forward, crashing through the bushes, and shouting as I went:

"'The Lord fights for Mad Ann, and she must slay all before her!'

"But I like to have spoke with the vain boast of a silly

woman, for I 'spected the t'other Injuns to run. One did, but t'other didn't; and when I jumped forward into his camp, the snap of his gun, with the muzzle not more'n ten feet from my breast, showed me how nigh I'd been to death without knowing it.

"Then, with a yell of fury, he threw down his gun, and leaped on to me with his tomahawk. I hadn't time to guard, or parry, it was so quick and sudden and surprising; but I did the best I could, and the blow came down without splitting my skull, as you see here, though it grazed the bone and stunned me some, and fetched me down on to my knees. Ag'in the weapon was whirled aloft, and another blow was coming; but, with all my might and strength, I jumped forward and wrenched the legs of the savage from under him, and he fell heavy by my side. He never got up ag'in—for my right arm was quick raised in wrath, and *my* tomahawk came down on to his skull and laid him quivering.

"I got up then, and took the scalps of the two, to prove my words—but the coward that run I didn't see ag'in. I went back for my horse, and here I am; and if you want to see the bodies of the savages, and get their arms, go out to-morrow and do so."

Such was one of the most remarkable adventures and exploits of Mad Ann, told, in her own peculiar manner, to a group of excited listeners. A search which was made by a party of hunters the next day, and which she herself guided to the scene of the tragedy, proved the truth of her statement so far as regarded the killing of the savages.

Mad Ann remained for a number of years in the vicinity we have named, even after the Indian wars were over, and spent her time in roving about from place to place, and hunting for wild beasts, whose skins supplied her with the means of procuring the few necessaries that her somewhat primitive mode of life required. She was, in the true sense of the word, a border heroine. She subsequently removed to the frontier of Ohio, and died, as for many years she had lived, in the great wilderness, deeply lamented by those who had reaped the benefits of her eccentric life of border deeds and border heroism.

The Daring Scouts

In the spring of 1794, while General Wayne, in command of the Northwestern Army, was occupying Fort Greenville, which he had constructed the preceding winter, news was brought to him that a party of Pottawatomies had surprised and destroyed the block-house of a small settlement not far distant, and massacred all the inmates except a young female, whom they had taken prisoner and were then supposed to be conducting to their village. This female, a Miss Eggleston, was the daughter of an officer of some note, who was a friend of Wayne's, and he determined, if in his power, to save her. At that time he had some two or three heroic little bands of spies, or scouts, attached to his division; and he knew if a rescue could be effected at all, the men to entrust with that important enterprise could be found among them, and them only.

Now it so happened that a small party of these scouts were at that moment in the fort, having come in the night previous with important information, and were preparing to set off again immediately. Sending for one of the most daring of these, Robert McClellan by name, who, though not the regularly appointed leader of the band, sometimes acted in that capacity when his commander was absent, the general briefly informed him of what had taken place, and asked him if he thought there was a hope of Miss Egglesston being rescued.

"I can't say as to that, Gineral," replied the scout; "but this I will say, ef it kin be done, I kin do it."

"How many men do you want?" asked Wayne.

"How big is the party?" inquired the other.

"From the report, I should judge there were twenty or thirty of them."

"Then it'll never do for us to make a regular stand up fight on't, Gineral, unless we has the cap'n and the others all along; and as they won't be in afore to-morrow, ef then, I reckon it's best to operate by sarcumvention; and the two that's here with me—Hickman and Hart—will be jest as good for that thar as a dozen more. Only put me whar I I can git on their trail, and ef the red niggers arn't too far ahead, I'll soon fetch a good report of *them*, ef I don't of the young woman."

"But you must bring a good account of *her!*" rejoined Wayne, in a positive tone. "It's to save *her* I send you; for she is the daughter of my friend, and her life and rescue are above price."

"Then we'll save *her*, Gineral," replied the hardy scout — "that is, ef the butchering varmints only save her themselves till we kin get to whar she ar."

General Wayne gave McClellan some further instructions, and then bade him set out immediately; and returning to his temporary quarters in the Fort, and informing his companions what was required of them, they at once set about preparing for their new adventure; and in less than half an hour, the three men were threading the intricate mazes of a great, dark forest, which then stretched away, unbrokenly, for many a long league before them.

With long and rapid strides—McClellan, the fleetest-footed hunter of his time, on the lead—they got over some twenty miles of ground, and reached the ruins of the block-house, where the massacre had taken place, just as the sun was setting. There was light enough to find the broad trail of the retreating Indians; and with no unnecessary delay they set out upon it, and advanced some two or three miles further, when the gathering night compelled them to encamp and postpone further operations till another day.

The night, however, passed off without any disturbance; and at the first streak of day they arose and resumed their journey; and ere the sun set again, they had travelled far upon the broad trail of their foes in a northerly direction.

It is not our purpose to follow them in detail. Suffice

it to say, that near the close of the second day, they reached a point where the trail forked, and it became necessary to make a careful examination, in order to decide which party had taken the prisoner with them. To the best of their judgment, the whole number of Indians was not much short of thirty; but they were not equally divided at the point of separation, as was evident from one trail being much larger than the other. They soon satisfied themselves that the girl had been taken with the smaller party; and this to them was a pleasing discovery, as it gave them more hope of being successful in her rescue.

This decided, they pushed on rapidly till night, and then encamped—proceeding on the following morning as before; and at the close of the third day, just as night was setting in, they came within view of the camp-fires of their foes. Waiting some two or three hours, until they thought the venture perfectly safe, they carefully proceeded to reconnoitre the Indian camp, which was in a small, pleasant, but heavily wooded valley, through which flowed a branch of the Wabash. Creeping up cautiously, under cover of some bushes, they beheld six Indians carelessly disposed around the fire—three of them lying down as if asleep, and the others sitting near together, conversing in low tones, occasionally laughing, and evidently totally unsuspicious of danger. A little apart, and bound to a tree, was the poor captive—a young and beautiful female—whose now pale and dejected features bespoke the despair of her heart, and, combined with her disheveled hair and torn and disarranged garments, rendered her an object of pity even to men hardened to almost every scene of suffering and distress.

Having fully ascertained the number and position of their enemies, and the fact that the prisoner, whom they had come to rescue, was still alive, the scouts drew stealthily back to a safe distance, and held a whispered consultation upon the manner of their future proceedings.

"I don't exactly like either of your plans," said McClellan, who had quietly listened to the propositions of the others. "It's our business to git the gal away—that's the Gineral's orders—and the way that we kin do that the best, is the best way. Now, instead of trying to steal thar guns, one o' you jest creep up and cut her cords, and start her off toward us as easy as you kin; but ef thar's an alarm, tell her to break for the nearest thicket, and we'll stand atween her and harm. I don't think thar'll be any trouble 'bout our coming out all right, for we've fout bigger odds afore to-day, without the 'vantage of a surprise, and licked 'em too."

After some further discussion, the plan of McClellan was acceded to as the best, and Hart was selected to enter the camp and release the girl—the others to be in readiness to pour in their fire in case of an alarm—which, to say the least, would be likely to throw the Indians into confusion, and give our friends so much the advantage—while the girl would be almost certain to escape, and her escape was what they now sought rather than the lives of the savages.

Having thus arranged the matter, the three scouts kept perfectly quiet and silent some two or three hours longer, and then began the execution of their final scheme. The fire, which the Indians had fed while astir, had now gone down to mere embers; but this only the better served McClellan's idea, as it would render Hart less liable to be seen in his approach to the prisoner.

Some quarter of an hour more was spent in arranging everything for perfect action, and getting into position, which they finally did in that stealthy and noiseless manner peculiar to men of their profession. Then leaving his two companions where their fire would be sure to be effective, Hart as cautiously and stealthily drew back, and glided round to the captive. He reached her without causing any alarm, but found her fast asleep, sitting on the ground, her back braced against the tree to which she was bound. To wake her, and warn her, and assure her that deliverance was at hand—without causing her to start, or cry out, and so arouse her captors—was a delicate task. He began, however, by whispering in her ear; and so continued till she gradually awoke, and heard, and comprehended his words; when her rare presence of mind came to his aid, and he was greatly rejoiced and relieved at her whispered reply:

"I understand you—I thank you—God bless you, whoever you are! Have no fear! I am a soldier's daughter, and will do whatever you bid me."

"Then jest as soon as I cut your cords," whispered Hart, in reply, "git up and foller me, and don't make a bit o' noise; but ef the Injuns do happen to rouse, don't get too skeered, but run for the nearest thicket, and leave me and my comrades to settle them."

He then cut her bonds; and quietly, but with trembling eagerness, she arose to comply with his directions; but the first step forward, her long-corded and benumbed limbs partially giving way under her, she stumbled upon a dry branch, which snapped beneath her feet.

Instantly one of the Indians nearest the tree started up into a sitting posture—when Hart, feeling himself called upon to act, suddenly presented his rifle at the breast of his foe, and lodged the contents in his body. As he fell back, the scout, with a yell of triumph and defiance, bounded over him to attack the next, the whole party being now fully aroused and alarmed. Snapping his pistol at the breast of the second, and finding it miss fire, Hart struck out with his tomahawk, but stumbled at the same moment, and, missing the warrior in the act of rising, fell heavily against him. The latter staggered, and was really much alarmed and confused; but comprehending withal that he had an enemy within his reach, he quickly grappled him, whipped out his knife, and plunged it several times into his body. He was in the very act of doing this, in fact, when a ball from the rifle of McClellan pierced his brain, and he fell dead over the dying form of Hart—Hickman at the same instant shooting down another—for with loud, terrifying yells, both had rushed upon the Indians at the same moment with their unfortunate companion.

There were now three unwounded Indians to two whites; and had the former known of their advantage, the day might have been their own; but they were surprised, alarmed, and half paralyzed with the thought that they were attacked by overwhelming numbers; and before they had time to recover, the smaller weapons of our heroes had done their work upon two more of them, the sixth one only making his escape with a yell of terror. The skirmish, from first to last, scarcely exceeded a minute; and probably no regular battle in the world ever showed such a proportion of the killed, to the number engaged, in so short a time.

But it was a dearly-won contest to our two surviving friends, and sad and gloomy were their feelings as they lifted their poor comrade from beneath his foe, and listened to the irregular breathings, which were soon to cease in death. The girl, who had not fled far, now returned and joined them in their grief, for she felt that the poor fellow had fallen in her rescue and defence. An hour later, the dying man expired in the arms of McClellan, rousing a little at the last moment, and speaking a few words, faintly:

"Good bye, boys," he said, "and remember me wherever you see the red niggers."

"We'll do that, Hart, you may rest assured," replied McClellan, in an unsteady tone; and over his mortal remains those two hardy scouts swore undying revenge against their savage foes.

Drawing the fair girl apart from the bloody scene, and assuring her that they were as ready to yield their lives in her defence as the one who had so fallen, they gave her a blanket, and persuaded her to lie down and get what rest she could, that she might be prepared for the long journey homeward, which would commence on the morrow. Then scalping their slain, and making prize of whatever they considered of any value, they sat down by their dead comrade, and passed the night beside him, rehearsing tales of adventures in which he had taken a part, and renewing their oaths of eternal vengeance against the whole Indian race.

At daylight the following morning they dug a rude

grave with their hatchets and knives; and having shown their final respect to their late companion, by interring his remains as well as their circumstances would permit, they set out on their return to the fort, which they eventually reached in safety, and where they delivered their rescued captive into the hands of General Wayne, who not only kindly thanked, but liberally rewarded them, and expressed a soldier's regret for the loss of their brave companion.

It may interest the reader to know that this same young lady—so providentially preserved at the general massacre of her friends, and so gallantly rescued at the expense of the life of one of those brave heroes of the wilderness—subsequently became the wife of an officer under Wayne, and the mother of one who now holds a distinguished position in the councils of the nation..

The Gamblers Outwitted.

The following story was narrated by a gentleman who desires his name withheld from from the public:

"Any man living on the lower Mississippi twenty years ago, who was not in favor of playing all sorts of games for all manner of sums, would have been at once pronounced no gentleman or a minister of the Gospel. I was myself not a little scandalized, on my first going South, at being asked by a gentleman to play cards for money; but universal custom is every thing in settling a man's mind upon the matter of right or wrong; and I regret to say I soon found myself as much disposed for the exciting sport as the most ardent of my companions, though never at any time so much attached to it as to play with a professional gamester.

"In this latter respect I materially differed from a friend of mine—a young planter by the name of Paul Rathbun—who, having become a great adept in the handling of cards, rather prided himself on the belief that he could outwit the most adroit gambler to be found; and he never went aboard a passing steamer without trying his hand with one or more of the chance-operating fraternity.

"Now Paul Rathbun and myself had agreed to take a trip to New Orleans, to enjoy a few week's pleasure and recreation in that great city of the South; and as he was going to take down a large sum of money, to meet some notes of country merchants falling due, his father, knowing his *penchant* for cards and adventure, called me aside, and requested me as a friend to have an eye to him and restrain him from carrying his proclivities to the extent of ruin.

"It was a cold, dark, stormy night that we embarked on board a downward steamer, from the then pleasant little town of Grand Gulf; and though we were in fine spirits, exhilarated to a highly talkative degree by a few parting glasses with the jovial friends who had seen us off, yet I felt nothing like intoxication, and was very much astonished and mortified to discover that my friend did, and within fifteen minutes after our appearance in the splendid saloon of the boat.

"What could it mean? Was it the effect of the liquor he had drank on shore? or had he been imbibing since? I had left him but a few minutes only; and now, on my return to the saloon from the guards, I found him almost reeling, and surrounded by a group of four or five dark-visaged, villanous-looking fellows, whom I believed to be pick-pockets, or gamblers of the lowest order, and with whom he was conversing with a familiarity that both astonished and vexed me. Whether sober or otherwise, I felt in duty bound to withdraw him from such company, and immediately approached him for that purpose.

"'Come, Paul, my dear fellow,' said I, quietly running my arm through his, 'let us retire to our state-room; I have something important to communicate to you.'

"'*You* have?' he replied with a strong emphasis on the pronoun, and partially turning his face to me, with a drunken man's quizzical leer. '*You've* got something to communicate, have you, old boy?'

"'Yes, Paul, I have something very important to tell you.'

"'That's a (hic) lie!' returned he, straightening himself up with drunken dignity, and winking at his delectable companions, who laughed approvingly, at my expense. 'You've got nothing to tell me—you only think I'm drunk, and want to be a father to me. But I'm not drunk yet, and you're not a going to be a father to me. Ain't I right, (hic) gentlemen, eh?'

"'Of course you are,' chorused the villanous group, with a general laugh. 'You want no father at your age.'

"'Ha! ha! ha!' laughed my friend, in drunken glee; 'it's funny enough, and I know you'll hic) laugh; but this old fellow is my paternal progeni- hic)-tor.' And griping my arm in a manner to cause pain, he began to push me around from one to the other, remarking to each 'I want you to know the old chap that's a father to me.'

"'Paul,' said I sternly, attempting to force him away, 'come with me.'

"He threw me from him with force, and made use of an insulting expression that I need not repeat.

"'Paul Rathbun,' I angrily rejoined, 'if you were sober, that remark should cost your life or mine.'

"'Oh, don't be afraid!' he rejoined, with a hiccough; 'I'm not so drunk as I look. I know exactly what I'm saying, and hold myself responsi-(hic)-ble for it."

"Grieved, angered, and mortified, I left him abruptly, and went out upon the guards. A furious northeaster was blowing, bringing wintry airs to a summer clime, but they felt delicious to my heated brow and burning temples.

"For half an hour I stood there, looking off upon the blackness, listening to the howling wind, driving sleet, coughing steam, and gurgling waters, but thinking that the whole pleasure of my trip, if not of my life, would be marred by the misfortune that had turned the brain of my friend. Suddenly it occurred to me that it was my duty to stand by and protect him till sober, let him be never so insulting, and forthwith I returned to the saloon.

"I found him, as I did not wish to find him, seated at a table, with a large pile of money before him, engaged in playing cards with the five villanous fellows in whose company I had left him. What could result from such a condition of affairs but his entire ruin, and the ruin perhaps of others?—for, as I have mentioned, he was taking down to New Orleans large sums for his friends, which would probably be as freely staked as his own money. And should I not, to a certain degree, be held accountable for this loss, since I had been empowered by his father to restrain him from the excess of ruin? It was certainly my duty to act, and my resolution was soon taken. Advancing to the table, I laid my hand upon his shoulder, and said, calmly but firmly:

"'Paul Rathbun, if you are intoxicated, this is no place for you, and I shall take you away by force; and if you are sober enough to comprehend the words of a friend, permit me to inform you, that you are in the hands of the lowest order of Mississippi gamblers.'

"The five strangers simultaneously started to their feet; and the one nearest to me said, in a low, threatening tone, fixing his eyes sullenly upon mine, as he thrust his hand into his bosom for a weapon:

"'Take that back, sir, and acknowledge us to be gentlemen, or I will have your heart's blood!'

"'Wait a moment,' said I, returning his gaze with an unquailing eye; 'wait a moment, and I will show you how I recant. Now you dare not touch me, let me say what I will, and for two reasons: first, you would lose your victim, and a few thousands; and secondly, what is of less consequence, you would all lose your unworthy lives; therefore, I boldly defy you to do your worst, and deliberately repeat here that you are gamblers and no gentlemen.'

"These remarks were made impulsively, under the excitement of anger, and with my hand upon a pistol, which I intended to use should I perceive the least attempt upon my life. What the consequences might have been, had not Paul Rathbun interfered, I cannot say; but he started suddenly to his feet, and, reeling forward a step, thus effectually covered my person with his.

"'Gentlemen,' he said to the gamblers, 'sit down, and don't mind this (hic) boy! If there's to be any quarrel with him, I'm the man for that. Don't let us spoil our night's sport to please him. There, that's (hic) right, gentlemen—sit down. And now, boy,' turning to me, 'go to bed, and don't bother (hic) yourself about matters too old for your compre-(hic)-hension. Here,' he added, producing a large pocket-book, as I stood looking sorrowfully into his face, considering what course was best to pursue: 'take this, Frank, and don't bother (hic) me. In there you'll find all the money that don't belong to me; and the rest's my own, and I'll do as I (hic) like with it. Take that, now, and go to bed—that's a (hic) good fellow!'

"I seized the pocket-book with avidity, thankful that I could get possession of what would save my friend from

"Hold! The first man that lays his hand on a dollar, I will kill as I would a dog."

See page 131.

after ruin and disgrace; and finding I could do nothing with him in his present condition, without resorting to force, I left him, as it were to his fate.

"But I did not retire to bed; it was impossible, under the circumstances, for me to sleep; and I spent hour after hour in alternately clambering over the cotton-piled deck, exposed to a cold, furious storm—in standing on the guards, dripping with rain—and in walking up and down the saloon, pitying the weakness of my friend, who still drank and played with men who had the same regard for him that so many wolves would have for a lamb.

One round after another of liquor was brought and drank, pack after pack of cards disappeared under the table, large sums of money changed hands continually, and still my poor, demented friend, as I considered him, sat among five human fiends, the victim of all.

"Almost wearied out with long-continued excitement and loss of rest, I had at last taken a seat some distance from the players, and, with my head upon my hand, was just giving way to an overpowering somnolency, when I was suddenly aroused, and much astonished, at hearing my friend exclaim, in that sharp, clear, cold, determined tone peculiar to him when carrying his point at the point of a Bowie-knife or the muzzle of a pistol:

"'Hold! The first man that lays his hand on a dollar, I will kill as I would a dog!"

"I started up, and beheld an unlooked-for tableau: The gamblers were all upon their feet, standing around the table, three with hands extended, as if to grasp a large pile of money, which one hand of my friend carelessly covered, while his other held death for the most daring in the shape of a loaded pistol. He was still seated in his chair, his cold, penetrating gray eye looking up unflinchingly from under his massive brow, and turning deliberately with his pistol from one to the other of those dark men, whose swarthy features expressed astonishment, rage and fear.

"'It's a swindle!' said the boldest, suddenly, with his hand still extended as if to grasp the money. 'You never got them cards honest; that money's ours, and we'll have it!'

"'Take it!' said Paul Rathbun, quietly, without the change of a muscle; and with the words there came a sharp click, as his thumb drew back the hammer of his pistol.

"By this time I was standing at his back, with a Bowie-knife in my teeth, and a cocked and levelled pistol in either hand.

"'Be modest, fellows, and only claim what is your own,' said I.

"'Ah, Frank, are you there?' cried Paul, with animation, partly turning his head to me, though without removing his eyes from his antagonists. 'A thousand pardons, my dear fellow, for the way I abused and insulted you! So you thought I was in liquor, eh? Ha! ha! you may be pardoned for that, considering that these shrewd sharpers thought the same. But it was necessary to deceive you, my boy, in order to deceive them—and so forgive me! Drunk, eh? I tell you, old gamblers, you are caught for once, and by a mere boy—for I am only a boy; and so if you were to play with *men*, where would you be? It is a swindle, is it? and no honest hand? Look there, Frank!—four aces against four kings! Is not that honest, eh? And see, my dear fellow, what those four aces won— seventeen hundred dollars all the money these rascals have, and enough to pay our trip to New Orleans and back. Go to, for shame! five against one, and that one a youth! Do me the favor to play next with a mere child, and never pride yourselves on being the equal of *any* Southern gentleman of *any* age.'

"While Paul Rathbun continued to rattle on in this manner, sometimes addressing me and sometimes the gamblers, several gentlemen came out of their state-rooms and gathered around us. On learning the true state of affairs, they greeted with a laugh the discomfited villains, who, in attempting to fleece my friend, had themselves been fleeced by him.

"Though at first evidently determined to fight for their

money, the gamblers soon became cowed by the appearance of numbers, gradually slunk away, with crestfallen looks, and finally left the boat at the next landing, swearing vengeance.

"Paul Rathbun hugely enjoyed what he termed his practical joke, but promised me he would never attempt the like again.

"Poor fellow! I believe he never did. At New Orleans he spent most of his downward winnings in charity, and was suddenly recalled home by a letter from his father, announcing the illness of a beloved sister. He left the city a couple of days before me, but I arrived first at his father's mansion. In fact he never arrived; and what became of him is not certainly known to this day. He had a state-room to himself on his upward trip, and one morning he was found missing, with blood on the sheet of his berth. It is supposed he was stabbed in his sleep, and his body thrown into the river. The murderer or murderers rifled his baggage, and probably robbed him of a large amount in money and jewels.

"But whether or not his death indirectly arose through revenge of any of the parties who figured in the scenes I have described, is a matter I have never been able to decide. All is mystery, and will probably ever remain so. Peace to his ashes!"

A Fight on the Prairie.

'It is a wild, glorious life for those who love the sports of the chase—the life of the mounted hunter on the great prairies of the Far West!" enthusiastically exclaimed a friend of mine, who had passed a portion of his life beyond what was then known as the borders of civilization.

"But then it has its perils and unpleasant passages, which sometimes make one wish himself safely at home!" I ventured to reply.

"True, we have our storms as well as sunshine," he rejoined; "but all joy has its sorrow, all good has its evil, all sweet has its bitter, else perhaps the first would pall Life is made up of variety and contrast; and so a man has more pleasure than pain, he is entitled, as things go in this world, to lay claim to happiness. Speaking of perils, though, by-the-by, and unpleasant passages, suppose I give you a rather striking incident in my chequered career?"

"By all means," said I; "the very favor I would have asked—nothing could please me better."

"Well, then, as I am one who always likes to come to

the facts, without any tedious preliminaries, suppose I jump at once into the very heart of my story?"

"All right—proceed."

"Well, then," pursued my friend—who, by the way, was a finely-built, athletic fellow, some thirty years of age, and one of the best horsemen I ever saw—"the incident I refer to, occurred during a buffalo hunt on what is known as the great prairies, up near the head waters of the Arkansas. A party of eight of us had opened our day's sport upon a small herd of buffaloes, and had begun the slaughter in the regular Western fashion—that is to say, by each singling out his animal, dashing up alongside on his fiery steed, discharging his holster pistols into the most vital part, and so following up the cow or bull to its final fall and death, and then immediately skinning it, taking a few select pieces for our camp fare, rolling up the hide, strapping it to the back of the saddle, mounting our horse, and dashing on again as before, leaving the remainder of the carcass to the cowardly *coyotes*, or small prairie wolves, which, with an instinct like that of dogs, seldom failed to follow in our steps,—we were thus engaged, I say, and I had become separated from all of my companions save one—whose animal, alike branching off from the herd, had taken the same direction as mine—when suddenly we were both startled by the cry of 'Indians!' and looking behind us, we saw, far away, some eight or ten mounted savages, bearing done for us with all speed, with similar parties chasing our friends in the distance, who were also scattered and flying in every direction.

"'By heavens! here is something more than fun!' cried young Summerfield, my companion, in alarm, instantly turning off from his wounded buffalo, and dashing up alongside of me. 'What shall we do, Leland—eh?'

"'Run or fight, I hardly know which!' said I, drawing up my horse for a momentary consideration, and sweeping the prairie with my eye.

"'Let it be a run, by all means!' he returned, in an eager, excited tone; 'it is our only chance.'

"'And what chance have we then?' said I, thoughtfully. 'These savages are doubtless better mounted than we, and will soon run us down; and it will only be fight or death at last—perhaps both. Doubtless if we were to dismount, make a kind of breastwork of our horses, and stand firm, the savages, after a few circles round us, a few grand flourishes, and a fascinating display of their equestrian skill, would leave us to ourselves—especially if, with a careful aim, we should happen to unhorse one or two of the most daring. Come! what do you say? We have our rifles already loaded; and we shall have time to load our pistols also before they get up; and the latter will serve us even better than the former should it come to a close encounter.'

12*

"'I think we can escape by flight, Leland,' returned Summerfield, in a nervous, agitated tone; 'and flight is my choice. But whatever we do, we must do quickly; for see! they are coming up furiously; and if we stand here three minutes longer, it will be too late to choose—there will be no alternative. If these were all, I would remain and abide the consequences; but if we permit ourselves to be surrounded, there is no knowing what moment the others yonder may join this party; and even you, sanguine as you are, cannot hope to long withstand such odds.'

"This last remark struck me with force; it would be the height of folly to think of holding out against a larger party than the one in chase; by flight we should probably draw them off from their companions, and thus have them to themselves, even if it came to a fight at last; and so I decided for flight.

"Our conversation had been very rapid, and our halt had not extended beyond a minute, during which time I had constantly employed myself in sweeping the broad, level plain with my eyes, and considering the chances of a successful run.

"Far, far as my sight could reach, in every direction save one, the blue horizon shut down to the level earth—the exception being a black point in the distance, not unlike a small cloud, which I believed to be a wooded elevation—one of the lower ranges of the great Rocky chain, thrown forward like the vanguard of an army.

"Over this plain, less than half a mile distant, but in a direction opposite to the black point in question, our mounted foes were swiftly advancing, yelling like demons; while away to the right, with horses and buffaloes mingled in strange confusion, our scattered friends were flying in terror, each hotly pursued by a small band of mounted savages. It was indeed a moment of peril, and a scene to make the hair rise with excitement, and the blood to course swiftly through the veins.

"'On!' I shouted—'to yonder distant wood! Our lives may depend upon our reaching that before our enemies.'

"And instantly setting our horses' heads in the proper direction, we buried our rowels in their flanks, and bounded forward like lightning, the Indians yelling even more furiously as they witnessed the result of our determination, and pressing even more eagerly forward in pursuit.

"Could we reach the point at which we aimed in advance of our pursuers? It was a long distance—many a long league; but then our horses were comparatively fresh; and though not, perhaps, all things being equal, of the same speed and bottom as those of our foes, yet sufficiently so, with the start we had, to give us hope.

"'At all events,' said I, 'we can shoot as quick, and as far, and as certain as the best of them.'

"'But not so many times,—for they outnumber us four to one!' returned my companion, who seemed more alarmed than it pleased me to perceive.

"'But once for each mark will do,' I rejoined; 'and if we find them gaining on us, it must be tried These savages are a cowardly pack, whenever they see certain death before them; and my word for it, if we can draw them away from the main body, and send a couple to their master, the rest will leave us to ourselves. Meantime let us load our pistols, and be prepared to take advantage of all the chances.'

"Accordingly, casting our bridle-reins over the high pommels of our saddles, we proceeded to put all our weapons in order, still spurring forward and keeping an eye to our enemies, who were pressing rapidly on, almost in a body, and, as I fancied, gaining on us slightly.

"We each had a brace of holster pistols, which would carry a large ball for the distance of thirty or forty yards, with the trueness and almost the force of a rifle; and having loaded these, reprimed our rifles, loosened our knives, and thus seen every thing in order, and well disposed for action, we somewhat quietly settled down, and gave our whole attention to the race.

"On, on, we flew! our gallant animals straining every

nerve, doing their duty nobly, and seeming as it were to take part in our hopes and our fears; and on came our pursuers, at the very top of their speed, eager for our destruction, and now and then causing us to thrill strangely with their fierce, demoniacal yells

"On, on, we sped—minute after minute—mile after mile; the dark spot, the haven of our hopes, rising a little to our view, but still seeming interminably distant; and our savage pursuers gaining on us perceptibly, and seeming to yell more triumphantly as they grew more certain of securing their victims.

"'Oh, my God! we are lost, Leland!' cried poor Summerfield, looking around in horror. 'Already the savages have shortened the distance one-half! and they will certainly be upon us before we can reach yonder wood, or even bring it fairly into view. See! Leland, see! our poor horses are blowing and foaming even now—while those of our blood-thirsty pursuers seem almost as fresh as when we started. We can do no more; and an hour, or even half an hour, will bring them up to us. Ha! those yells again! those horrid yells! they know we are at their mercy now! And such a death! shot down—butchered in the very prime of manhood—our mutilated bodies left to the ravenous wolves—our fates for ever unknown to our friends—oh, God! it is terrible! terrible!'

"'But why talk or think of dying, with so many chances

of life before us?' cried I, roused to something like anger by what I considered the paltry fears of my companion. 'Cowards are ever dying—the brave man falls but once.'

"'Oh, Leland,' replied Summerfield, turning upon me the most wretched, ghastly, wo-be-gone countenance I ever beheld—'do not blame me for what I cannot help! A horrible presentiment is on me, that my hour is at hand; and I have that to live for which makes life desirable; and my wandering thoughts have taken in the misery my friends will suffer when they shall discover that time brings not the wanderer back.'

"'Pshaw!' returned I, sharply, though not a little touched by his singular appearance and the peculiar melancholy of his tone; 'let us think of any thing now rather than the sentiment of a love-sick swain or a school-girl! With such fancies in your head, the savages will kill you, sure enough; but if you will only be the man I have always taken you for, you will live to go back and tell your own story.'

"'How can we escape—what can we do?' he dejectedly inquired.

"'Fight!' said I—'just what I intended to do in the first place. Our foes are gaining on us, as you say; we cannot outrun them; there is no alternative. But we have drawn them too far from the main body for them to get assistance; and now, if we act quickly, in concert, and with determination, the day may be our own.'

"'Yours it may be, Leland—but not mine!' he rejoined; 'for I know I shall not survive. However, do as you think best, and I will stand by you while I do live.'

"'See!' said I; 'there are two of our pursuers already some rods in advance of the others. Let us slack up gradually—so that they may suppose they are overtaking us from our exhaustion—and, when near enough to make our aim sure, wheel suddenly and try our marksmenship.'

"'I am ready,' replied my companion, with a melancholy shake of his head.

"We continued on about a mile further, by which time the foremost of our pursuers were yelling fiercely within the distance of a hundred yards.

"'Now is our time!' cried I. 'Rifles ready!—halt!—wheel!—fire!'

As the words were uttered, each was acted upon with promptness and decision, and at the last our pieces spoke together.

"We were both good marksmen, and had long practised the art of shooting on horseback, even when under full headway; so that the result astonished us less, probably, than it did the savages; who, not aware of our intentions, were not prepared for so sudden a shot. The one I had selected for my mark immediately fell from his beast, with a loud yell of rage and pain; but my companion, being not so sure in his aim, merely lodged his ball in the brain of the other's horse. The animal dropped suddenly, and would probably have have seriously injured any rider less expert than his own; but the agile savage cleared his back before he touched the ground, and immediately ran howling back to his advancing comrades.

"Fearfully wild and savage were the yells with which the Indians greeted our sudden display of heroism; and quickly spreading out on either side, they began to circle round us—bending over, keeping their persons concealed behind their horses, and letting fly their arrows from under the necks of their rushing animals.

"I now saw there would be little chance for us, if we dismounted, as we could not guard ourselves on all sides; and so telling Summerfield to load up as quick as possible, and then take a better sight than before, I proceded to do the same—we keeping our enemies at a distance, meanwhile, by a display of our pistols—and occasionally dodging our heads as an arrow whistled closer than usual past our ears.

"Just as we had succeeded in getting our rifles loaded, primed, and brought to our shoulders, ready for the first certain mark that should offer, one daring fellow came swooping round on the side of my companion. The next moment there was a flash, a crack, and the twang of a bow; and both marksmen fell; the Indian howling and rolling in the dust—poor Summerfield silently, alas! with an arrow drove through his brain between his eyes.

"I saw at once that he was killed—that his presentiment had proved too real—that I could no longer be of any service to him—and instantly I resolved to escape upon the horse of the Indian I had shot, which was still running at large between me and my foes.

"I had reserved my fire, and the savages knew it; and, warned by what had occurred, they took care to give me a wide berth—though still circling round, and sending their arrows from a distance; and suddenly spurring my horse forward, my foes retreating as I advanced, I was soon by the side of the animal I sought. Grasping his halter, I threw myself upon his back; and the next moment I was dashing swiftly across the plain—too swiftly for pursuit—to the utter chagrin of my enemies, who could only impotently howl forth their rage at the loss of their best racer and the foe they had counted as a victim. When fairly clear of them, I turned—gave a loud yell of triumph—fired my rifle in defiance—and then sped onward like the wind.

"At nightfall I reach Fort Bent, where I found two of my companions, who reported all the rest killed. But the next day, one by one, the others dropped in—all save poor Summerfield—the only victim of that day's chase—to whose memory we all sadly paid the tribute due to a companion and a friend."

An Arkansas Duel.

Some years ago, when horse thieves, negro stealers, gamblers, *id est omne genus*, were much more common in the Arkansas country than they are to-day, a party of six or eight borderers were one cool evening in November collected around the bar-room fire of the Jefferson House, in a place well known, but which it suits our purpose not to name. They were rather a rough-looking set of fellows, take them all in all; and at the moment we introduce them, were attentively listening to the wonderful exploits of one Kelser, who was known in those parts as the leader of a gang of bullying scoundrels—though the persons to whom he was talking, being comparative strangers, permitted him the rare enjoyment of telling his story, spreading his fame, and making himself a hero in a new quarter.

Winding up the detail of his sixth bloody duel and rencounter with an oath, he added, by way of a climax:

"I'm one of them as is never afeard of anything—white, black, or red—and all I want is, (displaying the hilt of his

Bowie-knife) for anybody to show me the fellow as says I is."

As he spoke, he straightened himself up, bent his round, bullet-head forward, and brought his face, with its pug nose, thin, sneering lips, and small, black, somewha bloodshot eyes, to bear upon each of those present.

No one made any answer; and each eye, if it did not quail, at least fell before the contemptuous glance of the braggadocio.

"Yes," he repeated, with another oath, "I'm one of them as is never afeard of anything, as I said afore; and to prove it, I'll tell ye of my fight with Dexter—Rash Dexter, as we used to call him."

And then, with the air of one perfectly satisfied that he was a hero, which no man dared dispute, he was proceeding with his story, when a tall, slender individual, in the dress of a Northern traveler, somewhat dusty, and with a pair of saddle-bags thrown across his arm, quietly entered the inn.

Approaching the bar—whither the landlord, who was one of the party at the fire, immediately repaired—the stranger mildly inquired if he could be entertained for the night.

"Certainly, sir," returned Boniface, with a cheerful air "A horse, I reckon, sir?"

The traveler nodded; and while he proceeded to divest

himself of his overcoat, and deposit his traveling equipments with the host, the latter called to a black servant, and ordered him to attend to the gentleman's beast.

"Supper sir?" pursued the landlord, with an eye to usiness.

Again the traveler nodded; and perceiving the fire was surrounded by the party already mentioned, and evidently not wishing to intrude himself among strangers, he quietly took his seat by a table near the wall.

Meantime he had not escaped notice—as no new-comer in such a place does; but while most of the company scanned him somewhat furtively, Kelser, the egotistical hero of his own bloody exploits, angered by the interruption, stopped his narration and regarded him with a savage scowl.

"Another —— Yankee—I'll bet high on't!" he said, in a sneering, grating tone, intended to disconcert, irritate, and insult the traveler.

The latter, however, seemed to take no notice of the remark; but turning to the table, upon which there chanced to be lying an old paper, he picked it up, as it were mechanically, and soon appeared to be deeply absorbed in its contents.

This quiet, inoffensive proceeding served to irritate the ruffian still more; but contenting himself for the time by muttering something about all Yankees being cowards, he turned to the others, and proceeded with his story—speaking somewhat louder than usual—especially when he came to the bloody details of his narrative—as if to arrest the attention of the stranger, and impress him unfavorably.

Finding the latter was not in the least disturbed, however, Kelser closed with a tremendous oath; and then, turning to the landlord, who had once more joined the party, he inquired, in a loud tone if he thought there were any "cussed thieves amongst 'em from abroad?"

"Hush!" returned the host, in a low, cautious tone; "don't go for to make a muss here, I beg of you—for such things ruin a man's house!"

"Do you want to take up on that fellow's side?" sneered the bully, fixing his black, snaky eyes upon the host, with an expression that made the latter quail.

"Oh, no, Kelser - I don't want to take anything up: and so I beg you won't say nothing to him. Come! let's take a drink all round, and call it quits."

"In course we'll take a drink," returned the other, with a coarse laugh; "and as it's to be all round, why, we'll have it all round."

Saying this, and rising as he spoke, he walked over to the inoffensive traveler, with a swaggering air, and, slapping him somewhat heavily on the shoulder, said, roughly:

"How d'ye do, stranger?"

The man looked up with something like a start, and displayed features in striking contrast with those of his interrogator. He seemed about five-and-twenty years of age—had a smooth, broad, high forehead—a rather Grecian slightly effeminate, and almost beardless face,—and mild, soft, pleasant blue eyes—the general expression of the whole countenance denoting one of a naturally timid, retiring, and unobtrusive disposition. Fixing his eyes upon the bully—rather with the air of one who did not exactly comprehend the cause of being so rudely disturbed, than with any thing like anger or resentment at the harsh, unceremonious interruption— he seemed to wait for the latter to volunteer some explanation of his uncivil proceeding.

"I said, how d'ye do, stranger?" repeated Kelser; "but you don't seem to understand the civil thing."

At this the crowd, in expectation of a quarrel, at once started up and silently gathered around the bully and the traveller. This seemed to startle the latter a little; and glancing quickly from one to the other, he replied:

"I am very well, if that is what you wish to know; but really I do not comprehend why you should be so solicitous about my health."

"There's a great many things that you —— Yankees

don't comprehend!" rejoined Kelser, with a chuckling laugh.

"What does this mean, gentlemen?" inquired the traveler, turning a little pale—his mild, blue eye beginning to gleam with a strange, peculiar light—at the same time rising and glancing from one to the other, till his gaze rested upon the troubled visage of his host. "What have I done that any one here should seek to insult me? Do you permit this, sir?" he added, addressing the innkeeper.

"He can't help himself," interposed the bully "If there's any body as wants to insult you, it's me; and Bill Kelser always does what he likes—any where, and with any body."

"And why do you seek to quarrel with a man that never saw or exchanged a word with you before?" quietly asked the stranger, his lips slightly quivering, either with fear or suppressed anger—a soft glow diffusing itself over his whole face—and the pupils of his eyes seeming to expand, and grow dark, and gleam even more strangely than before.

"Because I hate all you cussed Yankees; and whenever I sees one of your tribe, I always feel like cutting his heart out! for I am one of them as never knowed what it was to fear eyther man or devil!"

"Come!" interposed the landlord taking the bully by the arm—"we was going to take a drink, you know!"

"Yes, I'm in fer that, too!" said Kelser; "always good at eyther a drink or a fight, I am. You hear, stranger?" he continued, taking hold of the latter's arm somewhat roughly. "You hear, don't you? We're going to take a drink with the landlord; and if you can prove you're a decent white man, we'll *honor* you by taking another with you afterwards."

"I shall have no objection to treat, if the gentleman here think I ought to do so," returned the traveler, drawing himself up with dignified firmness, and speaking in a more positive manner than he had yet done; "but as for drinking myself, that is something I never do."

Nothing at that moment could have pleased the bully better than to hear the stranger refuse to drink; for he had long since resolved upon a quarrel with him; first, from natural malice; secondly, because he believed him one to be easily disposed of; and thirdly, because he might thus make a grand display of his fighting qualities, with little or no risk to himself—a very important consideration, when we bear in mind that all such characters are arrant cowards at heart.

"So you don't drink, eh?" he said to the stranger. "D'ye hear that, gentlemen?" appealing to the crowd. "Now every body round here has to drink or fight! And so (walking up to the traveler) you've got to do one or t'other—which shall it be?"

"I do not wish to do either," was the reply; "but drink I will not!"

"Then fight you shall!" cried the other, closing the sentence with a wicked oath, and at the same time laying his hand upon the hilt of his Bowie knife, and partly drawing it from its sheath.

"Do you intend to murder me? or give me a chance for my life?" inquired the stranger, with a coolness that astonished those who, looking upon his fine, delicate features, and slender figure, expected to see him shrink back in alarm and dismay.

"Give you a chance, in course!" returned the bully, in a less confident tone—for he too had expected to see the other succumb at once.

"Do you challenge me to a fair combat?" inquired the other.

"In course I does," blustered Kelser; "we don't do nothing else, in this country, but the fair thing."

The affair now began to look serious.

"Gentlemen," said the traveler, with a polite bow to the company in general, "you know how quietly I came in here, and how inoffensively I conducted myself afterwards; and you have seen how this man has ventured beyond all rules of good breeding and stepped out of his way to insult and fix a quarrel upon me. Now, then, as I am a stranger here—though one who has always heard much of Southern chivalry—I wish to know how many of you will agree to stand by and see fair play?"

"All! all of us!" was the almost simultaneous response. "You shall have fair play, stranger!"

The bully turned slightly pale, and seemed more discomposed and uneasy.

"I thank you, gentlemen, for convincing me, by your offer, that you are governed by justice and honor!" pursued the traveler; "and now I will prove to you that this man is a cowardly braggadocio, or else one of us shall not quit this place alive! It is understood that I am challenged to a single fight, is it not?"

There was a general affirmative response.

"The challenged party, I believe, has the choice of weapons, time, and place?"

Another affirmative response—the bully looking still paler and more anxious.

"Well, then, gentlemen, not being handy with the Bowie knife, and wishing an equal chance for life, I propose to leave the result to fate, and so test the courage of my opponent. Any man can stand up for a fight, if he knows he has the best of it—but only true courage can coolly face uncertainty—and my insulter boasts of fearing nothing. My proposition is this: Let two pistols be selected—one be loaded—and both be concealed under a cloth upon this table. Then my fighting friend and myself shall draw one by lot, point the drawn one at the heart of his foe, and pull the trigger—the unarmed one standing firm, and receiving the charge or not as Heaven shall will! Is not this fair?"

"Perfectly fair!" coincided all except Kelser, who demurred, and swore that nobody but a Yankee would ever have thought of such a heathenish way of doing business.

"Did I not tell you he was a coward—this fellow—who a few minutes ago feared neither man nor devil?" sneered the stranger, thus drawing a laugh from the company, who now seemed to be all on his side.

The landlord now objected to the affair taking place in his house—but on one of the company taking him aside, and whispering in his ear, he made no further opposition.

Accordingly, Kelser reluctantly consenting, one was chosen to prepare the pistols, which were immediately produced; and in less than ten minutes they were placed under a cloth upon the table.

"I waive all right to the first choice," said the stranger, as he and Kelser were brought face to face in their proper positions.

The bully, who was really very much alarmed—and who showed it in his pale face, trembling limbs, and quivering muscles—at once seemed to brighten at this concession; and thrusting his hand under the cloth, he drew forth one of the weapons, presented it at the breast of the other, and pulled the trigger.

It did not fire; but the stranger, who knew not that it was unloaded, neither blanched nor changed expression. The crowd applauded, and the bully grew ghastly pale.

"It is my turn now!" said the traveler, in a quiet, determined tone, fixing his blue eyes steadily upon the cowering form of Kelser.

This was more than the latter could stand.

"No, I'll be —— if it is!" he shouted; and instantly drawing the other pistol, he presented it, and pulled the trigger also.

But with a like result—for neither pistol was loaded—the company having secretly resolved to test the courage of both without bloodshed.

Throwing down the pistol with a bitter curse, amid a universal cry of "Shame! shame!" Kelser whipped out his knife, and made a rush for his antagonist. But the latter, gliding quickly around the table, suddenly stopped, and exclaimed:

"Three times at my life—and now once at yours!"

And with these ominous words he raised his arm quickly; the next instant there was a flash, a crack, and the bully fell heavily forward, shot through the brain.

The verdict of the jury, who sat upon the case, was justifiable homicide—and the blue-eyed stranger resumed his journey as if nothing had happened.

Would you know who he is? If we named him, we should name one who now holds a high official position; and for many reasons we prefer he should be known only by those who are already cognizant of the incident we have recorded.

The Poisoned Bride.

A NUMBER of years ago, a man by the name of Wallace, of Scotch descent, emigrated to Texas, and settled at a small inland village. His family consisted of himself, wife, daughter, and servant. This daughter, an only child, was then about eighteen years of age, and very beautiful—of a graceful figure, regular features, dark hair, and bright, merry, sparkling black eyes. She had received a good education, was well accomplished, and soon became the belle of the place. She had one fault, however—a fault common to most pretty women—she was a coquette.

Among her numerous admirers was a man some thirty years of age—tall, dark, and sinister of aspect—of whom report did not speak altogether favorably. He had come to the place a short time subsequently to the settlement of Mr. Wallace, and located himself at the village inn, where he gave out that he was a man of wealth. Nothing was known of his history, and there were none who could say he was not what he represented himself; but there were many who believed, for various reasons, that he was a professional gambler. He seemed to have plenty of money, and, so far as could be seen, conducted himself in an upright and honorable manner; but still he was not liked; there was something too stern and forbidding in the man to make him popular with the people around; and hence he was regarded with suspicion and distrust, and many stories were set afloat derogatory to his moral character. James Vaughan, for so he gave his name, seemed not in the least disturbed by these evil reports, but continued to conduct himself as if he believed that all were satisfied with the report which he gave of himself.

How it was that he first became acquainted with Helen Wallace, was not known to the gossiping portion of the village; but they were suddenly surprised to find him received at the dwelling of her father as a welcome guest; and it was soon rumored that he was treated by Helen herself with marked favor.

Time passed on—six months glided away—and still Vaughan remained at his old quarters; and still his visits to the house of Mr. Wallace continued, gradually increasing in frequency, until it was known that scarcely a day passed without a meeting between him and Helen.

Meantime there were many other gentlemen who called to see her, and whom she received with polite courtesy; but Vaughan, it at length became whispered about, was the favored suitor. She did not deny herself to any; but

he, as a general thing, was her escort wherever she went
He frequently rode out with her alone, and almost invariably accompanied her to all the balls, pic-nics, and parties
in the vicinity.

This finally settled the matter in the minds of many;
and it was not strange that a report should go abroad,
whether true or false, that the parties were engaged to
each other for the journey of life. This Vaughan himself
did not contradict, except in a laughing way, which only
tended the more strongly to convince the others of the
truth of their conjectures.

But the persons who had made such wonderful predictions concerning the future of Helen Wallace, were soon
destined to meet another surprise, which did much to
shake their faith in their own foreknowledge of events; for
one morning it was suddenly discovered, and rapidly
spread abroad to all concerned, that James Vaughan, the
still unknown and unpopular stranger, had disappeared as
mysteriously as he came.

Eager and earnest were the inquiries set on foot, to
know what had become of him. None could tell. The
landlord of the inn, on being questioned, declared that he
had settled his account in good currency, and had stated
that business required his absence—beyond which he knew
nothing—except that he had departed on foot, in the
night, ostensibly for a neighboring town, to take a public

conveyance for parts unknown. The Wallaces could give no additional information; and Helen herself laughingly declared that she was not his keeper, and knew not for a certainty that he would ever return.

Some few of the more wonder-seeking gossips undertook to raise an excitement, by stating that he had probably been secretly dealt with, and that his body might sometime or other mysteriously come to light; but even this supposition, greatly to their chagrin, was speedily destroyed, by ending parties to the town in question, where it was found that James Vaughan mortal, and not James Vaughan's ghost, had stipulated for a conveyance, and had taken bodily passage to Nacogdoches. This was all that could be gleaned, and all that could be known concerning the man who had been so much talked about; and the rest, being simply conjecture, soon died out a natural death.

Three months more passed away, and Helen Wallace was found to be just as gay and lively as ever—the only difference to note being, that she now had more suitors than before. Among these latter there was soon numbered one, supposed to be more of a favorite than the others, and who, at the time of Vaughan's departure, was not known in the village. This was a young man, some five-and-twenty years of age, of a light complexion, prepossessing appearance, and agreeable manners who had recently

11*

come into the place and opened a shop for trade. In that little village he was dignified by the title of merchant, and was supposed to be well-to-do in the world, if not absolutely wealthy.

Henry Cleaveland was a very different personage from his supposed rival, and made himself popular with all classes. He, like all the rest, appeared to be smitten with the charms of the gay Helen; and this time the interested gossips declared that he ought to be the favorite suitor, and did all in their power to bring about "the consummation so devoutly to be wished;" and apparently with success; for in a few months the report went abroad that he and Helen were engaged.

He had now become as attentive as his absent rival had ever been; and at length Helen herself announced that he was the chosen one, and that a certain day, sometime yet in the future, was fixed upon for the wedding. This was confirmed by her own preparations for the great event, and it was generally believed that the wedding would be a brilliant affair.

Not to dwell upon the matter, we may briefly state, that the anxiously looked-for day at length arrived, and was as auspicious of a happy ending as the believers in omens could have wished. It was near the close of summer, and the morning beamed as fair and beautiful as the fair and beautiful bride herself, and the blithe birds sung as gaily among the leafy trees as if their music had been attuned to celebrate a day of happiness for all who heard them.

A wedding in those days, and in that section, was oftentimes a more public affair than in the older and colder regions of the North. It was a merry-making day, when both young and old might congregate for festivity, hilarity and joy. The residence of Mr. Wallace was decorated for the occasion with evergreens and flowers, and his doors were thrown open to receive the visitors of the bride elect. Many servants were called into requisition, and long tables were spread under arching trees around the dwelling, and laden with substantial and fanciful viands for the enjoy- of the guests. But one of these, more beautifully and elegantly set out than either of the others, stood a little apart from the rest, and was the table of honor, or the table of the bride and her immediate friends.

As the day in question advanced toward meridian, the clergyman appeared—the bride and grooms, with their immediate attendants, took their places—and then, surrounded by a large number of interested spectators, the solemn ceremony was performed which united the happy couple for life. After this, as soon as the many and cordial gratulations were over, the bridal train led the way to the festive board, and all were soon engaged in doing honor to the hospitality of the provident host.

In the midst of these festivities, when the wines were

beginning to circulate, and toasts were being drank with smiling faces, and joyousness was pervading the whole assemblage—at this time, we say, like a dark cloud crossing the bright sunlight, and casting a shade of gloom over all—there suddenly appeared upon the scene the unwelcome person of James Vaughan. Each looked at him in surprise and then at each other, with a sort of mysterious wonder; and then all who could catch a view of the face of the happy bride, perceived that she had suddenly become deadly pale, and slightly tremulous, as if through secret fear.

There was no perceptible change, however, in the appearance of the new-comer; his features wore the same stern, cold, forbidding, sinister aspect. With a slight nod of recognition, he passed one after another of the different groups, and advanced directly to the table occupied by the bride, her relatives and attendants. Mr Wallace arose, and received him with a sort of constrained politeness, and introduced him to such other of the company as he now beheld for the first time. He bowed to each with that same cold formality which was characteristic of the man; and then advancing to the bride, he extended his hand, and said:

"Permit me to congratulate you! You know it was always my desire to be present at your wedding!"

Her face flushed crimson; and it was observed that she

trembled more than ever as she took his hand and in turn presented him to him who had now acquired the title of legal protector. A few civilities were exchanged between the different parties, and Mr. Vaughan was invited to become a guest at the board of honor. Room was made for him on the side of the table opposite the bride, and matters once more resumed their natural course; but not with the same freedom and hilarity as before—all parties seeming to act under deep restraint. If Vaughan noticed this, he appeared not to do so, but now and then exchanged a few civil words with those around him, and altogether conducted himself as one who believed himself a welcome guest.

At length, taking up a bottle of wine—which, it was subsequently remembered, he for some time held in his hand in a peculiar way, though it excited no suspicion at the time - he said, looking directly at the newly-wedded pair :

"Will you permit me to drink a toast with you?"

Receiving a quiet assent, he reached over, filled their glasses, and then his own.

"My sentiment," he continued, "is one which I know you will not refuse. Here is happiness through life, and only separation by death!"

The toast was a little singular, and the word *death* seemed *mal apropos* Why should it have been uttered then and there? It was the last word of the sentence—was pronounced distinctly, though without emphasis—but it unpleasantly fixed the mind upon what nobody cared to think about during a wedding feast.

The wine was drank in a kind of ominous silence, the bride turning a shade paler as the ruby liquid passed her lips; but it was noticed that the giver of the toast only slightly wet his lips, and, making some apology for his abstemious habits, set his glass down nearly full.

For a few minutes after this, nothing unusual was perceived. Conversation in all quarters was resumed; and it was evident that, in spite of the new presence, the old feeling of convivality was gradually being restored; when suddenly Mr. Wallace started up and called out, in a tone that sent a chill to every heart:

"Good God! what is the matter with Helen?"

The words brought the attention of all directly upon her, and more than one cry of alarm arose as the different guests sprung up in confusion.

The bride was indeed deathly pale—her eyes were closed—her beautiful features were working almost convulsively—and she was gradually sinking back in her seat and falling therefrom.

Her husband, turning to her in alarm, was in the act of reaching out his arm to save her, when he himself was suddenly seized in the same terrible manner; and both would have fallen together, had not some of the excited and now terrified spectators rushed forward and caught them.

For a few minutes a scene of the wildest confusion ensued. Young and old came hurrying up from the different tables, and crowding around in horror; and then, in a tremulous, fearful, shuddering whisper, dark words began to float through the collected crowd, and gradually swell out into one long, loud, wild, chilling, heart-piercing wail:

"*They are poisoned! poisoned! poisoned!*"

Then suddenly uprose another, a louder, and a wilder yell—the out-bursting shriek for vengeance, quick and terrible, upon the inhuman author of the dark and damnable deed.

But he was gone—James Vaughan was gone,—amid the awful excitement and confusion he had suddenly disappeared. Yet he must not escape!—the very earth would groan to hold upon her fair bosom such a monster!

"Ah! then and there was hurrying to and fro," indeed! with sounds of joy all changed to shrieks of woe! and sounds of merriment to yells of vengeance! Some ran away in horror, some wrung their hands with irrepressible grief, some hurried to seek medical aid, and others flew to arm themselves and follow the damnable author of all this misery.

We need not prolong the tale of woe. Three days later a solemn funeral procession wound slowly through that mourning village, following that lovely bride and her noble husband to their last dark and narrow home. But long ere the clods of the valley fell upon their coffins—"united in life, and in death not divided"—the breeze of the forest swayed to and fro the dangling body of their inhuman murderer, whom summary vengeance had overtaken, and sent, "all unanointed and unaneled," to his awful reckoning in the eternal world!

Attacked by Indians.

GENERAL LEE, in his Memoir of the Southern Campaigns, makes frequent and honorable mention of one Captain Joseph Kirkwood, of the Delaware line, whose regiment, at the battle of Camden, was reduced to a single company, of which the latter remained the commanding officer. Owing to the fact that Delaware could not raise another regiment, Captain Kirkwood, though truly deserving, could not by military rule receive promotion, and therefore remained in command of a single company throughout the revolutionary struggle—taking a gallant and distinguished part, not only in the bloody encounter at Camden, but also in the battles of Hobkirk's, Eutaw, and Ninety-Six.

After the declaration of peace, there being no other military service for this gallant officer, he removed with his family within the limits of the present State of Ohio, for the purpose of a permanent settlement. He chose a locality nearly opposite the present city of Wheeling, on the right bank of the Ohio, and erected his cabin on a commanding knoll, where, though greatly exposed, he remained unmolested for a couple of years. It was his intention to have built a block-house for further security, and he actually commenced one; but, from one cause or another, it was still unfinished in 1791, when the events occurred which we are about to relate.

One evening, in the spring of the year just mentioned, a small party of soldiers, under the command of one Captain Biggs, on their way into the country, stopped at the humble residence of Kirkwood, and asked permission to remain through the night, which was cheerfully granted.

The evening was spent in a sociable manner, in talking over the various events of the times—Captain Kirkwood depicting some of the more striking of the military scenes which had occurred in his experience, and also speaking, with a soldier's sensitiveness, of his chagrin at seeing officers younger, and of inferior rank, promoted over him, simply because his little State could not furnish a sufficient quota of men to give him the rank to which he was honorably entitled.

When the hour came for retiring, most of the men were assigned the loft beneath the roof, where, with the aid of straw and blankets, they disposed themselves very comfortably upon the rude flooring—Captain Kirkwood, with his family and the officer mentioned, remaining below.

All gradually fell asleep, and the house continued quiet

for several hours, not a soul dreaming that a merciless enemy was even then stealing through the surrounding woods in the darkness, bent upon the destruction of the building, and the death of all it contained.

Sometime late in the night, Captain Biggs, being restless, concluded to get up and take a walk in the open air. Passing leisurely once or twice around the dwelling, he advanced to the block-house; and, after examining it a few minutes, and wondering why the captain did not complete it, he turned his steps to the bank of the river. Here he stood a few minutes longer, in quiet meditation, looking down upon the dark, gliding stream—the rippling of whose waters, the slight rustling of the leaves, the plaintive hoot of the owl, and now and then the far-off cry of some wild beast, being the only sounds that broke the otherwise solemn stillness.

Once he fancied he heard a movement, as of some heavy body in the bushes near him; and knowing he was in a region of country not safe from Indian molestation, he started and turned quickly in the direction of the sound, looking steadily for some moments, and prepared for sudden flight, should he discover any further grounds for his partially aroused fears. But he neither saw nor heard anything to justify alarm; and turning away, he quietly repaired to the dwelling, re-fastened the door, laid himself down, and fell asleep.

Soon after this the whole house was startled by a loud cry of fire, which proceeded from one of the men who lodged in the loft. Captains Kirkwood and Biggs instantly sprung from their beds, and, rushing up the ladder, made the startling discovery that the roof was all in flames. A scene of the wildest confusion now prevailed—the men, thus suddenly aroused, and half choked with smoke, not fairly comprehending their situation, and the wife and children all shrieking with terror.

As soon as he could make his voice heard, Captain Kirkwood ordered the men to push off the burning slabs; and while in the act of doing this, a volley of balls rattled in among them, followed by those terrific yells which ever proved so appalling to those awakened by them in the still hours of night. Two of the men were wounded by the first discharge of the Indians—whose position, on the top of the block-house, situated still higher on the knoll, commanded the roof of the dwelling—and being greatly terrified, they all drew back in dismay, and some declared that their only safety was in immediate flight.

"Your only safety is in throwing off the roof before the whole house takes fire!" returned Captain Kirkwood, as he pushed in among them, and put his own hands actively to the work.

"We'll risk all that," said one, as he hurried to the

ladder. "I'm not going to remain cooped up here to be shot at."

"By heavens! you shall remain here till I give you leave to go down!" cried the enraged captain, as he sprung forward, seized the fellow, and threw him back violently.

"Let us pass!" cried two or three of the others, advancing toward the captain—the shots of the Indians meanwhile rattling like hail against the walls and burning roof, and their wild yells now and then resounding afar through the gloomy wilderness around.

"What! mutiny!" exclaimed Captain Kirkwood. "For shame, men! for shame! Turn back this moment, and do your duty! Is it not enough that we have a common enemy without, but we must have a civil strife within!"

"Who dares rebel against Captain Kirkwood's orders?" shouted Captain Biggs from below, whither he had gone for his rifle. "Shoot down the first rascal that attempts to escape, Captain, or refuses to obey you!"

"Quick, then, pass me up my rifle!" shouted Kirkwood, who kept his position at the head of the ladder.

"Ay, here it is," returned Captain Biggs.

Just as he was in the act of reaching it up, a ball passed through a small window, and, striking his arm, so disabled it that he let the weapon fall. Ripping out an oath, he picked it up with his other hand, and passed it to Kirk-

15*

wood. The moment the latter got hold of it, he turned to the mutinous men, and exclaimed:

"Now let me see who will refuse to do his duty! Back, there, and finish your work of throwing off the burning roof! The first man that attempts to leave this house, I swear to send this ball through his brain!"

The more mutinous of the number, finding the captain determined, and that there was no chance for them to escape, at once began to take an active part with those who were already doing their duty; and in a very short time the burning portions of the roof were dislodged and thrown to the ground—the Indians all the while keeping up a steady fire, and slightly wounding one or two more.

Thus far our besieged party had no opportunity to return the fire of the enemy; but now the latter, finding that their first attempt to burn the house was likely to prove unsuccessful, rushed forward in a body, with still wilder and more terrific yells, and at once began a vigorous assault upon the door and windows, the former of which they nearly forced open at the first onset.

The danger now being chiefly below, Captain Kirkwood hurried down, and ordered the greater portion of the men to follow, leaving a few above to defend the open roof, in case the savages should attempt to climb the walls and make an entrance there.

At once tearing up several puncheons from the floor, a

party of men proceeded to brace the door in the most effective manner, the others keeping watch near the two small windows, and firing whenever they could get a glimpse of an Indian.

In this manner the attack and defence was continued some little time longer—another of the party inside being slightly wounded—when suddenly the sound of a heavy gun came booming through the air.

"Courage, men!" cried Captain Kirkwood, in an animated tone; "they already hear us at Wheeling, and doubtless assistance will soon be here."

"Let us give three cheers!" said Captain Biggs; "just to show the attacking scoundrels that we are not the least intimidated."

Three cheers were accordingly given; and were answered by the Indians, by the loudest, wildest, and fiercest yells of furious rage.

"Ay, yell away! you mean, cowardly, thieving vagabonds!" shouted one of the men, tauntingly, as he recklessly advanced close to one of the small windows, which had not been so boarded up inside as to render his position safe from the balls of the enemy.

"Have a care there, Walker!" exclaimed his commander, in alarm.

Scarcely were the words spoken, when the man, clapping

his hands to his breast, staggered back, reeled, and fell to to the floor, groaning out:

"Oh, God! the fiends have killed me!"

Some two or three of his companions immediately lifted the poor fellow, and placed him upon a bed, while the two officers hurried up to examine his wound, which with deep regret they discovered to be mortal. As they turned sorrowfully away, the firing and yelling of the Indians, which up to this time had been almost continuous, suddenly ceased.

"Ah! they are about to depart," said Captain Kirkwood, joyfully; "probably they fear a reinforcement."

"More likely they have stopped to plot some new deviltry," said Captain Biggs, who was more familiar with the Indian mode of warfare.

All kept silent for a few minutes—waiting, hoping and fearing—so that the suspense itself was not a little painful. Suddenly one of the men uttered an exclamation of alarm; and on being questioned as to the cause, replied:

"Listen! Don't you hear the devils piling brush around the house? They're going to burn us out!"

"In that case we may be compelled to make a sortie," returned Captain Biggs.

"It must be at the last moment, then," said Captain Kirkwood; "for once beyond these walls, my wife and children would stand little chance of escape. If they set fire to us, we must endeavor to put it out. We have considerable water in the house, thank Heaven! and before they can burn through these thick logs, I trust assistance will arrive from the Fort.

Almost as he said this, a bright sheet of flame shot up round the cabin, shedding a lurid and fearful light upon those within. This was accompanied by a series of terrific and triumphant yells, and a general discharge of fire arms on the part of the savages.

There was not sufficient water in the house to justify the inmates in throwing it over the roof; and all they could do, therefore, was to wait, in the most gloomy suspense, till some presence of the fire could be seen between the crevices of the logs, and then attempt to check its headway within.

Some half-an-hour was passed in this manner—the Indians continually fetching and piling on more brush, until the lapping and writhing fire had ascended to the very roof—keeping up the while their yells of triumph, and occasional shots of musketry; which, combined with the lurid and ghastly light in which each saw the other, the loud and awful roaring of the flames, and the groans of the wounded, made a most terrible scene for the imprisoned inmates—a scene that cannot be fully described, and the horrors of which can only partially be comprehended by the most vivid imagination.

At length the fire began to dislodge the heated clay—which had been used to stop the chinks and crannies between the logs—and the furious flames to send in their devouring tongues in search of new material for destruction; and then all who were able set eagerly to work, dashing on water, and so checking in some degree the progress of the consuming element.

This was continued until the water became entirely exhausted; and then recourse was had to what milk there chanced to be in the house; and, after this, to some fresh earth, which they dug up from beneath the floor—the Indians still keeping up their yells, and firing through every crevice, (by which some more of the inmates were wounded, though none mortally,) and Captains Kirkwood and Biggs moving about from point to point, and animating all parties with their own heroism and the hope of speedy deliverance.

The attack began about three o'clock in the morning, and lasted till dawn; when the Indians, finding they could not succeed in their fell purpose without carrying the siege far into the day, and probably fearing they might suddenly be surprised by a large party from the Fort, uttered another series of wild, discordant whoops, poured in upon the building one regular volley, and then suddenly retreated—the men inside calling after them in the most taunting manner—the voice of the poor fellow mortally wounded being heard among the loudest.

About an hour before sunrise the whole party, having succeeded in subduing the flames, ventured forth cautiously, and immediately crossed the river to Fort Henry—Walker, the only one who lost his life, expiring on the way. Here all the living were properly cared for, and the gallant soldier was buried with military honors.

A few days after, Captain Kirkwood set out with his family for his native State; but meeting on the way some Delaware troops, who were marching to the Indian country, and who offered him the command of their body, he took leave of his family and turned back. In the November following, he took part in the bloody action known as St. Clair's Defeat; "where he fell," says his chronicler, "in a brave attempt to repel the enemy with the bayonet, and thus closed a career as honorable as it was unrewarded."

The Trapper's Story.

"Boys," said old Reuben Hardinge, as, with three of his companions, he sat before his camp-fire in the deep wilderness of the Far West, "it's right amazing how old recollections will plump down on a feller every now and then, and make him about as fit for his business as a turkey-buzzard is for a singing bird."

"What's up now, Rube?" inquired one of the others, as he lazily inhaled and puffed out a volume of tobacco smoke.

"Well, Joe, I war jest thinking back to the time I fust put out for these here diggings, and the right smart chance of a muss that made me do it."

"I never heerd the story, Rube."

"I reckon none of us ever did," said another.

"S'pose you tells it, ef you're in the mood for't," put in the third.

"Wall," rejoined Rube, "I s'pose I mought as well tell it as think about it—though thar's mighty few as ever heerd it—for it arn't one o' the things as I likes to hev cut across my track pur y often.

"Let me see now!" pursued the old mountaineer, musingly; "thirty year, I reckon, would take me back to a right smart-looking young man. Now you needn't grin so about that, boys—for it's a fact, by thunder! I warn't al'ays the scarrified, stoop-shouldered, grizzly-faced, gray-headed, grunting old beaver you sees me now, I can tell you—but a right smart chance of a sapling—six foot high in my moccasins, hair as black as a crow's, eye like a young eagle's, and with everything about me as limber and supple as a two-year old buck. Yes, that's what I war thirty year ago—but that thirty year has tuk it all down, amazing."

The trapper paused for a few moments, as one lost in contemplation, and then resumed:

"Yes, thirty year ago,—it don't seem a great while, nyther, though I've done a heap o' tramping and seen a heap o' rough and tumble sence then,—thirty year ago it war; and yit I can fotch it all back as cl'ar as ef it war yesterday; and the way *he* looked, and the way *she* looked, and the way I *felt*, all stand out afore me as plain as the nose on your face, Joe—and your wost enemy'll be apt to allow that you've got some nose.

"But you won't understand me, boys, onless I begins a little back o' that partickerlar time, and so I'll do it. You see the way of it war this: I war raised down in Tennessee, on to a plantation that would hev been my

16

father's ef he'd only had all his debts paid, which he hadn't; and on another plantation, about a half a mile off, thar lived Neil Waterman, who war a colonel 'n the militia, and a squire-in-law, and some punks giner.lly all round.

"Now Colonel Squire Waterman had a darter named Lucy, that war the purtiest speciment of a duck in them parts—slim, straight, plump-lipped, rosy-cheeked, and silky-haired, with two blue eyes that 'ud fotch the tallest brute of a human right down on to his marrerbones afore he knowed what ailed him.

"Wall, to git along into the meat of the thing, I fell head over heels in love with Lucy, from the time I war big enough to say boo to a b'ar; and I kept on that way, only gitting wusser as I growed older; and ef Lucy didn't love me back agin, she made believe to do it, and that did me jest as well for the time.

"But the difference 'tween me and Lucy, as we both growed older, war, that I'd only one to pick from, and she'd everybody—for every scamp in the diggings war arter her—and some o' the fellers I used to think monght be a heap better looking to her than Rube Hardinge— though I could out-run, out-jump, out-shoot, out-holler, and out-lick the hull kit, and stood ready to do it any minute that anybody wanted to try it.

"Wall, the p'int I'm coming to, ar' this: Things had

gone on one way and t'other purty considerable—and me and Lucy had quarrelled and made up agin about a hundred times—and I'd kicked the clothes off o' my bed every night for two months, in dreaming as how I war kicking some mean sneak as war trying to get on to the blind side o' the gal of my affections: things war gitting on this way, I say, when Colonel Squire Waterman he gin a corn-husking, and axed in all the boys and gals around them parts.

"I war thar, in course; and I went thar determined to keep poor Lucy from being bothered with palavers from .hem as she mou'tn't like; but, for some reason or other, the gal had tuk a notion jest then that nobody war no bother to her 'cept me, and that I war al'ays in her way when I happened to git along side o' her. That thar sort o' thing naterally riled me up and made me feel wolfish; and when I spoke, I ginerally said so'thing that didn't altogether set well on the stomachs of the crowd—though as to who liked it, and who didn't, I never stopped to ax.

"Now, amongst the ugly mugs as war trying to tote off the affections of Lucy, thar war one called Pete Blodget, that I'd tuk a mortal hate to; and jest as ef they'd both planned out how they could best fotch the catermount into me, he squeezed himself up along side o' Lucy; and she talked and joked and laughed with him, jest as ef no sech a man as me had never been born

"Wall, for me, I reckon I stood it purty well for a good while; but I felt Satan coming into me as I husked away; and I sometimes pitched the corn on to the pile, and sometimes over my head amongst the stalks and husks—for somehow blood war dancing afore my eyes, and I couldn't al'ays see right well what I war doing. At last the boys and gals all round me began to titter and laugh, and nod and wink, and I knowed it war all about me. Still I husked away, and didn't say nothing often, and then al'ays so'thing sharp and sassy.

"Now ef Pete had jest a minded his own business and treated Lucy respectful, and hadn't said nothing aggrawating to me, it's like he mought be living now to laugh over his triumph; but he couldn't be contented, the fool! when he war well off; and began to ax ef anybody had seed anybody as had chawed a green persimmon lately, meaning me. All the fools, Lucy amongst the rest, laughed at this, and pretended to wonder who he could mean; and as I still held myself down, (though I felt the seat gitting powerful hot, and seen little red things dancing afore my eyes,) he still kept on, gitting wusser and more p'inted like, till at last he says, says he, 'I'm the chap as goes in for ripe persimmons,' and he throwed one arm around Lucy's waist and drawed her over and kissed her.

"Now, boys, I've come to a spot that's al'ays been kind o' blank to me. I don't remember gitting up—but I 'spect

I did—for I remember finding myself standing up amongst a mighty excited crowd, with Pete lying down, his head all bloody, and a stove-in whiskey keg along side o' him, that all said I'd jest smashed agin his upper story; whilst Lucy, all fainted and stretched out limpsy, war being toted off by her father and two others, and follered by all the rest o' the gals, crying and screaming.

"The boys around now tuk different sides, and some said I war right and some said I warn't. But I soon fixed the matter. Stepping out from the crowd, I says, says I :

"'Let them as thinks I've done right, foller me; and them as don't, stay and take keer of Pete, till he gits well enough to ax for a settlement with rifles, which I s'pose he'll do ef he arn't a coward.'

"Wall, as I said, the party divided off, and some went home with me, and some staid and tuk keer o' Pete. I got my rifle down and cleaned her, and run some balls, and filled up my powder-horn, so's to be ready and not keep any body waiting as mought want to hev the thing settled arter a gentleman's fashion.

"By the time I'd got this done, a friend of Pete's comes over, and says as how he'd 'spect me to meet him at a place he named at daylight next morning.

"'I'll be thar!' says I : 'tell him I'll be thar, and give him so'thing wusser'n a whiskey-keg to git over!'

16*

"Wall, I war thar; and so war Pete, and everybody else round about them diggings, 'cept the women folks; and they'd a been thar, too, ef they'd only been allowed to come. It didn't take long to fix things for the fight—for all we wanted war a level piece o' ground and a chance to blaze away.

"Rifles at forty paces war the word in them times to settle all such trifles as ourn; and arter measuring off the ground, they sot me and Pete face to face, with the butts o' both our pieces standing by our feet; and then all drawed back out o' the way, and some one gin the word to fire.

"Up went our rifles at that word, and both pulled trigger at the same time. I felt so'thing queer about my neck; and putting up my hand, I found Pete's ball had gone through within a hair's breadth of my life; and I seen Pete at the same time clap his hand to his breast, and knowed by that he'd got so'thing to look arter too.

"But thar warn't no time to be spent in hunting balls— for it war a fight till death; and the fust man that could git his rifle loaded now, would hev the best chance o' talking about the muss arter it war over; so I went in for loading as fast as I could.

"Now I claims to be some at loading a rifle, and you'd better believe I done my best jest then; but in spite o' all I could do, Pete got ahead o' me, and I begun to feel that

Pete, lying down, his head all bloody, and a stove-in whiskey keg along side of him.

See page 185.

my time had come. Pete I knowed war a dead shot; and ef he could hev ten seconds for an aim, it war all up with this coon; and so when I seen him shaking in the priming, whilst I war only ramming down the ball, I jest looked round to the rising sun to say good-bye to daylight.

"I don't think I'm any more o' a coward than any other man; but when I seen Pete steadily raising his piece, and knowed when it come to a dead level that I'd not know nothing, I'll own up I felt powerful queer; and ef the little money and traps I had, could hev bought me about ten seconds, I don't think I should hev waited long afore making the trade.

"Wall, boys, that thar rifle come up slow and steady; but jest afore it got so as I mought hev looked straight into the muzzle, it war jerked one side, and went off in the air; and Pete Blodget fell down dead in his tracks, killed by my first shot, jest when two seconds more o' his life would hev ended mine.

"As soon as I found he war dead, I knowed I'd hev to quit them diggings sudden—for he'd got friends enough to set the sheriff arter me, and it warn't pleasant to think o' being cooped up in jail. So I broke round to Colonel Squire Waterman's house, and got a sight o' Lucy, who war jest about as white as a snow-bank.

"'Lucy,' says I, 'you're a critter as has kicked up a good deal o' mischief with me—but I forgive you. I come tell you that Pete Blodget won't trouble nyther of us no more, and that I'm jest a breaking for tall timber. Good-by, Lucy—I'm bound to quit—I've got to go—and on this here 'arth we'll never meet agin.'

"I war going on with so'thing more; but Lucy fell down fainty like; and so I left her, and put off for strange parts. I got to the Massissip that day, and got a passage to St. Louis, whar I soon got in with some old trappers, and started out for the life I've follered ever sence."

"And what became of Lucy?" inquired one of old Rube's interested listeners, as the trapper ceased and dropped his head upon his hands.

"Ah me, boys! that's what I can't answer!" sighed the old mountaineer; "and when a spell comes over me like thar done to-night, I ginerally sets and wonders. Ah! Lucy—poor, dear Lucy—nobody never loved you like this here old grey-headed beaver done when he war a kitten—never—never, Lucy—never!" and the old trapper dropped his head still lower, and drew his rough, hard hand more than once across his eyes.

A Miraculous Escape.

It was just after General Wayne's great victory of the Fallen Timbers, (said an old pioneer,) that I became acquainted with Captain Robert Benham, who had been quite a prominent actor in all the principal battles of the frontier. His name had long been familiar to me in connection with a very peculiar and remarkable affair which had occurred on the Ohio, at the mouth of the Licking river, as far back as the year 1779; and as I had heard his singular adventures at that place related differently by different parties, I felt no little curiosity to arrive at the exact facts; and therefore took an early occasion to get the particulars from his own lips; which I now give, as near as I can recollect, in his own words:

"It was in the autumn of 1779," began the captain, "that quite a party of us left the Falls of the Ohio, in keel-boats, under the command of Major Rodgers, for the purpose of making an attack upon the Indians at the old town of Chilicothe. On our way up the river, we met with no remarkable adventure till we approached the mouth of the

Licking, which we did about sunset of a delightful day; when we observed a few Indians standing upon a projecting sand bar, at the point where the two streams unite, apparently watching some companions in a canoe, who were crossing to them from the opposite bank of the smaller stream. If they saw us, there was nothing in their manner to indicate the fact; and thinking it possible to take them by surprise, Major Rodgers ordered the boats to be run up under some bushes along the shore, and all the men save five—some seventy in number -to advance cautiously through the wood, and completely surround the spot where the savages were.

"We all set off in fine spirits, thinking only of the surprise we should give the enemy, and never once dreaming of the surprise they might give us in return. Quietly, stealthily, we pushed onward, spreading out as we advanced, till at length we reached and fairly encircled the fatal spot; when, just as the order was being given to rush in upon the foe, we were startled and thrown into the greatest confusion by the uprising on every side of us of several hundred yelling Indians.

"We had been drawn into a complete ambuscade—had been taken by our enemies in the very trap we had set for them. Instantly they poured in a destructive fire, and then fell upon us with knife and tomahawk; when the panic on our part became fearful, and the slaughter tremendous.

A MIRACULOUS ESCAPE.

Like frightened sheep we huddled together; and then, finding ourselves hemmed in by our foes, who hewed us down as fast as they reached us, we turned at bay, and poured back a volley from our side. Then, with yells as wild and savage as their own, we broke through their lines, and rushed for our boats. But the Indians, comprehending our design, reached them before us, and made a capture of all save one, in which the men left in charge had made their escape. Our only chance now was to break their lines again, and start through the forest to the station of Harrodsburg. Favored by the gathering shades of night, some twenty of our whole party escaped, though hotly pursued by our blood-thirsty foes.

"But I was not one of that fortunate few; for, as I was in the act of clearing some five or six of the enemy, who barred my way to a dense thicket, and just as I had cut down a couple of the nearest, a ball passed through my hips, shattering the bones. At once I fell, but luckily among some thick bushes which for the moment concealed me; and the others, probably thinking me dead or escaped, immediately darted off in pursuit of my flying friends. I had my rifle still in my hands; and wounded and suffering as I was, I proceeded to load it as I lay on the ground—my only hope now being that I should succeed in killing one or more of the bloody wretches before a terminus should be put to my own existence.

"As minute after minute went by, however, and the yells of the savages grew more and more distant, and night began fast to envelop me in her welcome pall of darkness, a new hope sprung up in my breast, that I might possibly o secrete myself as to escape the observation of the enemy altogether. Slowly dragging myself through the bushes to a fallen tree, which lay within a few feet of me, I, with the most excruciating pain, crept up under the branches, which I disposed above my person in the best manner I could.

"Here for hours I lay, suffering agonies of body and mind which no language has power to describe. I dared not stir again, scarcely to breathe. I heard the Indians return, and I could tell by the sounds that they were going over the ground and butchering all the wounded they could find. About midnight, as near as I could judge, they once more drew off and lit their camp-fires, the glimmering of which I could faintly perceive through the thick foliage which surrounded me.

"Let me pass over that night of horror. If any one would have the faintest idea of what I suffered, he must imagine himself in my situation—there—in the branches of that tree—with both hips shattered—surrounded by my dead friends—and, worse still, my living foes. I dared not change my position, nor give vent to a single groan, and at times it seemed that nature must compel from me some expression of pain, in spite of my utmost will. Oh, it was a horrible night! and may God deliver me from ever passing such another.

"But the end was not yet. Horrible as that night was, I dreaded to see the morrow. How could I expect to escape the lynx eyes of so many savages, when they should begin to beat over the ground for plunder? And at times the thought of this so worked upon my feelings, that I was more than once tempted to shriek out, and let my position be known, and thus bring upon myself the relief of a speedy death—for I knew, from my disabled condition, that the Indians would not think of taking me prisoner, but butcher me at once. And yet the instincts of life were greater than the temptation I speak of. And these same instincts, by the way, seem wisely set for our preservation—to act when reason tells us that all hope is lost and we had better end our woes at once.

"How painfully I watched the dawning of the day! how eagerly and tremblingly I listened to every sound! At length I could hear the Indians astir; and soon after they began to traverse the scene of slaughter, and gather up the arms of my companions, and strip their bodies of every garment. They were hours at their work—and to me those hours were ages. At times, when some of them drew near the spot where I lay, I felt my heart in my very throat, and it seemed as if I should die of suffocation

Twice a small party of them came so close that I could see their half-naked, hideously-painted forms through the leaves; and once a single warrior stalked by me, within reach of my rifle. Up and down, and over the ground they passed and re-passed many times, till they were evidently satisfied that none of the dead or the wounded had escaped their notice. They then drew off in a body along the bank of the river, where they remained for hours—in fact, till late in the day—when, being joined by the rest of their companions, who had probably made a long journey in pursuit of the fugitives, they repaired to the boats.

"With a feeling of thankfulness which I cannot express, I heard them put off from the shore, and every sound gradually die away to silence. And yet, shortly after, there came an awful revulsion of feeling; for I now felt that I was alone—alone in the wilderness—afar from friends—so crippled that I could not walk—could only move my body, in fact, by a great effort—suffering all the time the most excruciating agonies, and in danger of perishing from starvation. Had I been able to move about, even though never so slowly and feebly, I could have rejoiced in my good fortune; but situated as I was, I felt that only an overruling Providence, such as had so far preserved me, could still save me from even a more terrible doom than I had escaped.

"As I thus lay on my back, in a position which had

scarcely been changed for more than twenty hours, I looked up through the leaves, and, to my surprise, I might almost say joy, I beheld a raccoon in the act of descending the trunk of a large tree, some of whose branches even canopied the spot where I lay. Was this poor animal a messenger of hope? Had Providence directed it hither for my preservation? I fancied so then—I almost fancy so still. At all events, I cautiously raised my only remaining friend, my rifle, took a quick but certain aim, and fired. The ball sped to its mark, and the animal dropped dead within a few feet of me; and as I raised myself among the limbs, with the intention of dragging myself to it, I was startled by hearing a human cry.

"Fearing the Indians had not all gone, I hastily reloaded my rifle, and then remained perfectly still, fairly trembling at the thought of what I might next behold, but determined to sell my life dearly, and shoot the first human figure I should see approaching me. Presently I heard the same loud, startling cry repeated, but this time much nearer than before. Still I kept silent, my rifle firmly grasped, for I could recognize nothing like the voice of one of my race. Again I heard the same singular sound, but still nearer yet, and a rustling among the underbrush, apparently at a distance of twenty yards. I now cocked my rifle, and poised it, resolved to shoot the first object that should appear But fortunately nothing did appear, till my heart had been made to leap for joy, by the utterance of words, in my native tongue, which fell clearly and distinctly upon my ear, and assured me it was a countryman, perhaps a companion.

"'Who are you? where are you? for God's sake, speak!' cried the voice.

"I now gave an answering shout; and soon I was gratified by the sight of a human figure, pushing rapidly through the bushes, whom, notwithstanding his haggard and blood-stained features, I at once recognized as Peter Brent. On getting sight of me, he stopped and exclaimed:

"'My God! Captain Benham—is this you? How did you escape? I thought I was the only being left alive by the butchering wretches!'

"'Alas!' I returned—'I'm as good as dead—for I'm badly wounded in my hips, and cannot walk a step.'

"'See!' he rejoined—'I'm no better off—*both my arms are broken!* and I've no power to use a weapon, and couldn't feed myself if I had any thing to eat. I think, of the two, Captain, you're the *best* off, after all—for you at least can shoot game, and so won't starve.'

"'Aye,' said I, 'but how am I to get it when I have shot it?'

"'I see,' he replied, with a sort of laugh, 'the *two* of us only make *one* decent man. You've got arms and I've got legs; and if ever we get out of this infernal scrape at all, I reckon we'll have to work out together. And if Heaven is willing, and the red devils will let us alone, we'll be able to do it yet, and cheat the howling imps of two scalps any how!'

"It was a very singular and remarkable occurrence, that only two men should have escaped from that scene of slaughter; and of these, the one with his hips broken, and the other with his arms. Brent, like myself, had had nothing to eat for more than twenty-four hours. And like myself, too, he had escaped, after being shot, by crawling into a thicket, and laying flat upon the earth, at a point where the Indians had passed and repassed within a few feet of him. Here he had remained concealed through the night, and the day, till the savages had departed; when the pangs of hunger had brought him forth in search of food; which he had little hope of finding, and knew not by what means he might get it into his mouth if obtained.

"On hearing the report of my rifle, a faint hope had sprung up in his breast that a companion might be near; but whether it should prove to be a friend or an enemy, he determined to make himself known, and risk captivity, or even death, rather than remain in his helpless condition.

"We now began our singular mode of living, which probably has never been paralleled in the world's history. The first thing Brent did, was to search for the raccoon

I had shot and push it along to me with his feet. I then dressed it; and kindling a fire with dry sticks, which he also pushed up to me in the same manner, I broiled t, and on this we made our supper—as hearty and as palatable a meal as I ever ate in my life - I feeding him as he sat beside me. Our hunger appeased, we felt more sensibly the pangs of thirst; and at first we could devise no means for obtaining the water so near us. Necessity, however, is the mother of invention; and luckily bethinking me of my hat, I placed the rim in my companion's mouth, and told him to wade into the river, until he should be able to dip the hat under; and then, by returning quickly, I fancied a good portion of the water might be retained after allowing for the leakage. The plan succeeded; and taking the half-filled hat from his teeth, I held it for him to drink, and then drank myself, the most refreshing and invigorating draught that ever passed my lips.

"The immediate wants of nature being now fully supplied, we began to be more cheerful and hopeful, though still suffering extreme pain from our shattered limbs, which I next proceeded to dress as well as our circumstances would permit. Making some rude splints with my knife, I took off my shirt and tore it into strips; and then putting the bones of Brent's arms together as well as I could, I bound the splints around them. This done, I proceeded to dress my own wounds in the same incomplete way.

"Another night now set in, which we passed together, lying close in the thicket, and suffering a great deal of pain. We slept little, but spent the tedious hours in talking over the dire events which had happened, and mourning the loss of our brave companions.

'The second day, beginning early in the morning, and keeping a sharp lookout for game, I was fortunate enough to shoot two squirrels and a wild turkey, the latter being quite numerous in that region. This served us for food through the day; and on the third I succeeded in shooting a couple more squirrels and a few birds; my companion always kicking the game to me with his feet, and pushing up sticks and brush in the same manner, and I dressing and cooking the animals and feeding him.

"So matters went on for several days, the game gradually becoming scarcer, and requiring a great deal more labor on Brent's part to drive within reach of my rifle. Days thus passed on, and even weeks, before my wounds were so far healed as to permit me to hobble about on crutches; and during all this time we saw not a human soul, though anxiously watching for some chance boat to pass down the river and take us off.

"Our garments being thin, and our shirts torn up for bandages, and the weather setting in cold, our future prospects looked cheerless enough, and we were much concerned lest we should be obliged to winter where we were. To be prepared for any emergency, we, with much labor, put up a rude shanty, which served in some measure to protect us from the almost wintry blasts which now began to sweep over the desolate scene.

"As the season grew colder and more inclement, the game became so scarce that my companion with difficulty drove enough within rifle-shot to give us a single meal a day; and, with all the rest, our powder got so low in the horn that I could count the charges, and dared not fire except when certain of my mark: then it was we began to feel the horrors of despair, and sometimes to regret that we had outlived the dead around us. Almost naked, with unshaven, haggard faces, hollow cheeks and sunken eyes, we now indeed looked pitiable, even to each other; every day, too, our condition seemed to grow worse instead of better; and at last, with a sinking heart, I informed Brent we had but four charges of powder in our horn.

"'God help us!' was his reply.

"Matters were thus at their very worst, when, one day, Peter burst suddenly into our shanty, where I sat shivering over a few embers, and, with tears in his eyes, exclaimed:

"'Blessed be God! Captain Benham, we're saved! there's a flat boat just turning the bend above us!'

"Who shall describe my feelings then! I started up and hobbled down to the bank of the river, shouting wildly as I went, lest the boat, scarcely yet within sight, should pass us ere I could reach the beach.

"Oh! how painfully anxious we watched its slow approach! continually shouting, to attract the attention of the men too far distant to hear us, and making every kind of signal we could possibly think of for the same purpose.

"Gradually the boat neared us; and at length we could see its crew gathered together, and pointing toward us. But, oh Heaven! imagine, if you can, our horror, when we saw them suddenly betake themselves to their oars, and push over to the Ohio shore, and then row past us with all their might, notwithstanding our frantic gesticulations and piteous prayers for help! On they swept down the river; and then Brent and I, looking at each other with silent horror, sunk down together upon the cold beach, and mentally prayed for death to end our sufferings.

"Suddenly—oh, sight of agonizing joy!—we saw a canoe put off from the larger boat and approach us; and then we got up, and fairly screamed and begged for assistance. When the rowers had come near enough to converse with us, they stopped, and told us they feared we were decoys, put there to draw them to the shore, that the Indians might fall upon and murder them; and it took no ittle time, and the most earnest asseverations and piteous appeals, to convince them to the contrary.

"At last, after rowing past us two or three times, and closely inspecting the shore, and getting us to come far out on a sand bar, they ventured to take us aboard. We were kindly treated by these men, when they came to hear our story; and being taken by them to the garrison at the Falls, (now Louisville, Ky.,) we were placed under the care of a skillful surgeon, and soon restored to our usual health and strength."

Such was the remarkable story of Captain Benham—remarkable for the fact that two men should so singularly escape from the savages, and live six weeks in the wilderness—the one with useless arms, and the other with useless legs—the two together making as it were *only one whole man!*

Whoever shall to-day stand upon the levee of the now large and flourishing city of Cincinnati, and glance his eye across the beautiful Ohio, shall behold the very spot where these remarkable events occurred, at a time when all around, on either shore, was a wild, howling wilderness

A Mother's Courage.

It was in the spring of 1785, and on a clear, beautiful day, that a party, consisting of two men, a woman and a child, were passing down the Ohio in a conveniently-sized boat, for the purpose of joining some friends at a settlement below. This party bore the surname of Marston, and the relationship of husband, brother, wife, and daughter. They had come from the interior of Pennsylvania, transporting their goods by horses to the Alleghany, and thence descending that river and the Ohio in the boat they now occupied.

The eldest of the four was a large, tall, fine-looking man, some thirty years of age, and the husband of the female and father of the child. The wife appeared to be some six or eight years the junior of her partner, was small, slender and graceful, and possessed a countenance of more than ordinary intelligence and beauty. The brother was younger than the husband, and inferior in size and strength, but comely of feature, and evidently a man of considerable muscular power. The youngest of the party was a sweet, chatting, blue-eyed, golden-haired little girl of four summers, the favorite of all, and especially the idol and joy of its fond and almost girlish mother, both of whom seemed much out of place in journeying through that wild, unsettled, and perilous region.

Thus far our adventurers had met with no material accident or misfortune; nor had they seen any of those fierce enemies of their race, who were then known to be prowling through the great forests which stretched away on either hand for hundreds of miles; but now they were more directly entering the country inhabited by their swarthy foes, and which had been more distinctly marked by the aggressions of the latter upon their white invaders; and as they turned their eyes toward the green and flowery banks of the delightful stream, upon whose placid bosom they were floating, it was less to admire the solemn beauties of nature, than in dread of what those mighty forests might conceal. Yet the men, as was natural they should, relying upon their strength, and their skill in the use of weapons, seemed less uneasy than the girlish mother, who, at every unusual sound, would clasp her offspring to her heart, and glance around her in fearful apprehension.

"Mary," said her husband, approaching her on one of these occasions of alarm, which became more frequent as she advanced on her journey, "how is it that you, who have been so courageous all along, have now of a sudden become so timid?"

"I hardly know myself, William," she replied, in a sweet, musical tone, looking up with a smile, "unless it is that we are entering a more dangerous region, and that I am every moment growing more fond of our pretty little Ada, and more fearful on her account;" and bending over the child, which she now held in her arms, she imprinted a mother's kiss of love upon its ruby lips.

"But I'm not afraid, mamma, when you and papa are with me," prattled the blue-eyed pet; "for I know nobody'll hurt me where you are."

"Ah, God bless your trusting innocence!" cried the father, impulsively catching her up in his arms and covering her cherub face with kisses. "No one shall hurt you where I am—and may the good God keep us all from harm!"

During their voyage down the river, it had sometimes been necessary to lay up at night, especially in foggy weather; but they had generally managed this matter with great caution; securing their boat near, rather than at, the shore, by making a line fast to some overhanging branch and dropping a sort of rude anchor. At these stopping places our voyagers had been the most apprehensive; yet it was not at these that they were really most in danger, but while floating along in the bright light of day, as the sequel of our narrative will show.

On the very day that we introduce them to the reader, but some two or three hours subsequent to the conversation recorded, the little girl, in looking toward the Ohio shore, became much attracted to a long line of beautifully-flowered shrubbery, which so overhung the stream that a branch might easily be broken in passing; and with infantile glee she clapped her hands and exclaimed:

"Oh, papa, do get little Ada some pretty flowers!"

The boat was not far from the land, and the current set in close to the bank, so that it was an easy matter to comply with her wish; and the fond father, giving directions to this effect, and himself taking an oar, was about to push in toward the thicket, when the mother, with what seemed to be a premonition of danger, quickly interposed, saying, eagerly and earnestly:

"Nay, William, do not think of such a thing, but keep further out in the stream! From some cause I am frightened—I feel that danger lurks in every thicket, and I know we cannot be too cautious."

"Pooh, Mary, you are too easily alarmed!" replied her husband; "no one would be more cautious than I, if I thought there was danger; but there is none here, surely; and little Ada might as well have a bunch of flowers to please her."

So saying, and without heeding the remonstrances of his more timid companion, he, assisted by his brother, turned the boat up alongside the shrubbery; and both were in the act of plucking a flowering branch—the little girl, meanwhile, in her mother's trembling arms, clapping her tiny hands with delight—when suddenly two sharp reports, almost blended into one, rung out upon the still air; and the brothers fell back together, the one shot through the heart and the other through the brain.

At the same instant there came a series of terrific yells, a rustling among the bushes, and two hideously-painted savages came leaping into the boat. First making sure of their victims, by plunging their knives several times into their bodies, they next tore off their scalps, and tauntingly shook the trophies in the very face of the now petrified and horror-stricken wife and mother, who stood like a statue of marble, as motionless and seemingly as cold, her eyes glaring wildly, and the little girl clinging to her in a terror she could not comprehend. Then attaching each his scalp to his girdle, they made a flourish of their tomahawks over the head of the mother, rather as it seemed with the intention of terrifying than of striking her. But finding her unmoved—for she was still paralyzed with horror—one of them rudely snatched the child from her arms, and made as if to dash out its brains on the gunwale of the boat. This he might indeed have done—for his basilisk eyes were gleaming with fiendish malice—but the other interposed, and said something in their native tongue; when, turning to the still immovable mother, he struck her a blow with his fist, knocked her down, and threw the shrieking child upon her.

The two Indians now proceeded to secure the boat, by working it up under the overhanging bushes, and so disposing of them as to completely conceal it from the view of any party passing up or down the river, or looking out from the opposite shore

By the time this was completed, poor Mrs. Marston had in some degree recovered the use of her faculties, and had begun to bemoan her hard fate in low, choking sobs, the while straining her trembling child as tightly to her anguished bosom as if she thought that her maternal arm could shield it from her merciless foes.

One of the Indians now advanced to her side, and, rudely pushing her with his foot, made signs that she must get up and follow him ashore. She understood and complied with his desire—for she had now some little hope that her child would be spared to her—and with a mother's undying love, she felt that she would willingly struggle through any thing, endure every thing, for its sweet sake.

We may not dwell upon her feelings, for none but a mother so suddenly and terribly afflicted, and so hopelessly placed, could comprehend the bitter anguish of her heart.

At a little distance back from the river, the Indian bound his prisoner to a sapling, leaving the child free beside her, and then returned to his companion, and assisted him in securing their captured spoil.

They now seemed disposed to be merry—those grim, inhuman monsters—as they gloated over their not invaluable prize—stripping the dead of their garments, securing their weapons and amunition, and reveling, like hungry beasts, in the palatable edibles which their explorations exposed—chatting glibly in their native tongue, and now and then laughing merrily, but cautiously, as here and there they fell upon what they considered a prize of more than usual value—the last of these being no other than a mysterious-looking keg, which they were not long in discovering to be fire-water, and over which they not only laughed, but around which they fairly danced, in fiendish glee.

At length, placing the keg in the middle of the boat, they knocked in the head with their hatchets, and began to indulge in the exhilarating poison, gradually increasing their at first light potations to a kind of drunken carousal, which lasted for several hours, and finally ended in a state of comple intoxication.

Meantime the poor mother had remained bound to her

tree, listening to the fierce revelry of her captors, and all the time in trembling apprehension lest something might direct their thoughts to her, and she and her darling Ada become fresh victims of their now liquor-maddened passions. But as time wore on, and their potations grew deeper, and their carousal more drunken, if not less boisterous, a wild hope sprung up in her breast, that through their final inebriation she might providentially effect her escape; and from that moment she became more intensely excited than ever, and listened with a still more wildly palpitating heart, hushing the very murmurs of her poor child by looks and whispers of terror that it seemed instinctively to comprehend

At last, just as the bright sun was setting, the long wished-for moment seemed to arrive, the drunken sounds having gradually died away to silence; and she reasoned that her foes were now no longer in a condition to prevent her escape, which peradventure she might effect, provided she could immediately get free of her bonds.

But how was this to be done? Her hands were corded behind her back, and her body made fast to the tree. She tried to work herself loose, but her efforts only served to tighten the cords and give her pain; and she was upon the very point of uttering a shriek of despair, when she remembered in time that the sound of her voice might fall upon the obtuse senses of her drunken foes and mechanically arouse them to action.

But stay! another strange, wild hope enters her breast! Can she make use of Ada? Can she venture the poor child to the fearful risk of returning alone to the boat, and procuring a knife? It is a thought as trying as death itself, though less fearful than a long and hopeless captivity, and it seems to be their only salvation. Time is passing—her captors have become still—and something must be done! Shall she risk the only alternative in her power? Something seems to urge her to do so; and finally, wrought up to a pitch of desperation little short of madness, she explains to the trembling little creature what she needs of her, and gives her directions how to proceed.

And that innocent little thing comprehended her, and finally set out on her fearful mission. Oh! what a trial was that to the tender nerves of that poor mother! and from the moment of her departure, till that of her return, the brief suspense was to her an age of horror. But the child went, and returned in safety, and brought back a knife, which she had stealthily taken from the very side of one of the murderers of her father and uncle, and which was even yet red with their blood.

The poor captive shuddered as she looked upon the fearful weapon; and yet she experienced a faint gleam of joy, at the thought that it would be the means of setting her free, and thus, under God, the means of saving herself and child.

Little Ada, by her mother's direction, soon cut the binding cords; and the moment Mrs. Marston found herself at liberty, she caught the heroic little girl in her arms, covered her sweet face with kisses, and then, with an almost bursting heart, knelt upon the ground, and poured forth a fervent prayer of thanksgiving to the Great Unseen.

Strengthened by this, she arose and prepared to act; but the thought of what was before her, and the still slender thread upon which her own life and that of her child depended, brought back a sinking of the heart, and a trembling of every nerve. What was to be done now? She was alone in the great wilderness—a weak, feeble woman—far from home and friends, and surrounded by dangers of every imaginable description. Could she escape on foot with her child? Impossible! they would either starve or fall a prey to wild beasts or Indians. What course then? for they *must* escape. There was the boat—but then there lay the murderers of her husband and his brother—and what could she do with them? Should she in turn murder them, while they slept their drunken sleep? A cold, icy shudder crept through her veins at the bare thought! But then her child *must* be saved! and to save that, by any means, was imperatively her duty.

We will not follow her thoughts. Enough that she at last, carrying the child in her arms, resolutely but cautiously returned to the fearful scene, where still lay the dead bodies of her friends; and, almost beside them, but upon some bales and boxes, nearly on a level with the gunwale, their now drunken murderers.

With the knife firmly clasped in her hand, that widowed mother reached the boat; she entered it; she stood over her foes; they were in her power; she raised the knife; should she strike? She hesitated—trembled—grew faint of heart—her hand fell. She thought of her child, and the arm was again nerved, and again raised, but again fell powerless.

Ha! another thought! She hurried forward, placed the child near the bow, and warned it not to speak or stir; and then, seizing an oar, pushed the boat from the shore, and set it drifting down the stream. Then darting forward and securing the weapons of her enemies, she nerved herself for the great trial, and, using all her strength, suddenly rolled them both into the river.

On striking the water, one of the two Indians sunk almost immediately; but the other, who perhaps had drank less deeply, and was not so much intoxicated, began to struggle for life, and soon appeared to recover sufficient consciousness to comprehend what had happened, and struck out fiercely for the boat. But that girlish mother, nerved by the thought of her child, her own wrongs, and the instinct of self-preservation, prepared to defend herself even at the cost of life. She had pushed the Indians over, because it was not in her heart to slay them in cold blood, if she could escape by other means; but she was firmly resolved not to be taken again; and bringing a rifle to bear upon the struggling savage, she waited till she saw him about to make a lodgement astern, and then pulled the trigger. A flash, a report, a groan followed, and the bubbling waters grew red above the grave of her foe.

All that long, terrible night that heroic mother watched by her living child and its dead and gory father, and labored hard to keep the boat from drifting to either shore; but what pen may portray her mingled emotions of grief for the dead and joy for the living—her hopes and fears—her horror and despair? She lived through her trials, however, and the next day was discovered by a party of hunters, who, at her cries of distress, came to her relief, and thus she was saved.

We will simply add, that that heroic little ch'ld, Ada Marston, in after years became the wife of one of Kentucky's most distinguished and chivalric sons.

A Daring Exploit.

That the names of brave and noble heroes are sometimes allowed to sink into oblivion—while others, far less meritorious, but far more vain-glorious, are permitted

"To fill the speaking trump of future fame——"

the following most gallant exploit, performed by one whose memory should have been more honorably preserved, is a striking case in point. What we here present is but a narration of simple, though thrilling, facts, which we have obtained from a strictly authentic source, and to which a few still living can bear testimony.

On the twenty-third day of October, 1812, Daniel Stellwagen, as Master of the brig Concord, received his instructions from Francis Jacoby, the owner of the vessel and sailed from the port of Philadelphia, bound for Lisbon, Portugal. War between the United States and Great Britain had even then been declared; but the blockading squadron of the latter power had not yet taken possession of American ports; and Captain Stellwagen made a safe and peaceful voyage out; and entered Delaware Bay, on his return, sometime in March of the following year, heavily freighted with a valuable cargo.

Little intelligence of what was actually taking place had reached him on the ocean; but enough to make him anxious concerning his safe arrival at the port of Philadelphia, and doubly cautious and watchful as he neared the mouth of the Delaware, where he had reason to believe the enemy would have a small fleet stationed for the purpose of intercepting and overhauling all vessels either outward or homeward bound, and making prizes of such as should lay claim to the protection of the American government.

Drawing near the dangerous point under cover of darkness, the captain took soundings, hugged the Jersey shore, and signalled landward for a pilot to run him through the Cape May Channel. Toward morning the signal appeared to be answered; and at the first gray touch of dawn, a little skiff was seen bounding over the waves, bringing the long-looked for pilot, who received a cordial greeting from the master of the brig.

In reply to a dozen eager questions concerning the most important news, the pilot informed the captain that affairs looked dreary enough. A British blockading squadron—composed of the Poictiers, seventy-four, Admiral Beresford, and several smaller vessels—even then had possession of the bay, almost within gun-shot, and stopped every thing going out or coming in, and it was rumored that they would soon attempt to burn Philadelphia.

"This is serious news, Pilot—very serious news!" rejoined Captain Stellwagen: "I was afraid of this, and took good care to keep my signal lights from the observation of the enemy. But what chance have we of escaping the blockade?" he anxiously inquired, peering eagerly about him in the dull, gray, foggy light, but catching no glimpse of the fleet.

"A mighty slim chance, I'm afeard, Captain—but I'll do my best. If we was only an hour earlier, I reckon I could take her safe through, and I may do it yet—though I'm afeard daylight will expose us before I can show the thieves a clean pair of heels. But fill away, lads!" he continued, turning to the anxious crew, and assuming the full command: "make sail and brace in the yards! It's a little past high water, and we've got to run her through the Cape May Channel, and hug still closer the Jersey coast, to keep out of notice of the ships as long as we can."

His orders were promptly obeyed; and in a few minutes, guided by that seemingly intuitive skill which a good pilot seldom fails to possess, the heavily-laden brig began to thread the narrow and winding passages before her; while he, as one master of her fate, took a commanding position, and eagerly watched every oil-spot and tide-rip, and now

19

and then glanced at the yet dimly seen shore for his familiar landmarks.

Meantime a fair breeze sprang up, and the Concord began to make good headway; and calling the anxious captain's attention to the fact, the sympathetic pilot added:

"Don't be down-hearted! we may pass the heavy ships without being discovered after all; and if it wasn't for a smart little craft called the Paz, of some five or six guns, which it's like is above us—though she may be in at Lewistown Roads, as I hope she is—I'd be willing to insure her for a small per centage."

"May Heaven favor us!" said Captain Stellwagen, solemnly; "for setting aside the loss of my vessel, I have a dear wife and children in Philadelphia; and the thought of being taken prisoner, and parted from them for years, almost unnerves me."

"Well, keep a stout heart, and we'll get through all right yet!" returned the pilot, encouragingly.

For a few minutes after this, a deep and anxious silence was maintained by all—the Concord gliding slowly but steadily onward, still hugging the Jersey shore, and passing unharmed over the deeper portions of Crow Shoal. But every minute it was growing lighter and more light; and presently the tapering masts and spars, and the dark, sullen-looking hulls of the British squadron, could be clearly perceived away to the left, quietly riding at anchor near what was termed the Brown Buoy.

"There they are, and my curses on 'em, for a mean, kidnapping, robbing set of Johnny Bulls!" muttered the pilot, in the same breath that he issued some rapid orders concerning the management of the brig. "But they don't see us yet, the sleepy heads!" he added, in a more hopeful tone; "and if they'll only fool away their time a half hour longer, I'll show 'em a Yankee trick that'll give 'em something to swear about for a month."

Great was the anxiety of the gallant Captain Stellwagen and his men for the next fifteen minutes — every breath they drew, while unperceived, seeming to add to their security and hope; but suddenly, to their dismay, a wreath of white smoke was seen to issue from the gun-deck port of the seventy-four, followed by the heavy boom of a gun, and then by another and another, together with the flutter of several flags from her fore-royalmast, and a repetition of the signals from the rest of the fleet—all proclaiming that the escaping Concord had all at once become an object of interest to those who hoped for gain by her capture.

"There they go! they have discovered us, and are signalling their Tender to give chase!" said Captain Stellwagen, with a deep sigh, but firmly compressed lips.

"Let 'em blaze away, gall-blast 'em!" cried the now excited pilot; "we don't mind no such barking as that;

and if their confounded jackall is only down near Henlopen, it's little she can do now to hurt us eyther."

"Send a man with a sharp pair of eyes to each masthead, to look about for the man-of-war schooner, Mr. Rawlins!" cried the Captain, turning to his mate. "Be awake now, and move lively!"

Several minutes of intense anxiety were now passed by those on board the Concord, in keeping a sharp lookout for the dangerous schooner—and a faint hope was beginning to spring up in every breast, that she was at anchor at some place below them—when suddenly the pilot, who was carefully surveying the scene with a glass, exclaimed, with an oath:

"There she is, with her two bare poles run up so innocent like, (the —— thief!) just above the Brandywine, where she's playing 'possum, pretending to be dead or asleep, like a spider watching a fly, and calculating to take us as soon as we git up to her! Yes, I'm afeard they've catched us finely, after all, Captain!" he added, looking down the stream; "for the fleet is pouring out its armed boats to cut us off from the sea, and this sneak is waiting to nab us as we go up."

"What we cannot cure we must endure!" said Captain Stellwagen, in a seemingly calm tone of resignation, as he took the glass, and for a few minutes quietly surveyed the scene around him. "She does not move yet," he added, with some slight degree of hope, as he once more brought his glass to bear upon the schooner, "and we are almost on a line with her. Perhaps——Ha! there she goes!"

As he spoke, the fore and topsail yards of the schooner were suddenly swayed aloft and crossed; her sails, one after another, were run up and set; and almost immediately she began to fill away and run before the breeze, in a direction to cut off the more heavily-laden Concord.

"Well, Pilot, there is but one course for us now!" said the Captain, in a firm, even tone of voice, as he glanced around upon the gloomy faces of his disappointed men, with an expression of mingled determination and desperation; "we must face this she-devil and stand her fire—for, while a chance remains, I will never surrender."

This determination met with a hearty approval from all; and the pilot hopefully suggested that, by keeping among the shoals and flats, where the schooner could not safely venture without a native of the coast to guide her, the brig might even yet go clear.

The chase, which was now fairly begun, was excitingly maintained for some considerable time—the Paz gliding steadily up the more smooth and open channel, into which the fugitive Concord must eventually turn—and the latter essaying every art to escape, by crossing ridges and banks, or boldly ploughing the deeper water of narrow channels between dangerous shoals.

As the space occupied by the dividing shoals and sand-spits gradually narrowed, it brought the two vessels nearer together, till at length the schooner opened her fire, and sent her shot whistling around the brig and through her rigging and sails, though without inflicting any material damage

Crow and Deadman's Shoals were safely passed by the Concord, and good fair sailing might have given her the victory; but the time had now come for her to find her way into the main channel, or run aground; and in attempting to do this, her heel suddenly caught and ploughed the sand beneath her; she stopped - started — caught again; and then, with every timber groaning, she thumped hard aground, and fell partly over on her side.

All was over now, and so groaned the disappointed Captain, as he gloomily surveyed the faces of his disappointed men. The Paz, perceiving the discomfiture of the Concord, at once ceased firing, and dispatched some twenty men in cutters to take possession of what was now her prize.

"Steward," said the Captain, addressing a bright-eyed mulatto, as the foremost cutter, containing an admiralty's mate, came alongside the brig, "hand the officer the man-ropes!" and he himself walked quietly to the gangway, to receive his captor with the same polite dignity he would have welcomed him as an honored guest.

"Who commands this brig?" demanded the officer, as he sprung on deck from the rail.

"I did, sir, before you came," returned the Captain, with a polite bow.

"Your papers, if you please," said the other.

"They are American, sir," replied the Master, as he quietly handed them to his captor.

"Then," returned the midshipman, merely glancing at the manifest, clearance, and crew-list, "I take possession of this vessel, and lay claim to her as lawful prize, in the name of His Britannic Majesty."

He then proceeded to give the necessary orders for securing the crew of the Concord, furling her sails, hoisting English colors to her main peak, and preparing her to float off with the next tide; and as soon as these commands were executed, he dispatched the cutters back to the schooner Paz, bearing the pilot and crew of the Concord prisoners, and a hasty report to the lieutenant-commanding—he himself remaining as master of the prize, and retaining Captain Stellwagen as his guest, the mulatto steward as a general waiter and cook, and seven of his own men to make every thing secure.

The day passed off with no remarkable occurrence—the Concord being got afloat at the next high tide and anchored in the main channel—where she remained till the second morning after; when, there springing up a fresh breeze from the south-east, with a flying mist, indicating the commencement of a "smoky south-easter," she was got under way, and beat down the bay to within some quarter of a mile of the fleet, where she was again brought to anchor, directly under the guns of the seventy-four.

Here, feeling himself perfectly secure, and the storm which had sprung up rather increasing than abating, the young officer gave himself up to the enjoyment of good eating and good drinking, and the happy illusion that he was supreme commander of all he surveyed, and might perhaps be sent home with the prize, to receive a lieutenant's commission and be made a lion of for his distinguished services.

The crew, too, became rather elated at their good fortune; and the rigid discipline of the service being somewhat relaxed, and good wine, direct from Lisbon, being easily procured from the stores around them, they gradually became careless to a degree that at length awoke a strange, wild hope in the breast of Captain Stellwagen, that perhaps, with the assistance of his steward, he might yet, by a bold, desperate step, retake his vessel and escape from the very clutches of his foe.

Till this thought and this hope entered the mind of the captain, he had been very much cast down and depressed; as indeed he well might be; for he had by this capture not only lost his all of worldly goods, his position as commander of a goodly ship, but his own personal liberty, and the ardently-cherished hope of soon meeting with the dear beings of his fondest affection and solicitude; and though he had seemingly appeared cheerful and resigned when conversing with his polite and gentlemanly captor, it had been the cheerfulness which one sometimes assumes to cover grief, and the resignation which as often springs from the very depths of despair. But now, with the bare hope of escape—the bare hope of regaining all he had lost, and again greeting, with the fond kiss of a husband and father, all he loved on earth—a new life seemed infused into his veins—a new spirit seemed animating his body—and he felt as if, in some bold attempt for freedom, he would have the physical strength of a dozen men.

He now, though apparently indifferent and at his ease, began to watch closely everything taking place around him; and it was with a secret joy he could scarcely conceal, that he observed the remissness of the officer in command, who spent most of his time below in eating, drinking, and smoking—and the careless negligence of the men, who, with their arms rolled up in a tarpaulin and placed under the long-boat, passed a large portion of the day under a temporary awning, which they had stretched along the deck to secure themselves from the fine, driving Scotch mist, and where, with plenty of wine and small chat, they appeared to be both happy and oblivious.

Under pretence of giving his faithful steward, Richard Douce, some directions about his supper, Captain Stellwagen easily found an opportunity to touch him upon the matter nearest his heart. Briefly mentioning what he had seen, and what, if Heaven favored them, they might hope, he added, in a low, earnest tone:

"Richard, how much are you willing to risk for your freedom and mine?"

"My life, Captain Stellwagen, for *my* freedom—and my life, twenty times over, for *yours*, sir—God bless you!"

"Thank you, Richard; you are a brave, noble lad, and I trust will have your reward. I have a plan in view, which, should it succeed, will perhaps give us both our liberty, and restore us to our friends."

"Ah! Heaven bless your honor!" said Richard, his eyes sparkling with hope.

"But if it fails, Richard——" and the captain paused and fixed his dark eye steadily upon the other.

"What then, sir?" asked the steward, holding his breath and turning somewhat pale.

"We shall either be cut to pieces by yonder men, or be swung from the yard-arm of a man-of-war!" rejoined the other, with impressive solemnity. "So, Richard, my brave lad," he gravely added, "think well and seriously before you decide upon what must result in liberty or death!"

"Captain," said the brave mulatto, after a momentary pause, "I'm with you for life or death! What you dare, I'll dare—and what you suffer, I'll suffer—and God bless you for the kindest master I ever sailed under."

"Your hand, Richard!"

The captain then briefly made known his plans, which would not require action before the flood tide of the following morning, and established signals between himself and faithful servitor, by which the latter would know exactly when and how to act, even should there be no further communication between them.

The following was a trying night to the two prisoners—a night of alternate hopes and fears—but the next morning, to their unspeakable delight, they found everything favorable to their purpose. The wind was blowing almost a gale in their favor; the rain was fine and misty, the tide was running up; the men were under their awning, with their arms, as on the previous day, rolled up in the tarpaulin and placed under the bow of the long-boat; and the Prize Master was below, thinking about anything rather than the capture of himself and the escape of his prisoners.

Soon after this, the Midshipman came on deck, and exchanged a few words with his prisoner, on the state of the weather, and the prospect of their being left unmolested by the Admiral for at least another day; and then the Captain went below, and was followed by the steward, with some hot coffee, as was previously agreed upon.

The Midshipman's pistols and cutlass were in his berth; and these Richard Douce now hurriedly secured, handing the former to his master and hiding the latter. This done, he again went on deck, and took his station by the cook's galley, to await the final signal of life or death; while the captain, hastily swallowing a cup of coffee, called to the officer to come down and take his ere it should cool.

As the latter complied, the captain made an errand on deck; and on reaching it, he remarked that he would draw over the hatch, to keep out the rain; and having done so, he quietly fastened it with the hasp, and thus secured the officer a prisoner without his being aware of it.

Glancing quickly around, and perceiving that everything was favorable to his desperate purpose, the captain now gave the signal agreed upon, a twist of his neckcloth; and the mulatto, bounding upon the tarpaulin, caught it up in his arms, and darted back to the quarterdeck, where he succeeded in arming himself with another brace of pistols before the astonished crew had time to take any action whatever.

Both the captain and steward, pistols in hand, now rushed forward together, the former exclaiming, in a voice of thunder:

"Down into the forecastle, every man of you, before I blow your brains out!"

Three of the surprised and astonished men fled precipitately down the fore-castle hatch—two seemed irresolute—and two, the boatswain's mate and quarter-master, made a show of resistance. Instantly each was covered by a pistol in the determined hands of Stellwagen and Douce, and the captain again thundered forth:

"Back, I tell you, and down with you below, or, by the living God above us, I will scatter your brains where you stand! I am a desperate man, and will have possession of this vessel or die!—so down with you—down—ere I send your souls to your Maker!"

As he uttered this threat, his fine commanding form seemed to tower aloft; and the bright, stern gleam of his dark, eagle eye, proclaimed that his was an oath that would not be broken. The petty officers, awed by his look, began gradually to quail before him; and then, exchanging glances, they sullenly turned on their heels, and slowly followed those who had preceded them. The moment their heads were below the deck, the hatch was closed and secured by some heavy coils of rope, which the gallant captain and his steward now drew upon it.

"Quick, now, Richard!" exclaimed the captain; "cut the hempen cable, and let her drift beyond the guns of the fleet! The wind is in our favor—the tide is running up—

and if they do not perceive us in this cloud-like mist, we shall soon be beyond their reach. God send we may! for our lives depend upon it."

He had scarcely finished his order, when the mulatto severed the cable, and the laden brig was once more in motion. A few minutes of the most intense anxiety followed; and then there boomed a signal-gun from the seventy-four, to warn the Prize Master of the Concord that something was wrong. It was of course unheeded, and was presently followed by another.

"Now then for our lives!" cried the captain, as he sprung forward and seized a rope. "Cut loose the jib, Richard! Now hoist away! There—there—up she goes! Now, my brave lad, spring up and cut the gaskets of fore-sail and foretopsail, while I take the helm and keep her off before the wind!"

The two men both worked hard and fast; and in a few minutes the sails were spread and sheeted home, and the noble vessel was speeding away from her foes, favored by wind and tide. Gun after gun now thundered from the Poictiers, and shot after shot came whistling past the brig and through her rigging; but in fifteen minutes more she was beyond the reach of her enemies, and bearing safely homeward the brave master and steward, who had recaptured her by one of the boldest and most daring exploits on record.

We need only add, that in due time she safely arrived in Philadelphia, where Captain Stellwagen had the honor of transferring to the legal authorities the first prisoners brought thither during the war of 1812—a commissioned officer and seven men—captured by himself and colored steward, and taken, together with the vessel which contained them, right from under the guns of an Admiral's fleet.

History does not furnish a bolder or a braver deed than this.

Captain Daniel Stellwagen subsequently entered the United States Navy, and commanded the Third Division of Galley's at Commodore McDonough's celebrated victory on Lake Champlain. He was afterward honored by Congress with the presentation of a sword and a vote of thanks, and died at Philadelphia in 1828, respected by all who knew him, and beloved by those who knew him most.

Rocky Mountain Perils.

The life of the trapper in the Far West, in earlier times, was one of almost constant peril. Setting off alone, or with only a companion or two, into the great, lonely wilderness, whose only denizens were wild beasts and savages, and pursuing an occupation which led him into the wildest and gloomiest retreats among the mountains, he was compelled to be ever on the watch, night and day, to protect his life against foes who often lurked in deep thickets, or behind projecting rocks, awaiting an opportunity to cut him off and carry his scalp and effects in triumph to their barbarous homes. This wild life naturally made the trapper wary, suspicious, and ferocious—a sort of semi-savage; and regarding his rifle as his truest friend, and the Indian as his greatest foe, he took care to keep the former ever by him, and kill the latter whenever opportunity presented.

One of the most daring, and for many years successful, of these mountaineers, was a man by the name of Markhead. He was a finely-built, athletic fellow, and was probably as devoid of fear as it is possible for any human being to be and retain the natural instincts of life. There was no personal risk, at one period of his career, that he seemed afraid to venture; and probably, the renowned Kit Carson alone excepted, there never was so bold and reckless a hunter, trapper, and guide, who lived so many years to boast of his almost incredible exploits. He managed for a long time to escape with life; though his body and limbs were covered with ugly scars, which told the tale of many deadly conflicts, and how near he had more than once been to the very jaws of death itself.

As a single instance of what he had been known to dare, it is related of him, that, while accompanying Sir William Drummond Stewart in one of his expeditions across the mountains, a half-breed absconded one night with several animals; and Sir William, being greatly vexed and annoyed at the occurrence, remarked that he would give five hundred dollars for the scalp of the thief. Soon after, it was discovered that Markhead was missing; but the next day he rode into camp, with the scalp of the half-breed dangling at the end of his rifle.

Markhead was by profession a trapper, and boldly ventured into every region where he thought he might be most successful in taking the beaver, having no regard whatever to the dangers he would be compelled to encounter in his lonely explorations. On more than one occasion he was himself taken by outlying savages, who were only prevented from immediately dispatching him by their fiendish desire of burning him at the stake; but he always succeeded, sometimes in an almost miraculous manner, in effecting his escape, and always embraced every opportunity of a vindictive revenge upon the hated race.

The Yellow Stone and its numerous branches, from its source among the mountains to its junction with the great and turbid Missouri, was the favorite trapping-ground of this daring individual; and one of his most remarkable adventures in this region of country it is our present purpose to record.

Setting off alone, as was frequently his custom, with his riding-horse, pack-mules, "possibles," "traps," and camp-utensils, himself well-armed and equipped in mountain style, Markhead penetrated far into the territorial possessions of his savage foes, and at last fixed his camp in a wild, romantic valley, and set about his vocation with the same careless indifference to danger that the angler would cast his line in the tranquil waters about his peaceful home.

Here he remained unmolested for several weeks, and found beaver so plenty as to gladden his heart at the thought of the "glorious time" he would have when he should return to the "rendezvous," that paradise for such mountain men as happen to bring sufficient "peltries" to indulge largely in its luxuries, its games, and its general dissipations.

But going one morning to examine his traps, the gallant mountaineer, to his great annoyance, discovered the fresh print of a moccasin a little distance back from the stream; and the sight so roused his ire, that he at once gave vent to it in a very uncomplimentary apostrophe to an individual he had not yet seen; and using all due caution to guard against a surprise, he continued on down the stream to his different traps; and found to his great delight, that each one held a prize, in the shape of a plump, fat beaver. Having dispatched the animals, and reset his traps, he cautiously, but proudly, returned to his camp, muttering as he went along:

"The sneaking fool! to come and put his foot into my mess in that way, and think to outwit me! But I'll fix him yit, and every son of an aboriginee that comes with him; for whilst I find beavers coming in this handsome, and begging to be tuk by a gentleman what appreciates, I'll be dogged ef I'll be druv from my position by all the greasy, copper-colored rascals in North America!"

Markhead spent much of the day in hunting for "Indian signs," but without discovering any thing to excite fresh uneasiness. He found a few more moccasin prints, it is true, but evidently made by the same feet; and he came to the conclusion that some stray Indian, perhaps a solitary hunter, had been near his camp and departed—it might be with, and it might be without, the knowledge of a white man being encamped in the vicinity. If the former, and the savage had friends near, he thought it more than likely an attempt would soon be made to waylay and kill him; and if the latter, that he had nothing unusual to fear; but as he could not determine this point satisfactorily, he permitted prudence for once to have entire control over his actions; and he took the trouble to secrete his peltries, lead his animals to a new grazing spot, and pass the following night in another place himself.

The next morning, Markhead, by a new and roundabout course, went down to his first trap most cautiously, reconnoitering the ground as he neared it; and much pleased was he with himself at having taken this precaution; for right in the very path along which he would otherwise have approached the spot, he now discovered three Indians, crouched down among some bushes behind a projecting rock, patiently awaiting his appearance. By the course he had prudently taken, he had come upon the stream a little below, and consequently behind them; and he now, without being himself perceived, had them in fair range.

"That's the way you painted heathens watch for a white gentleman, is it?" chuckled the trapper, as he slowly and deliberately brought forward his long, unerring rifle, and took a steady aim at the nearest, who nearly covered the one beyond him

Markhead recollected the old proverb of "killing two birds with one stone," and a grim smile partially relieved the harshness of his vindictive expression as he pulled the trigger. True to its duty, the piece sent forth its leaden messenger, and with such force as to drive the ball clean through the first savage and mortally wound the second. The instant he fired, the daring mountaineer grasped his long knife, and bounded forward with a ferocious yell; while the unharmed Indian, starting as suddenly to his feet, with a wild yell of surprise and terror, darted quickly away, leaving his wounded, floundering, and groaning friends to the mercy of a foe who was never known to spare one of the hated race.

On coming up to the wounded savages, neither of whom was dead, Markhead proceed to dispatch and scalp them with the same ferocious satisfaction that he would have butchered and skinned two wounded wild beasts; after which he coolly reloaded his rifle, without the least compunction of conscience, and with a self-complacent chuckle at his own caution and triumph.

"Wonder how fur that thar other skeered Injun 'll run afore he stops!" he grinned, as he spurned his dead enemies with his foot, and gathered up, as further trophies of his exploit, the weapons with which they had intended to destroy him. "Thar!" he continued, as he moved away from the dead bodies; "I reckon I'll see to my traps now, without axing no leave of you, whilst you stop here to feed wolves and buzzards, that maybe is wanting a breakfast this fine morning."

He then, believing there was no further danger set off boldly, and somewhat carelessly, down the stream, to visit his traps. As on the preceding day, he found his success had been somewhat remarkable; and, fairly loaded with beaver he returned toward his camp in fine spirits. On his direct route, was a wild, romantic glen, with steep, high, rocky hills on either hand, and between which dashed, foaming and roaring, a clever mountain stream. He had reached nearly the centre of this valley, and was walking leisurely along, when he was startled by the sharp report of several muskets, instantly followed by the fierce exultant yells of a small party of savages, who sprung up suddenly from behind different concealments and darted toward him in a body.

The instant the Indians fired, Markhead felt a sharp twinge in his left arm; and glancing toward it, he perceived the blood streaming through his garments, and knew he was wounded; but finding, on trial, he could use his arm, he gave no further heed to it, and concentrated his every thought upon the saving of his life.

The Indians, some six or eight in number, were now bounding forward to finish their work; and instantly throwing down his beaver, the trapper brought his deadly rifle to bear on the foremost; and he was in the very act of firing, when the latter, perceiving his danger, uttered a short cry of surprise, and dodged behind a tree—an example which his cowardly companions took care to imitate as speedily as possible.

This gave the intrepid hunter a moment to look about him and calculate his chances of escape; and perceiving, on the hill to his left, an opening among the rocks, as it might be the mouth of a cave—and knowing if he gave his foes time to reload, they could certainly kill him where he stood—he suddenly turned, and dashed across the stream, and up the steep acclivity; his enemies immediately bounding after, with yells of triumph, but being deterred from venturing a too rapid pursuit by a wholesome fear of his deadly rifle, which every now and then was steadily brought to bear upon the nearest.

In this way Markhead reached the point at which he had aimed, some considerable distance ahead of his pursuers; and for a few moments he stood and debated with himself whether he should secrete himself within the opening, which appeared large and deep, or continue his flight over the mountain ridge. He decided on the former, as the readiest means of giving him immediate time for cool and deliberate calculation; and the next moment he disappeared from the sight of his yelling foes; who, fearing his ultimate escape, now sprung up the hill more nimbly and boldly.

The opening, as the trapper had conjectured, was the mouth of a cave of considerable dimensions; and was so guarded, by winding passages among projecting rocks, as to secure to him, from the moment of entering it, a feeling of safety; and darting back a few paces, he ensconced himself behind a sharp angle, and waited for his foes to come up.

Presently he saw the Indians appear, one after another, at the mouth of the opening, and cautiously peer into the gloom within; but neither seemed possessed of courage sufficient to lead the way to what would probably be certain death to the foremost. From where they stood, the savages could not discern the fugitive, though he could perceive them distinctly; and it required all his self-control to restrain his desire of firing upon them, and trusting the rest to chance.

Soon after, the Indians withdrew from the view of the trapper, and for a few minutes all was silence within and without. He conjectured they were now holding a consultation; and when he thought that his very life might depend upon the result, he could not but feel anxious to have an end put to his suspense by an attack or retreat.

Suddenly, while he was wondering how he should get safely out of his present "scrape," even with the loss of his animals and furs, the mouth of the cave was darkened by several Indians, and lightened by the flash of several muskets, while half a dozen balls flattened themselves against the rocks, and the reports reverberated strangely as the sounds were thrown back from the farthest recesses of his subterranean retreat.

Markhead was untouched by their fire, but enraged at what he considered their audacity; and, with a yell of defiance, he instantly raised his own rifle and poured back its contents. His shot, fortunately, took effect in the breast of a warrior, who fell over, and rolled yelling down the rugged hill, to the great chagrin and dismay of his companions, who made haste to get beyond the reach of so dangerous an enemy.

After this, the savages, though remaining in the vicinity, and keeping a close watch upon the mouth of the cave, to prevent the escape of the prisoner within, took good care to keep out of his sight. And so the day wore away—Markhead fretting and swearing at what he termed his ill-luck, in being "cooped up in sich an infernal hole," but not caring to venture out in the face of almost certain death.

At last, toward night, he was suddenly surprised by seeing a large pile of brush thrown down in front of the cave, and was not slow in comprehending that his foes intended to smoke him out, as he himself had aforetime smoked out some wild beast. This pile was rapidly augmented by fresh combustibles; and in the course of an hour it had become quite formidable—the trapper sitting and watching, and considering which might be the safest proceeding for him—to remain and let them fire it, or attempt an escape by suddenly breaking through it.

"But I'll let the cusses do it," he muttered, at length; "for I can break through arterward as well as now, and night'll soon be here to kiver me as I run."

Had the savages thought of this plan and acted upon it sooner, the history of the trapper might have ended with that eventful day—for an escape in daylight would have been almost impossible; but fortunately for him, they did not set fire to the combustibles till the forest had begun to grow dusky with the advancing shadows of night. The materials they had collected being old, dry brush, ignited like so much tinder; and in a minute after the application of the match, the whole pile was a crackling and roaring flame—the heat and smoke at once penetrating far back into the cavern, and soon rendering it an untenable place.

Seeing the time had come for him to make another desperate effort for his life, Markhead secured his powder-horn in his bosom, wrapped the skirt of his hunting-frock around the lock of his rifle, grasped his knife firmly, drew in his breath for a start, and concentrating his whole will upon his single purpose, suddenly bounded forth, directly through the scorching flames.

So sudden was his exit from the cavern, that the Indians, though looking for the event to take place, and standing prepared to fire at and fall upon him with their knives and tomahawks, did not even get their guns to bear till he was half way down the dangerous declivity; and then they discharged their muskets almost at random, and set yelling after him with a degree of uncertainty and confusion that gave him an additional advantage.

On reaching the bank of the stream, Markhead turned quickly down it, darted into a favoring thicket, thence into the water, and threw himself flat down close up under the overhanging foliage. Here he quietly remained, favored by the fast gathering shades of night, till his enemies, who believed he was still in flight, had run yelling past in fierce pursuit; and then, as they gradually grew more distant, he started up and ran in an opposite direction.

An hour later he had reached in safety the spot where he had deposited his pelts. Gathering up as many as he could carry, he next sought and found his horse, mounted him, and escaped—leaving his mules, traps, and camp utensils as the spoil of his foes.

Three days after this, he boldly revisited the spot, and found the remainder of his furs; but all the rest of his property had been discovered and taken away by the savages. At this Markhead sought relief to his feelings by what in Western parlance would be termed "some pretty tall swearing;" but concluded at last to make the best of what he possessed, and set off to the nearest station o get a new outfit.

That same season, notwithstanding all his misfortunes, Markhead might have been found trapping along the different streams, in the vicinity of his losses and thrilling adventures; and when he repaired to the "rendezvous," in the following autumn, no single trapper could out-count him in peltries, or out-talk him in exploits.

But this man of daring finally met a terrible fate. At the fearful uprising of the treacherous Mexicans, in the Valley of Taos, at the time of the massacre of Governor Bent and other Americans, Markhead, and a companion named Harwood, who had gone thither to exchange some peltries for whiskey, were captured by the blood-thirsty mob, and shot down like dogs.

So perished, in the full vigor of manhood, one of the very bravest, boldest, and most reckless of that hardy and daring little band known as the Trappers of the Far West.

The Dead Alive.

"WE Doctors sometimes meet with strange adventures," once said to me a distinguished physician, with whom I was on terms of intimacy.

"I have often thought," I replied, "that the secret history of some of your profession, if written out in detail, would make a work of thrilling interest."

"I do not know that I exactly agree with you in regard to detail," rejoined my friend; "for we medical men, like every one else, meet with a great deal that is common place, and therefore not worthy of being recorded; but grant us the privilege of you novelists, to select our characters and scenes, and work them into a kind of plot, with a view to a striking *denouement*, and I doubt not many of us could give you a romance in real life, comprising only what we have seen, which would equal, if not surpass, any thing you ever met in the way of fiction. By-the-by, I believe I never told you of the most strange and romantic adventure of my life?"

"You never told me of any of your adventures, Doctor,"

I replied; "but if you have a story to tell, you will find me an eager listener."

"Very well, then, as I have a few minutes to spare, I will tell you one more wildly romantic, more incredibly remarkable, if I may so speak, than you probably ever found in a work of fiction."

"I am all attention."

"Twenty-five years ago," pursued the Doctor, "I entered the medical college at F—— as a student. I was then quite young, inexperienced, and inclined to be timid and sentimental; and well do I remember the horror I experienced, when one of the senior students, under pretence of showing me the beauties of the institution, suddenly thrust me into the dissecting-room, among several dead bodies, and closed the door upon me; nor do I forget how my screeches of terror, and prayers for release from that awful place, made me the laughing-stock of my older companions.

"Ridicule is a hard thing to bear: the coward becomes brave to escape it, and the brave man fears it more than he would a belching cannon. I suffered from it till I could stand no more; and wrought up to a pitch of desperation, I demanded to know what I might do to redeem my character, and gain an honorable footing among my fellow students.

"'I will tell you,' said one, his eyes sparkling with mischief; 'if you will go, at the midnight hour, and dig up a subject, and take it to your room, and remain alone with it till morning, we will let you off, and never say another word about your womanly fright.'

"I shuddered. It was a fearful alternative; but it seemed less terrible to suffer all the horrors that might be concentrated into a single night, than to bear, day after day, the jeers of my companions.

"'Where shall I go? and when?' was my timid inquiry; and the very thought of such an adventure made my blood run cold.

"'To the Eastern Cemetery, to-night, at twelve o'clock,' replied my tormentor, fixing his keen, black eyes upon me, and allowing his thin lips to curl with a smile of contempt. 'But what is the use of asking such a coward as you to perform such a manly feat?' he added, deridingly.

"His words stung me to the quick; and without further reflection, and scarcely aware of what I was saying, I rejoined, boldly:

"I am no coward, sir, as I will prove to you, by performing what you call a manly feat.'

"'You will go?' he asked, quickly.

"'I will.'

"'Bravely said, my lad!' he rejoined, in a tone of approval, and exchanging his expression of contempt for one of surprise and admiration. 'Do this, Morris, and the first man that insults you afterward makes an enemy of me!'

"Again I felt a cold shudder pass through my frame, at the thought of what was before me; but I had accepted his challenge in the presence of many witnesses—for this conversation occurred as we were leaving the hall, after listening to an evening lecture—and I was resolved to make my word good, should it even cost me my life: in fact, I knew I could not do otherwise now, without the risk of being driven in disgrace from the college.

"I should here observe, that in those days there were few professional resurrectionists; and it was absolutely necessary to have subjects for dissection, the unpleasant business of procuring them devolved upon the students; who, in consequence, watched every funeral eagerly, and calculated the chances of cheating the sexton of his charge and the grave of its victim.

"There had been a funeral, that day, of a poor orphan girl, who had been followed to the grave by very few friends; and this was considered a favorable chance for the party whose turn it was to procure the next subject, as the graves of the poor and friendless were never watched with the same keen vigilance as those of the rich and influential. Still, it was no trifling risk to attempt to exhume the bodies of the poorest and humblest—for not unfrequently persons were found on the watch even over these; and only the year before, one student, while at his midnight work, had been mortally wounded by a rifle ball; and another, a month or two subsequently, had been rendered a cripple for life by the same means

"All this was explained to me by a party of six or eight, who accompanied me to my room—which was in a building belonging to the college, and rented by apartments to such of the students as preferred bachelor's hall to regular boarding; and they took care to add several terrifying stories of ghosts and hobgoblins, by way of calming my excited nerves, just as I have before now observed old women stand around a weak, feverish patient, and croak out their experience in seeing awful sufferings and fatal terminations of just such maladies as the one with which their helpless victim was then afflicted.

"'Is it expected that I shall go alone?' I inquired, in a tone that trembled in spite of me, while my knees almost knocked together, and I felt as if my very lips were white.

"'Well, no,' replied Benson, my most dreaded tormentor; 'it would be hardly fair to send you alone, for one individual could not succeed in getting the body from the grave quick enough; and you, a mere youth, without experience, would be sure to fail altogether. No, we will go with you, some three or four of us, and help you dig up the corpse; but then you must take it on your back, bring it up to your room here, and spend the night alone with it!'

"It was some relief to me to find I was to have company during the first part of my awful undertaking; but still I felt far from agreeable, I assure you; and chancing to look into a mirror, as the time drew near for setting out, I fairly started at beholding the ghastly object I saw reflected therein.

"'Come, boys,' said Benson, who was always, by general consent, the leader of whatever frolic, expedition, or undertaking he was to have a hand in: 'Come, boys, it is time to be on the move. A glorious night for us!' he added, throwing up the window, and letting in a fierce gust of wind and rain: 'the very d—l himself would hardly venture out in such a storm!'

"He lit a dark-lantern, threw on his long, heavy cloak, took up a spade, and led the way down stairs; and the rest of us, three besides my timid self, threw on our cloaks also, took each a spade, and followed him.

"We took a roundabout course, to avoid being seen by any citizen that might chance to be stirring; and in something less than half-an-hour we reached the cemetery, scaled the wall without difficulty, and stealthily searched for the grave, till we found it, in the pitchy darkness—the wind and rain sweeping past us with dismal howls and moans, that to me, trembling with terror, seemed to be the unearthly wailings of the spirits of the damned.

"'Here we are,' whispered Benson to me, as we at length stopped at a mound of fresh earth, over which one of our party had stumbled. 'Come, feel round, Morris, and strike in your spade, and let us see if you will make as good a hand at exhuming a dead body as you will some day at killing a living one with physic.'

"I did as directed, trembling in every limb; but the first spade-full I threw up, I started back with a yell of horror, that, on any other but a howling, stormy night, would have betrayed us. It appeared to me as if I had thrust my spade into a buried lake of fire—for the soft dirt was all aglow like living coals; and as I had fancied the moanings of the storm the wailings of tormented spirits, I now fancied I had uncovered a small portion of the Bottomless Pit itself.

"'Fool!' hissed Benson, grasping my arm with the gripe of a vice, as I stood leaning on my spade for support, my very teeth chattering with terror; 'another yell like that, and I'll make a subject of you! Are you not ashamed of yourself, to be scared out of your wits, if you ever had any, by a little phosphorescent earth? Don't you know it is often found in graveyards?'

"His explanation re-assured me; though I was now too weak, from my late fright to be of any assistance to the party; who all fell to with a will, secretly laughing at me, and soon reached the coffin. Splitting the lid with a hatchet, which had been brought for the purpose, they quickly lifted out the corpse; and then Benson and another of the party taking hold of it, one at the head and the other at the feet, they hurried it away, bidding me follow, and leaving the others to fill up the grave, that it might not be suspected the body had been exhumed.

"Having got the corpse safely over the wall of the cemetery, Benson now called upon me to perform my part of the horrible business.

"'Here, you quaking simpleton,' he said; 'I want you to take this on your back, and make the best of your way to your room, and remain alone with it all night! If you do this bravely, we will claim you as one of us to-morrow, and the first man that dares to say a word against your courage after that, shall find a foe in me. But, hark you! if you make any blunder on the way, and lose our prize, it will be better for you to quit this town before I set eyes on you again! Do you understand me?'

"'Y-ye-ye-yes!' I stammered, with chattering teeth.

"'Are you ready?'

"'Y-ye-ye-yes,' I gasped.

"'Well, come here, where are you?'

"All this time it was so dark that I could see nothing but a faint line of white, which I knew to be the shroud of the corpse; but I felt carefully round till I got hold of Benson, who told me to take off my cloak; and then rearing the cold dead body up against my back, he began fixing its cold arms about my neck—bidding me take hold of them, and draw them well over, and keep them concealed, and be sure and not let go of them, on any consideration whatever, as I valued my life.

"Oh! the torturing horror I experienced, as I mechanically followed his directions! Tongue could not describe it!

"At length, having adjusted the corpse so that I might bear it off with comparative ease, he threw my long, black cloak over it, and over my arms, and fastened it with a cord about my neck, and then inquired:

"'Now, Morris, do you think you can find the way to your room?'

"'I–I–do–do–don't know,' I gasped, feeling as if I should sink to the earth at the first step.

"'Well, you cannot lose your way, if you go straight ahead,' he replied. 'Keep in the middle of this street or road, and it will take you to College Green, and then you are all right. Come, push on, before your burden grows too heavy; the distance is only a good half mile!'

"I set forward, with trembling nerves, expecting to sink to the ground at every step; but gradually my terror, instead of weakening, gave me strength; and I was soon on the run—splashing through mud and water—with the storm howling about me in fury, and the cold corpse, as I fancied, clinging to me like a hideous vampire.

"How I reached my room, I do not know—but probably by a sort of instinct; for I only remember of my brain being in a wild, feverish whirl, with ghostly phantoms all about me, as one sometimes sees them in a dyspeptic dream.

"But reach my room I did, with my dead burden on my back; and I was afterwards told that I made wonderful time; for Benson and his fellow-student, fearing the loss of their subject—which, on account of the difficulty of getting bodies, was very valuable—followed close behind me, and were obliged to run at the top of their speed to keep me within hailing distance.

"The first I remember distinctly, after getting to my room, was the finding myself awake in bed, with a dim consciousness of something horrible having happened—though what, for some minutes, I could not for the life of me recollect. Gradually, however, the truth dawned upon me; and then I felt a cold perspiration start from every pore, at the thought that perhaps I was occupying a room alone with a corpse. The room was not dark; there were a few embers in the grate which threw out a ruddy light; and fearfully raising my head, I glanced quickly and timidly around.

And there—there, on the floor, against the right hand wall, but a few feet from me—there, sure enough, lay the cold, still corpse, robed in its white shroud, with a gleam of firelight resting upon its ghastly face, which to my excited fancy seemed to move. Did it move? I was gazing upon it, thrilled and fascinated with an indiscribable terror, when, as sure as I see you now, I saw the lids of its eyes unclose, and saw its breast heave, and heard a low, stifled moan.

"'Great God!' I shrieked, and fell back in a swoon

"How long I lay unconscious I do not know; but when I came to myself again, it is a marvel to me, that, in my excited state, I did not lose my senses altogether, and become the tenant of a mad-house; for there—right before me—standing up in its white shroud—with its eyes wide open and staring upon me, and its features thin, hollow and death-hued—was the corpse I had brought from the cemetery.

"'In God's name, avaunt!' I gasped. 'Go back to your grave, and rest in peace! I will never disturb you again!'

"The large, hollow eyes looked more wildly upon me—the head moved—the lips parted—and a voice, in a somewhat sepulchral tone, said:

"'Where am I? Where am I? Who are you? Which world am I in? Am I living or dead?'

"'You were dead,' I gasped, sitting up in bed, and feeling as if my brain would burst with a pressure of unspeakable horror; 'you were dead and buried, and I was one of the guilty wretches who this night disturbed you in your peaceful rest. But go back, poor ghost, in Heaven's name! and no mortal power shall ever induce me to come nigh you again!'

"'Oh! I feel faint!' said the corpse, gradually sinking down upon the floor, with a groan. 'Where am I? Oh! where am I?'

"'Great God!' I shouted, as the startling truth suddenly flashed upon me; 'perhaps this poor girl was buried alive, and is now living!'

"I bounded from the bed and grasped a hand of the prostrate body. It was not warm—but it was not cold. I put my trembling fingers upon the pulse. Did it beat? or was it the pulse in my fingers? I thrust my hand upon the heart. It was warm—there was life there. The breast heaved; she breathed; but the eyes were now closed, and the features had the look of death. Still it was a living body—or else I myself was insane.

"I sprung to the door, tore it open, and shouted for help.

"'Quick! quick!' cried I: 'the dead is alive! the dead is alive!'

"Several of the students, sleeping in adjoining rooms,

For there, standing up in its white shroud, was the corpse.

See page 256.

came hurrying to mine, thinking I had gone mad with terror, as some of them had heard my voice before, and all knew to what a fearful ordeal I had been subjected.

"'Poor fellow!' exclaimed one in a tone of sympathy; 'I predicted this.'

"'It is too bad!' said another; 'it was too much for his nervous system!'

"'I am not mad,' returned I, comprehending their suspicions; 'but the corpse is alive!—hasten and see!'

"They hurried into the room, one after another; and the foremost, stooping down to what he supposed was a corpse, put his hand upon it, and instantly exclaimed :

"Quick! a light and some brandy! She lives! she lives!'

"All now was bustle, confusion and excitement—one proposing one thing, and another something else, and all speaking together. They placed her on the bed, and gave her some brandy, when she again revived. I ran for a physician, (one of the faculty,) who came and tended upon her through the night, and by sunrise the next morning she was reported to be in a fair way for recovery.

"Now what do you think of my story so far?" queried the Doctor, with a quiet smile

"Very remarkable!" I replied; "very remarkable, indeed! But tell me, did the girl finally recover?"

"She did; and turned out to be a most beautiful creature, and only sweet seventeen."

"And I suppose she blessed the resurrectionists all the rest of her life!" I rejoined, with a laugh.

"She certainly held one of them in kind remembrance," returned the Doctor, with a sigh.

"What became of her, Doctor?"

"What should have become of her, according to the well-known rules of poetic justice of all you novel-writers?" returned my friend, with a peculiar smile.

"Why," said I, laughing, "she should have turned out an heiress, and married you."

"*And that is exactly what she did!*" rejoined the Doctor.

"Good heavens! You are jesting!"

"No, my friend, no," replied the Doctor, in a faltering voice: "that night of horror only preceded the dawn of my happiness; for that girl—sweet, lovely Helen Leroy—in time became my wife, and the mother of my two boys. She sleeps now in death, beneath the cold, cold sod," added the Doctor, in a tremulous tone, and brushing a tear from his eye: "and no human resurrectionists shall ever raise her to life again!"

Fight with a Bear.

At Independence, Missouri—that grand rendezvous for traders, trappers, travelers, emigrants, Indians, and, in short, for all going to, or returning from, the Far West—I once met an old mountaineer by the name of Glass—John Glass—though he looked as little like glass as any substance I can think of. In fact, John clearly showed, in his weather-beaten, scar-disfigured face, that his had been "a hard road to travel." Indeed, on second thought, I hardly know as I am justified in saying that John Glass had any face at all; but he had a head, and the front part of that head much resembled one side of an overgrown, badly-whitewashed gourd—a portion of the nose and original skin having been removed, leaving in place a kind of cicatrized surface, which a great amount of weather, and a total abstinence of soap and water, had turned to a color that I find comparable with nothing except the aforesaid vegetable.

I was not at that time acquainted with John personally; but being somewhat fascinated by his appearance, I begged an introduction, which was readily accorded by one having the honor of some familiarity with this nondescript specimen of the wilderness.

"I say, old hoss, hyer's a settlement chap as wants to know you a few," were the words which brought the attention of John Glass fully upon myself, and was my only form of presentation to the scarified mountaineer.

"Wall, stranger, you kin know me a heap, ef you're civil," was the reply of my new acquaintance, spoken in a tone that sounded not unlike the gurgling of water from a jug. "Chaw, hoss?" he added, inquiringly, having, like many another individual I wot of, an eye to the profits which might accrue from my acquaintance.

I instantly took the hint, and a plug of tobacco from my pocket, and handing the latter to my new friend, I observed that he had better keep the whole of it, as I had a sufficiency left.

"Hurraw!" cried the old trapper "You're a trump, you ar, and I'd play you agin any amount of dandified jimcracks I ever seed. You're a hoss as has bottom, or else I'm a wolf—hurraw!"

I saw I had made a good impression on my *outre* friend of the wilderness; and I naturally argued, that if a plug of tobacco could do that much, a little whiskey would do more. So, after a few exchanges of civilities, in which I endeavored to compliment John as much as he had me, I mildly suggested that we might as well take a drink.

"Hurraw!" he cried, in his broadly accented dialect; "you're one on 'em, stranger! and old peeled Jack is one as likes to know you. Drink? In course I will—and ef you kin jest find the fellow as says John Glass ever was knowed to refuse to drink when ax'd, you'll see a fight."

Accordingly, we adjourned to one of that kind of institutions in which these rough borderers most do congregate; and having called together a few of John's friends, we chartered a corner of the shanty for that especial occasion. The whiskey having been brought forward, in due proportion to the number and quality of the guests, who at once paid their respects to it, pipes were next in order; and each man having loaded, prepared to fire—and did fire—and such a volume of smoke I never before beheld except at the discharge of a regular battery.

My sole object in this operation was to hear from the lips of John Glass himself how it had happened that his figure head had become so seriously damaged; and so, seizing the first favorable opportunity, I broached the subject in a quiet way.

"Wall, stranger," said John, "that was one o' tne scrapes. Hey, Bill," he added, turning to one of his companions, "you remember that thar, I reckon?"

"Wall, I does, hoss," returned the other; "and ef I

didn't think you war dead that time, may I never see the Rocky agin!"

"Yes, Bill," pursued Glass, "you thought as how I war dead; and it's like you wern't glad to find it different, for you'd got my hoss and gun all snug enough. But you see, when John Glass goes under, thar's gwine to be an 'arthquake; and thar warn't nary 'arthquake then. Stranger," he added, filling his glass and turning to me, "I'll just tell you how it war, for you're right decent for a settlement feller, and decency ought to be encouraged. You see, stranger, it war a good many years ago—I don't exactly remember how many—that me and a party war gwine out to the mountains. Wall, we'd fixed up for a reg'lar trapping expedition, and had our hosses and mules, and all the rest o' our kit along, for a reg'lar three months' hunt. We got over onto the Black Hills without any accident, which war some'at to talk about for us, kase we didn't often go fur without them things. I say we got over onto the Black Hills, and pitched our camp in one o' the purtiest places I ever seed, whar we kind o' spread ourselves to make beaver come. Me and Bill, here—the old hoss—paired off, kind o' partner like, and did business in our own way, and that thar way war some.

"One day, as we war off that thar way together, setting our traps along a stream whar the beaver rayther seemed to like the fun—for they allers kin smelling round and

FIGHT WITH A BEAR.

rushing pleased and curious—we got kind o' tangled up in a thicket o' wild cherry, which growed along the stream. I war pushing along a leetle ahead o' Bill, when all at once't, as I kim to a kind o' opening, I seed a big grizzly, as quiet as a kitten, turning up the arth with his nose for the roots as laid below.

"'Hurraw, Bill!' says I, 'hyer's fun, and thar's meat.'

"'What's the muss, Jack?' says Bill, hurrying up to me.

"I showed him the b'ar about twenty yards off, and we agreed as how we'd draw his blood.

"Now, stranger," continued the old trapper, turning to me, "them thar grizzlys is some."

"In a bear fight?" I quietly suggested.

"Exactly—haw! haw! haw!" laughed the mountaineer. "They're some in a b'ar fight—just so; and you're some punks, any whar. Wall, as I was a saying, we fetched our rifles to an aim, and both spoke together. We both hit old grizzly plum centre: but them is critters as don't mind hitting, and our shots didn't seem to do no more nor jest kind o' rile up his dander. He kind o' started up and looked round, as savage as Old Nick; and then, seeing our smoke curling up from the thicket, he know'd thar was some'at for him thar, and broke for us like a streak o greased lightning.

"'Hurraw, Bill!' says I; 'we're in for't now. We'll be made meat on, sure as shooting.'

"'Wall, we will, old hoss,' says Bill, 'onless our legs is longer nor the b'ars.'

"'It's a run now, any way,' says I, as we both on us made a break through the thicket.

"Bill was behind me afore, but he was ahead o' me now; and ef he didn't do some tall walking then, I naver seed snakes. Hey, Bill?"

"Wall, I did, Jack," grinned Bill, who was himself nearly as pretty a specimen of the wilderness as the narrator.

"We both on us tore through the bushes like mad," resumed the old mountaineer; "but they was awful thick together, I tell you, and we didn't get along not nigh so fast as I has afore now, tumbling down hill; and we didn't git along not nigh so fast as the cussed old b'ar, who kim plunging arter us like a mad bull, gaining on us at every jump. Maybe as how I didn't swear some at them thar old bushes, which stuck into me at every leap, and kind o' kept me from gitting any war, with old grizzly pulling up close behind.

"At last we got to t'other side o' the thicket, whar thar was a patch o' prairie, and a big steep bluff on t'other side on't, about a hundred yards off.

"'Hurraw, Bill!' says I; 'it's bluff or die; for old grizzly has got kantankerous; and he ain't so fur behind but what he m)ut hear us holler. 'Leg it, Bill!' says I; 'let your pegs do their duty.'

'And Bill, here, he did leg it, for he'd got the ¸gs as could leg it; and I didn't keep a great ways behind. But the old varmint, he gained on us all through the bushes; and when I struck that thar prairie, I hadn't more'n twenty feet the start o' him. I'd hev cleared old Bruin, though, easy enough; but jest as I got half way to the bluff, I struck my infernal foot agin a stone, and kim down headlong. I got up agin right sudden; but it war too late for running now; for jest as I got on my feet, the old scamp stood straight up alongside o' me, and reached out his paws for a hug, like some o' the old Frenchmen I've seed out thar. I know'd old grizzly's hug warn't for any good, though; but seeing as thar warn't no help for't, I kind o' made up my mind to it, and gin him the contents o' the only pistol I had, at the same time yelling to Bill to load up and settle him.

"I'd jest got the words out, when old grizzly got his paws onto me, and, with one infernal rake downwards, tore off skin enough for a leather apron. I drawed my knife, said some'at o' prayers, and pitched into him with all my might; and we went rolling over and over on the grass, sometimes the b'ar topmost, and sometimes me.

"That thar, boys, is purty much all I know about the fight," pursued Glass; "but some time next day I opened my peepers agin, wiped off the blood, and found I war the wust-looking human you ever seed. My old scalp hung clean over my face—the skin o' my face, and the most o' this here nose, war spread out all around me; I'd been dug into clean down to the ribs, which looked as ef they'd been peeled; and more'n all that, some thieving scamp—(Bill, here, kin tell you who that war)—had stripped off the most o' my clothing, and tuk my pistol, and rifle, and every —— thing away."

"Yes," said Bill, "I'll jest tell you how it war, boys—I jest thought as how Glass war dead, and I run down to camp and told 'em so, and old Sublette told me and Rube to go back and bury him. We went back, and tuk his things; but concluding thar warn't no use o' settling him into the turf, we put back and told the boys as how we'd done it; but we hadn't, and Jack warn't dead, he warn't."

"No, sir-ee!" chimed in Glass—"nor I didn't want to die, nuther. Wall, I kind o' looked around like, and seed as how old grizzly had got rubbed out, and that thar was some satisfaction, anyhow."

Here Glass took still another glass, smacked his lips, and continued.

"Ef I war to tell you all that happened arter that, I'd keep you here till morning—so I wont. The short on't is, I jest tore up my shirt, and did up my wounds as well as I could; and then lay round thar, feeding on old grizzly for a good many days, till I got strength to crawl away. The boys, I reckoned, had changed their camp, and so I sot out for a fort as I knowed was about ninety miles off; and I tell you what it is, that thar war one o' the wust tramps as ever this hyer old beaver seed; for I war all cut up, almost skinned, and had to feed on roots and berries all the way.

"At last I got to the fort, and some jimcrack of a doctor sot to work on me; and, stranger, I kim out as good as new, as you kin see for yourself. I managed to git another hoss, and then started for another fort, whar I knowed the boys would be coming in to winter. We both got thar about the same time; and a skeerder-looking set o' white niggers nor them war, when they seed me, as they knowed war dead and buried, coming up astraddle o' that thar old hoss, this hyer child never put his eyes on.

"'Hurraw, Bill!' says I, as I seed him quaking, and trying to git out o' sight—for the scamp knowed as he war guilty, and I guessed it—'I'll jest kind o' trouble you for that thar hoss, and gun, and the rest o' my fixings.'

"Bill handed 'em over, and I tuk my place amongst the boys, ready for the next thing as mought turn up.

"'Thar, stranger,'" concluded the old mountaineer, "you knows now why I looks so purty; and so now let's liquor agin, afore we spile."

I subsequently ascertained that this story of John Glass was true in every particular; and I give it as a specimen of what human nature—and especially human nature as found in the wilderness of the Far West—can endure and survive.

The Haunted House.

I ONCE had a friend—I say had, for he is dead now, poor fellow—by the name of Lance Walters, who possessed the most remarkable nerve of any one I ever saw. Nothing seemed to alarm him—nothing could frighten him. I have seen him, when the pestilential scourge was taking down nearly every other individual, as calm, collected, and apparently as cheerful as one at a wedding feast. I have seen him, when the lightning flashed with blinding vividness, and the thunder was crashing with a stunning power, sit coolly and collectedly by a window, quietly reading, apparently without being aware that any thing unusual was going on around him. When the cholera was here, in 1832, it gave him no uneasiness. When that wise savant of Europe startled the world with the prediction that all sublunary things were about to be brought to a close by an erratic comet, my friend laughed. When, a few years subsequently, all the stars of Heaven seemed shooting from their spheres and falling in one fiery shower, and hundreds were quaking with terror, believing the last day had come, Lance was one who stood looking at the phenomenon, and thought it a very pleasant and beautiful sight. When the day drew near which that *soi disant* prophet, Father Miller, had so rampantly preached as the end of time, and thousands of frightened fanatics were preparing to put on their ascension robes, for a glorious, saintly, aerial flight, Walters treated his friends to an essay on the philosophy of fools. In short, nothing disturbed him; he had an easy digestion, and slept soundly; and he could at any time—before meals or afterward, morning, noon, or night, or in the middle of the night—balance a glass full of wine on a single finger, and neither spill a drop of the liquid nor show a tremor of his own nerves. He had a good eye, and was a dead shot; and if he ever failed to put a ball in the bull's-eye at a hundred yards, without rest, the fault was in the rifle and not in him.

I think I have said enough to show that Lance Walters was a man of remarkable nerve; and a man of remarkable nerve, let me observe, is a man remarkable for never knowing what it is to fear—for real fear is something which always springs from a disturbed condition of the nervous system. Lance had traveled a good deal; and, in the course of his career, had met with a number of startling adventures. He had been in Texas in his earlier days, and had seen men coolly shot down as dogs; he had seen them fight with knives, and both fall in the contest, covered with ghastly wounds; he had more than once had a loaded pistol presented at his breast, and fully believed that the next moment would be his last; and yet in all these trials of nerve, his features had scarcely paled, his eye had never quailed, and not a quiver of a single muscle had ever been perceived.

The bravest, however, have their weak points, and Lance Walters had his, as my story, or perhaps I should rather say *his* story, will show.

"Were you *ever* afraid?" I once said to him, as we sat conversing upon kindred subjects.

"Once," he replied, "never but once—I never knew what fear was but once."

"And pray," said I, "on what particular occasion was that?"

"A particular occasion, indeed!" he rejoined, as he lit a fresh Havana and threw himself back in his easy chair, while the cloud of smoke which soon enveloped him seemed to indicate that even the recollection brought with it some little nervous excitement. "Do you know," he pursued, " I was never a believer in the supernatural!"

"You were never a believer in any thing, except a kind of iron immobility, which you were pleased to term courage," I replied.

"I say, my friend, I never *was* a believer in the supernatural up to a certain period; I do not say I am a believer in it now; but this much I shall say, that there are some things I have seen, belonging either to Heaven or earth, or both, which far surpass my comprehension, and seem unexplainable by any known law."

"Well, go on," said I, with interest, "and give me the particulars of that particular occasion, when for once, and only once in his life, Lance Walters was scared."

"Well, scared is a term I am not partial to," smiled my friend; "but no matter. To begin, then, you must know I was once traveling through the interior of Alabama; and being one day belated in reaching my destination, I concluded to ask a night's entertainment of a planter, whose dwelling loomed up invitingly on my way. I rode up to the door, and found the proprietor himself quietly sitting on the piazza, indulging in the luxury of what, had I been among the Choctaws, the original proprietors of the soil, I should unhesitatingly have pronounced a calumet of peace. Having passed the usual salutations of the day, and replied to his inquiry, that I was neither a pedlar nor a relation to one, I quietly made the proposition of passing the night beneath his roof. He gave a cordial assent, and some half a dozen negroes very speedily disposed of my horse and valise. I next proceeded to make myself agreeable to mine host—a hale, hearty man of fifty, of a pleasant and sociable turn of mind—and soon we were in full blast, chatting away on all sorts of matters pertaining to all parts of the country—east, west, north and south.

"A summons to supper interrupted our conversation; and forthwith mine host conducted me to a bountifully-supplied table, where I flatter myself I did ample justice to any quantity of broiled chicken, bacon, eggs, etc. After supper we took a smoke; and the feelings of my Southern entertainer having by this time risen to fever heat in favor of his Northern guest, he proposed that we should silently indulge in a stimulating distillation called peach-brandy. I assented; and I think I am justified in adding, that neither of us drank more than a quart. One thing is pretty certain, however; in the exact ratio that the liquor went down, our spirits and fancies went up; and from beginning with the practical, we glided into the poetical, advanced to the terrible, and wound up with the marvelous; that is to say, from talking of crops and cattle, we proceeded to quote Shakspeare and Byron, pushed on to duels and street encounters, and ended with ghost stories. I did not believe in the last—not even with the assistance of the brandy—but my Southern friend did. I could tell as marvelous tales as he; but then, unlike him, I could not swear to them; and I came near getting myself into trouble by doubting that he believed all he said he did.

"'So you are incredulous?' he queried, looking me steadily in the eye.

"'Most assuredly sir,' I replied. 'What! talk of ghosts, and believe in them? Upon my soul, that is a little too much for a man that has traveled! I have always heard of these things as being at a distance, or else as having happened in some demolished structure, and so I have pretty much settled it in my own mind that their ghostships are always a great way off from an enterprising mortal, or else have long since gone quietly and snugly to rest.'

"'Would you like to see a ghost?' he inquired.

"'If it is convenient,' said I.

"'Come! what do you say to my own house, here, being haunted?'

"'I should like to hear what you say to it first,' returned I.

"'Well, sir, I say then, that one room is nightly visited with something supernatural.'

"'I am very happy to hear it,' I rejoined; 'and if that room is to let, I should like to engage it, for one night at least.'

"'But are you really serious,' he inquired, 'in wishing to lodge in a haunted room?'

"'Serious as a judge, if not as sober as a priest,' laughed I.

"'Well, then, young man, I will try your mettle; you shall have the room, for one night at least—that is, if I can get my darkies into it long enough to attend to the sleeping arrangements.'

"'Do you really pretend to say,' pursued I, somewha quizzingly, 'that there is a ghostly performance there every night?'

"'Well, I will let you report in the morning whether there is one there this night or not.'

"'But it must really be ghostly,' said I, 'for any human performer will be likely to get what he will not want to keep.'

"'Use your weapons in any way you please,' he rejoined; 'only be careful and not damage my house and furniture more than is necessary.'

"After some further conversation, during which I puzzled myself not a little to ascertain whether my host was really in earnest or not, he ordered his head female domestic to see that the bed in the haunted room was in proper condition, and the furniture well dusted. I watched her, as he gave these directions, thinking to detect something like a covert smile; but so far from it, I even fancied that the wench turned a shade lighter; and her exclamation of, 'Oh, Marse John! ef de gen'lman's gwine to sleep dar, de Lord help him!' seemed to be spoken with something like horror. Could it be possible there was anything in it? Were they indeed in earnest? Was there such a thing as a real ghost out of Shakspeare? Pooh! pshaw! nonsense!

"All things must come to an end, and so did our smoking, talking, and drinking. At last I rose, with my nerves less steady than usual; and my host himself conducted me to my supernatural chamber, through a row of rolling eyes and ebony faces, which were turned upon me with the expression of beings who believed I had sold myself to the Evil One, and was about to hand him over his bargain.

"'Well,' said I, as my host set down the light upon the table, which I saw had recently been dusted, 'how soon is this performance to begin? for, thanks to that brandy of yours, I shall be asleep in something like a quarter of an hour.'

"'Young man!' solemnly replied my superstitious friend; 'you jest now—but if you jest to-morrow morning, I will give you the best boy on my plantation, and say you are the bravest man that ever rode through Alabama!'

"With this he very gravely shook me by the hand, wished me a safe deliverance from the woes to come, and retired with the dignity of a state functionary, leaving me in a frame of mind something between a grin, a yawn, and a horror.

"Finding myself entirely alone, I took a quiet survey of

the apartment, but discovered nothing remarkable. In one corner stood a bed, and near it an old-fashioned bureau; a table, a settee, and two or three chairs, were ranged along the walls; at the windows hung white muslin curtains, and the floor was covered with a sort of matting—the whole apartment, in fact, having the appearance of a genteel, country sleeping-room. I looked out of the windows, and found they opened upon the garden. I then examined the walls carefully, the matting, every corner, crack, and crevice, to be certain there was no chance of playing a trick upon me, though I hardly thought my host was one to sanction anything of that kind. I next locked the door, and then examined my pistols, and placed them with my knife under my pillow. Then, having arranged the means of striking a light in a case of emergency, I proceeded to undress and turn in; and finding all right, I finally put out the light. The room was now quite dark, and I looked to see my supernatural operators begin their nocturnal orgies; but having looked in vain till my heavy eyelids began to droop, I gradually yielded to the somnific influence, and a kind of forgetfulness succeeded.

"I am not certain whether I slept or not; but I was suddenly aroused by feeling something like a cold hand placed upon my mouth, followed by a kind of stifling sensation, not unlike that produced by nightmare.

"'Well,' thought I, 'this is cool, certainly. I am in for it now, at all events; and so let us see who will come out second best.'

'My first idea was to carefully raise my hand, and suddenly grasp the hand of the unknown; and then, if I found a body to it, to put that particular body in a condition not to play tricks upon travelers any more. But in attempting to raise my hand, I made the startling discovery that it was paralyzed.

"This was the first shock of any thing like fear which my system ever received; and I freely admit the sensation was not a pleasant one. What could it mean? Was it in reality nightmare, or something else? I knew nothing human could paralyze me, and for the first time I began to think there might be some foundation for the stories of my host. But, pshaw! it was a dream—I knew it was a dream—a kind of waking dream—a dyspeptic dream—superinduced by a hearty supper, some over-indulgences afterward, and the ideas fixed upon my mind when I went to rest.

"I made another effort—a stronger and more determined effort—and brought up my hand like lightning, but just as I grasped for the intruding hand, it seemed to be removed, and I felt something like a light blow upon my temples.

"'Have a care, whoever you are!' said I; 'for I am armed, and will not be trifled with!'

"As I spoke, I fancied I heard a low, mocking laugh; and at the same instant the bed seemed to be raised up from the floor, and rocked like a cradle.

"Nothing daunted, though somewhat mystified, I grasped my knife and pistols, sprung out of bed and under it, but found nothing. Then, strangely enough, the room, which had till now been very dark, suddenly appeared slightly illuminated, so that I could see all over it. I came out from under the bed, and heard a heavy jar, as if the latter had suddenly been lifted and then dropped back to its place. This was strange! very strange! but I would find out the secret; and I hurried about the apartment, examining every object by the new and gradually diffused light, which was not unlike that of early day.

"But, then, whence came this light, which was of itself as much a mystery as the rest? I hastily drew back the curtains of the windows – but all was dark without—not a ray came through the glass—and this astonished me exceedingly. Where *could* this light come from? and what could be the cause of it? If there was a lantern a lamp, or a fire, in an adjoining apartment, I knew I should more distinctly perceive the light through a crevice than in the body of the room itself—yet I could discover nothing to lead me to suppose that any other place was illuminated.

"I spent some quarter of an hour in looking over and under every thing I could find, and then went and sat down on the bed; but just as I did so, the apartment suddenly became dark again, and I distinctly felt a hand grasp my ankle. As I cautiously glided my own hand down to it, it seemed to be removed, and the same instant I felt a smart blow upon my forehead, followed by another low, taunting laugh.

"I now began to feel strangely. This was a species of jugglery that passed my comprehension. Had the room not been mysteriously lighted at all, I fancied I might account for the rest as a trick; but that light was something for which I could fix upon no rational cause; and not being able to discover the source of the light, the rest became alike mysterious and inexplicable.

"Next followed sounds, not unlike the rushing and moaning of winds—the very room itself seemed to rock— and I heard a slow, steady, measured tread, with a clanking noise as of chains. With my pistol and knife firmly grasped, and both ready for action, I waited for the steps to approach me; but though they seemed to be continually advancing, they apparently came no nearer. Presently I felt a cold air blowing upon my face; and believing that some trap-door had been opened near me, I reached for my matches, struck a light, and looked eagerly around me; but every thing was exactly as at first—nothing seemed to have been disturbed in the least.

"I now made another thorough search around the walls for a secret door; and then, lifting the matting by degrees, I also carefully examined the floor underneath; and having thus fully satisfied myself that there was no entrance to the room except through the door and windows—and the door was still locked, with the key remaining in it, and the windows I knew had not been opened—I threw myself down upon a seat, and pondered the mystery for more than an hour, occasionally pinching myself to be certain I was awake.

"At last, finding I could not settle the matter to my own satisfaction, I proceeded to make another thorough examination of every thing and every place—actually opening the drawers of the bureau to see that no one was concealed within—and then once more put out the light. The very instant I did so, however, I felt myself touched in twenty places at the same time, by what appeared to me to be twenty hands; while something like a brush was drawn rapidly up and down and over my face several times. I now began to grow uneasy—to be in some degree alarmed—to believe indeed there might be more things in heaven and earth than had been dreamed of in my philosophy.

"'In the name of God,' said I, solemnly—'if this be

aught from the other world, make known your wish, and depart to your rest!'

"From that moment, for something like half an hour, I neither heard a sound, nor felt a touch; and throwing myself once more upon the bed, I resolved to sleep out the night, let it be what it would, and make such a report in the morning as I might see proper.

"With this intent I closed my eyes, and gradually fell into a drowsy state as at first; but suddenly a bright flash, like that of the most vivid lightning, brought me up with a start, and I found the room illuminated as before, and heard several strange noises all around me. My feelings at that moment I can only describe as a kind of mingled impression of awe and terror—of something wild and weird-like—a secret sensation of something fearful and unearthly. A weak, faint, sickening feeling came over me; and closing my eyes, I fell back, completely exhausted On looking up again, the room was as dark as the blackest night, except in one single spot overhead, where there seemed to burn a kind of small, bluish light, that illuminated nothing around it.

"This was too much. I felt I would rather acknowledge myself vanquished, than courageously remain involved in such terrible mystery through the night; and tremblingly I rose, with the intention of finding my way out of the apartment.

"I had scarcely touched my feet to the floor, however, when I experienced a kind of paralyzing shock, followed by a sensation of being lifted and swung in the air. The next moment I seemed to drop heavily; and as I advanced a step, with my hair fairly standing on end, a cold, clammy hand grasped mine. Determined to know what it belonged to, my fingers closed upon it like a vice; while with the other hand I felt along an arm that seemed to end in air, without other form or body attached. The very acme of horror now seized me; this could belong to nothing human; it was indeed a creation of the invisible inhabitants of the invisible world; and with a long, loud, despairing shriek, I fell."

Here my friend, Lance Walters, brought his narrative to a pause.

"Well!" I exclaimed, in no little excitement; "what then?"

"I hardly know what then," he replied. "The next I remember, I found myself in bed, with the old planter and his wife and some half a dozen negroes standing around me, and a neighboring leech taking blood from my arm. I recovered in the course of the day, and in the afternoon took leave of my entertainer, fully determined never to spend another night beneath his roof. You perceive," he concluded with a smile, "I did not get a darkey for a present, nor had I the honor of being accounted the bravest man that ever rode through Alabama."

"But what was the mystery?" said I.

"Ah, what indeed?" mused Lance.

"Was it nightmare—a dream—a chemical trick—or was it something really supernatural?

"That is what I have been trying to settle ever since," replied Lance Walters; "but, till the day of my death, I fear it will remain a mystery to me. Enough that I was really frightened for once; and I was only too glad to get away, without asking or being asked any unnecessary questions. Let me trouble you for another cigar!"

Bill Lukens' Run.

Afar out in the great wilderness of the Far West, around their camp-fire, sat four mountaineers, one toasting his meat at the fire, one mending his torn moccasins by the flickering light, and the other two squatted upon the ground, quietly smoking their pipes, while their mules and horses stood feeding near. It was a wild picturesque scene—in a deep valley, near a mountain stream—a lurid light gleaming upon their hard, bronzed features, their rough, mountain costume, their packs and arms, their feeding cattle, the gliding stream, and the rocks and the trees around and above them.

"I say, Bill, old hoss," said one of the two who sat smoking, turning to his nearest companion, "'spose you gin us that thar scrape o' yourn with the Injuns! I'd like to smoke another pipe afore I turns in; and them kind o' things, you know, sarves to float the time along amazing."

"Wall, that thar war one on 'em!" returned Bill, emphatically, taking a long, steady pull at his pipe, and rolling out quite a cloud: "I never had sich a run afore, since I owned these hyer pegs."

The second speaker, Bill Lukens, was a tall, brawny fellow, some five-and-thirty years of age, with sandy complexion, light-blue eyes, and strongly marked features He had spent a great portion of his life in the wilderness, as hunter, trapper, and guide; and, like all who are continually exposed to perils, had passed through a great many scenes of adventure, and had had a great many hair-breadth escapes. He had recently joined the present party, to whom he was known by reputation; and having, on more than one occasion, alluded to his "scrape with the Crows," one of his companions had now asked him for the story, to while away the time around their camp fire.

"Wall, crowd her through!" said the first speaker, in reply to Lukens.

"Ay, that's the talk," said the one who was toasting his meat.

"Next to the fun o' being in a scrape," observed the fourth, "is the fun o' telling on't, or hearing on't."

"Wall," resumed Bill, "as you're all willing, and me, too, I'll go in. You see, it was just this hyer way:—Me and my pardner, old Fighting Pete—it's like some o' ye knows him?"

"I does that—easy," replied the first speaker, drawing two or three rapid whiffs from his pipe; "I knows the old beaver, jest like a trap. Me and him had a fight once, and I got licked!"

All laughed, and Bill Lukens proceeded.

"Wall, as I was a-saying, old Fighting Pete war my pardner; and me and him war setting our traps, up along the Big Horn, one day, about three or four year ago, when I seed some'at as I didn't like, and I pinted it out to Pete.

"'What does you call that thar, old hoss?' says I.

"'Why, that thar's as plain as shooting,' says Pete. 'That thar's a moccasin print, as had a Injun foot into it, and not many year ago nyther. Augh! it's allers the way,' says Pete; 'ef a feller happens to git whar he can do suthin decent, round comes the bloody red niggers to spile it all. I say, Bill, we'll hev to put out from hyer, and it goes agin me like sand in my eye.'

"'Wall, says I, 'thar's only one print, anyhow.'

"'As you *see*,' says Pete—'only one print as you *see*—but you arn't sich a confounded fool as to 'spose a Injun walks on one leg, I 'spect?'

"'Wall,' says I, 's'pose he has two legs?—that thar only makes him *one* Injun—and then we're two to one, any how.'

"'Augh!' says Pete, drawing himself up amazing, and looking as wise as an owl; 'does you know anything about hens?'

"'Not uncommon,' says I, 'but I've eat 'em to Independence.'

"'Shah!' says Pete; 'I don't mean that thar; but I means ef you know the principal upon which they works?'

"'Not particular,' says I.

"'Wall, then, I'll tell ye,' says Pete. 'They fust makes a nest, and then they lays a nest-egg, and arter that they lays more.'

"'But,' says I, 'I don't see the pint.

"'Why, you bat-blind crow,' says Pete, 'the pint is, that this hyer red nigger ar' the nest-egg; and whar you sees a sign o' him, you'll see more soon—for he ain't a egg as'll stay long alone—so it's my opine we'd better gather up our traps and put out from hyer.'

"'Wall,' says I, 'I don't know but that's safe advice.'

"'It ar' hoss, sir ee!' says Pete.

"So we tuk up the traps as we war putting down; and then we went to look arter some we'd sot afore—Pete going up the river, and me down—but both agreeing to meet at a place as we'd named Cedar Bluff.

"Wall, boys, I hadn't gone fur down the river, when, jest as I war passing along behind a thicket like, whiz, came two or three arrers—two of 'em so close as to graze the skin, and t'other one sticking into my arm a bit, and followed by some o' them thar yells as all the skunks knows how to do.

"'Hooraw!' thinks I: 'ar' that your game!' and making powerful quick tracks for a near bluff, I turned the corner of a rock, and, looking back, seed three o' the red niggers close arter me, still yelling like mad.

"I didn't know how many thar mought be; but I thought as how, ef the forward one war Fighting Pete's nest-egg, I'd make a cold chicken on him sudden. So fotching round my old rifle, I let him hev the nicest part into it—thinking, maybe, ef he'd git more'n he wanted, he'd let the next imp behind him hev a bit, too. And he did—yes, sir-ee! for the ball went plump through him, and into the one behind him; and sich a howling as they all set up together, you never heerd.

"Wall, I 'spected now to see t'other hound turn and run, and gin it up straight. But he didn't—nary once—no, *sir*—but come full bent arter me, drawing another arrer to the head, and letting it slide so close as to make me think o' what a preacher once said to me 'bout my prayers.

"'Oho!' says I, dodging around another corner o' the rock, and hugging it close; 'ef you're all, you'll be easy meat, too, afore long; and ef you thinks I'm a gwine to run from *one* sich a red nigger, jest wait till I git a chance to tell you I arn't.'

"Wall, round he come, blowing amazing—for he thought I'd gone on furder, case the place had that kind o' a look—out I soon tuk the conceit out o' him powerful; for jest as I seed his ugly mug agin, not more'n four feet off, I riz up and lit on to him, like a painter on to a deer; and afore he knowed particular what ailed him, he didn't know nothing—for I'd got my butcher into him a few, I tell *you!*

"Wall, I ripped off his scalp, and shook it in his face, to show my contempt for the beast; and then, t'aring off his b'ar-skin, and taking his bow and arrers, to help me out, in case thar war any more 'bout, I kicked him down into the water. Then I gin one reg'lar yell for old Wirgin'a, and sot to loading my rifle, all the time keeping my eye peeled, and looking two ways for Sunday.

"Jest as I war ramming down the ball, I heerd a few more yells, some distance off, and old Pete's rifle crack at the same time. Says I to myself: Pete war right 'bout that thar hen business, and thar'll be a nest-full round here soon, anyhow. Then I wanted to do two things. I wanted to git to Pete, and help him out; and I wanted to git to t'other niggers, and get thar scalps and traps. But I didn't do nyther: fust, bekase I knowed that ef old Pete war to be killed or tuk, it 'ud be over afore I could reach him; and second, bekase thar war some answering yells t'other side o' me, not fur off; and I felt as how, ef I stayed round there long, I mought know a feller, by the name of Bill Lukens, that 'ud want help the wost kind hisself.

"So I primed the old rifle quick as lightning; and taking along the bow and arrers, I plunged into the Big Horn, and made for the bluff on t'other side. I got over thar without ary accident, and crawled up under some bushes, whar I could look back; but when I did look back, I seed some five or six o' the niggers pointing me out; and then, whiz, came another lot o' arrers, (along with some o' the darndest yells,) and two on 'em stuck into me—one on 'em into my meat-trap, and t'other into my arm.

"One o' the arrers I pulled out, and t'other broke off in. 'But,' says I, 'you infernal old Crow niggers, I'll give another o' ye suthin as ye can't pull out;' and taking plum sight at the feller with the longest feather, I drapped him amazing The arrer in me now hurt me oncommon; but it war in the fleshy part o' my arm, and had nothing to do with my running pegs; and so I reckoned the next best thing to do war to use them a bit.

"Wall, I pulled up the bluff as quick and as zig-zag as I could—the infarnal imps all the while blazing away with thar arrers, and howling powerful over thar dead. I got up to the top o' the bluff safe enough; and from thar, about a mile off—or maybe half-a-mile—I could see a big bit o' prairie; and crossing that thar prairie, full bent, war a big crowd more o' the thieving scoundrels. I begun to think it war a gwine to be tight dodging, and broke for the nearest thicket; but jest as I reached it, my ha'r fairly riz for the yells as burst from it a'most stunned me—and the next breath I found myself surrounded and tuk.

"'Wall,' says I, 'Bill Lukens, your trapping ar' done for. You're wanted for a roasting-piece—'cept your scalp —and that thar'll rattle in some greasy nigger's lodge, to make glory for him and music for his squaw.'

"Not to spin the matter out too long, I'll jest say what they done with me, and how I got cl'ar of 'em. They tuk me down to the prairie as I seed from the bluff; and thar, arter a while, they all met—nigh a hundred on 'em—and thar I had my trial. I couldn't understand much Crow talk; but I made out enough to know that they war a-gwine to hev some fun with me, ayther by way of a burn or a run. I war in hopes it would be a run; but I didn't say so, kase it warn't likely they'd take my advice, anyhow, even ef I talked Crow to 'em with tears in my eyes.

"At last, arter a good deal of palavering, and some grumbling, it war decided as I should make a run for thar fun. But I took a good look at these hyer pegs, and then at thar spindle shanks, and made up my mind, ef t' ey'd keep off thar hosses and be decent, I'd show 'em a run as 'ud be more fun for me nor them.

"Wall, hollering and laughing, kicking and slapping

me, and making all sorts of a hullabaloo, which I 'spect they thought war fun, they tuk me way out into the prairie, 'bout five mile from any tree or bush; and thar, arter stripping off all my clothes, and tying my hands behind my back, they made me understand—some'at by words and some'at by signs—that when they gin the big yell, I war to run for my life, and every nigger on 'em arter me, and the first one as mought hit me with his tomahawk, war to hev my scalp for pay.

"'Thank you,' says I; 'but if it's all the same to you, you greasy niggers, I'd prefer to keep that thar same scalp my own self.'

"Still, I didn't think I had much chance o' doing it; for how war a naked man, with his hands tied behind his back, and placed in front of a hundred o' the red niggers, to git away from 'em? and then git away to some fort arterwards, afore he'd starve to death? But, anyhow, it war a chance for life, and Bill Lukens and me concluded we'd go in and do our purtiest.

"Purty soon they all stretched themselves out in a long row, way past both sides o' me, and about thirty yards behind, and I noticed as they all put aside all thar weapons 'cept their tomahawks and knives. That thar war some hope to me, and I looked a head to see the chances. Straight ahead I seed prairie, and nothing else; but off to the right, 'bout five mile, as I said afore, war the hills whar they'd tuk me from.

"Now I knowed them thar hills war my only chance; ut I know'd, too, it 'ud take a long and a fast run, forrerd, to cl'ar the hounds so as to double on 'em and shape my course that thar way; and I'd jest got these hyer things all thought over like, when up rose one tremenjus yell, like a young airthquake, and off I bolted, like a shot from a gun, and on come the hull yelling pack arter me.

"'Pegs,' says I, 'ef you've got any respect for Bill Lukens, do your duty now, for ef you gin in, he'll hev his har lifted amazing!'

"And pegs did do thar duty; and sich another run you never seed. I put on, and on, and on, as hard as I could tear; and all the time I could hear the yells behind just about as nigh; and I didn't dar to take a look back, for fear some tomahawk would settle me; for I knowed they could throw a few feet with a sartain aim.

"Arter running a good while, and finding myself still alive and kicking, and not hearing the hounds quite so lively-like, I jest turned my head a little, and seed as how I'd left all but six fur back; and out of them thar six, only one or two would be like to gin me any trouble, ef I could hold out at the rate I war going.

"I had more hope now, and I did my best, I tell you.

I strained every narve, and cord, and all the other fixings into me, and kept on for nigh a half hour, doubling so as to git my line towards the nearest wood. When I looked back agin, I seed all had gin in 'cept two; and out o' them thar two, one war a good way behind t'other; so I knowed it war only one arter all.

"'Oh, ef I only had my hands loose,' says I to myself, 'I'd bet a pound o' bacca yit, that I'd fix that thar varmint;' and so I begun to tug and pull at the thongs, till I thought I'd cut 'em clean into the bone.

"At last they gin way, and I thought that thar war the happiest minute I ever knowed. I hadn't nothing to brag on yit, for I war naked, and without any weapon o' any kind, and the devil behind me had both a knife and a tomahawk, and he now seemed to be gaining on me at every step. The nearer I got to the woods, the more I strained every narve to the very wo'st; but all at once the blood began to gush from my nose, and mouth, and ears, and then I knowed, ef I couldn't play possum and come the blind over the Injun, I war a gone beaver. So I kind o' turned one eye onto him like, and made believe as I war working harder'n ever; yit all the time slacking up a little, so as he mought come up by degrees and not suspicion me. Twice I seed him lift his tomahawk to throw, and twice I got ready for a dodge; but the hound calkilated he'd got me safe, and thought he might as well hold on to it, and sink it into my brain with a sartin stroke.

"As t'other one had gin out and turned back afore this, thar warn't but one that I could fear now, and I jest made up my mind not to die easy. I found I couldn't reach the wood, and that thar warn't no use o' trying; and so I kept drawing the nigger on like, till he came panting up to within about two foot, and had got his tomahawk raised for the blow; when fixing myself for a desperate stroke, I wheeled sudden, bent my head down, and struck him with it right in his meat-trap, doubling us both up together. He struck with his tomahawk at the same moment; but being tuk by surprise, he didn't hit me; and grappling him with all the strength I had left, I jerked the weapon away from him; and afore he could help hisself, I sunk it into his brain. As he fell back, wildly feeling about for his knife like, I drawed myself back, and keeled over on the 'arth, a'most as dead as him.

"Wall, I laid thar till I got rested some; and then I stripped off his b'ar skin, and wrapped it round myself, and tuk his scalp-knife and tomahawk, and crawled off into the woods, whar I slept over night. The next day I made tracks for the nearest fort, feeding on roots and berries all the way, and gitting in thar at last quite a starved-looking human. Thar I found Fighting Pete, the old hoss, who'd got away from the varmints with less trouble, and had told 'em all as how I war 'rubbed out.'

"But I warn't!" concluded Bill Lukens, knocking the ashes from his pipe: "no, sir-ee! And now, boys, as you've got my story, let's turn in, for we've got a heap o' 'ramping to do 'arly to-morrow."

The Faithful Negro.

Just before the breaking out of what is commonly known as Lord Dunmore's war, a man by the name of Jonas Parker settled in the western part of Virginia, on a small creek which emptied into the Ohio. His family consisted of his wife, three children, ranging from five to twelve, and a negro servant. The place where he located was some distance from any settlement or station, and the scenery around very wild and romantic, with lofty and heavily-wooded hills sloping back from the valley. He brought his family here early in the spring, built him a rude log cabin, and, by great exertions, succeeded in clearing and planting a considerable patch of ground the same season.

One day, near the close of summer, as Mr. Parker and his negro Tom were at work in the woods, about half a mile from the dwelling, the latter, who had gone down to a creek near by, came hurrying back, with an expression of alarm depicted upon his black features.

"Well, Tom, what now?" inquired his master, suspending his work to look at his frightened domestic.

"Oh, Marse Jonas," answered Tom, in a quavering voice, looking fearfully around him as he spoke, "I tink I seed suffin down dar."

"You are always seeing something wonderful," pursued the other; "but it generally turns out a very trifling affair. Did you see a black face in the water, when you stooped down to drink?"

"Oh, Marse Jonas, I seed suffin wossern'n dat. Dar, don't larf, Marse Jonas! Great golly! I seed eyes in de bushes—'relse I neber seed nuffin afore—nuffin—during dis life!"

"Well, eyes are not apt to hurt anybody, Tom," returned Mr. Parker, with a laugh; "I've seen a great many eyes in my time."

"Yes, but, Marse Jonas, it's a difference what they's 'tached upon."

"That is true, Tom. Well, what did your eyes belong to?"

"I tink dey was 'tached upon a Injin.

"Ah!" exclaimed the other, appearing for the first time a little startled. "Why did you not say so in the first place, you blundering fool! Pshaw! there are no Indians about here, except in your imagination. What makes you think it was an Indian?"

"'Case I tink de Injin was dar, dat's all," answered the black, looking timidly about him. "I tink, Marse Jonas, we'd bes' go down to de house, to 'tect missus and de chillren."

"I believe it would be folly to do so," rejoined Mr. Parker, "for I am almost certain you have seen nothing at all. Still, as you have made me uneasy, I will go back; but if you fool me many times, look out for a tanning."

"I's not de chile to fool you, Marse Jonas," said Tom, hastily gathering up the tools, while his master took up his rifle, which was leaning against a tree, and, keeping his eye warily about him, proceeded to examine the priming. "No, I's not de chile to fool you," pursued Tom. "If I didn't see the horriblest eyes—and dem dar eyes Injin's—den I nebber seed nuffin—neber—nuffin during dis life—dat's trufe."

Mr. Parker now suggested that it might be as well to go down to the creek and make a search through the bushes; but to this proposition the negro excitedly demurred—saying, that if there were Indians there, they would be certain to shoot him before he could find them.

"That is true, Tom," replied the other—"*if* there are Indians there, which I do not believe. However, as you seem so much alarmed, and as I am willing to admit the possibility of such a thing, we will return to the house."

Accordingly Mr. Parker and his servant set off, along the side of the hill, to a point whence they could get a view of the dwelling, he carrying his rifle so as to be ready for instant use, and the negro keeping close at his heels with the axes and other implements, and both looking warily about them, closely scanning every tree and bush.

Nothing occurred to justify the alarm of the negro till they reached the edge of the corn-field, which ran down to the house; when, just as Mr. Parker was in the act of reproving his servant for exciting his fears without cause, there suddenly came reports of some three or four rifles in quick succession—instantly followed by wild, Indian yells—and both Tom and his master dropped together, the latter struck by two balls, one in his side and the other in his leg.

"Oh, my God! my poor family!" he groaned, as he gathered himself upon his feet, and beheld the negro stretched out on his back, apparently dead, and the savages, with wild yells of triumph, in the act of bounding forward to finish their work and take the scalps of their victims.

Hastily staggering to the nearest tree, Mr. Parker now set his back against it, drew up his rifle, ready for the foremost, and so stood as it were at bay. Perceiving this, and knowing too well the certainty of the white man's aim—and also feeling themselves perfectly sure of their prize, and therefore not caring to throw away a single life—the Indians immediately took shelter behind different trees, and began to reload their pieces.

To remain where he was, Mr. Parker now saw would be certain death in a few moments; wounded as he was, and continually growing weaker from loss of blood, it was vain to think of flight; and yet, with death staring him in the face, and an almost maddening desire for self preservation, equally for his family's sake as his own, he felt that something ought to be tried for his salvation, though never so hopeless the attempt.

Looking quickly and searchingly around him, he perceived, about ten paces distant, a dense thicket; and believing if he could reach that, his chances of life would be increased—as the savages, without actually entering, could not make their aim sure—he gathered all his strength and nerve for the effort, and ran forward to the spot, falling in the midst of the bushes, and just in time to escape two balls of the enemy, which at the same moment whizzed over his head.

Seeing him fall, and supposing their last shots had proved fatal, the two savages who had just fired, uttering yells of triumph, darted out from behind their trees, and, flourishing their scalping knives, bounded forward to the thicket; but ere they reached it, Mr. Parker, who had succeeded in getting upon his knees, and his rifle to bear upon the foremost, pulled the trigger.

There was a flash, a crack, and a yell at the same moment; and springing some two or three feet clear of the earth, the Indian fell back dead, at the very feet of his companion; who suddenly stopped, uttered a howl of dismay, and for a few moments seemed undetermined whether to advance or retreat.

That momentary hesitation proved fatal to him also; for the negro, who had all this time been feigning death, but was really unharmed, now thinking there might be a possibility of escape, clutched one of his axes nervously, quickly gathered himself into a kind of ball, made two sudden bounds forward, the distance being about ten feet, whirled his weapon around his head, and, before the astonished warrior had time to put himself on guard, brought the glittering blade down like lightning, cleaving the savage through skull and brain, and laying him a ghastly and bleeding corpse beside the other.

"Dar, take dat, you tieving red nigger!" shouted Tom, with an expression of demoniac fierceness; "take dat dar! and don't neber say nuffin more 'bout shooting down white gentlem."

The words were not fairly uttered, when crack went the rifles of the other two savages, one grazing the left cheek of the negro, and the other causing his right ear to tingle.

"Great golly!" cried Tom, ducking his head; "dat dat was most nigh being de finishering of dis chile. But as you isn't got no more loads in, you ole varminters," he yelled, shaking his fist in the direction of the savages, "s'posen you doesn't shoot nuffin more afore us gent'em does."

Then seizing the empty guns of the two slain warriors, he rushed into the thicket, where Mr. Parker was concealed, exclaiming:

"Marse Jonas, I's hopes you isn't dead yet; but two of the Injins am; and here I is, wid dar two guns, dat only wants suffin in 'em to blow de oders to de debil."

"Ah, Tom," groaned Mr. Parker, as he lay on the ground, making every exertion to load his rifle which his failing powers would permit, "thank God you have escaped! I feared you were killed at the first fire."

"Not 'zactly, dat time, Marse Jonas; but dis chile was drefful skeered, dat's trufe; and seeing you drap, I t'ought I'd jest make b'lieve I's dead too, and wouldn't neber know nuffin more during dis life. But when I seed you get away, and shoot dat dar rascal dar, and t'oder stop so 'stonished to look at him, I conficluded I'd quit playing de possum, and get up and do suffin; and I did it—dat's trufe. Ah! dear Marse Jonas," he pursued, bending down by the side of the other, and speaking in a sympathetic tone, "you is hurt bad—berry bad—I know you is—and I's berry sorry; but you knows I tole you dar was Injin eyes in de bushes."

"You did, Tom; and had I then hurried immediately homeward, it is possible I might have escaped: though it is equally probable the Indians were on the watch to take us at advantage; in which case the result might have been no better than it is. Oh! that I was home with my family! for they must have heard the firing here, and be terribly alarmed; or, if not, they may be off their guard, and successfully attacked by another party; for it is more than likely these few have not ventured hither by themselves. Ah! God forbid," he ejaculated the next moment, fairly starting to his knees," that they should have been attacked and murdered first! But no! for then I think we should have heard their cries! and it is probable the savages would have wrapped the house in flames. I must get home, Tom—oh! I must get home. But how? how?"

"Why, Marse Jonas, ef you'll jus' let dis yere nigger tote you on his back, he'll fotch you dar."

"But what of the other Indians, Tom? have they fled?"

"Doesn't know—but guess dey am. I *axed* one on 'em to stop—and he did—but I guess de oders didn't want to."

"You are a brave fellow, Tom, for all!" said his master; "and if I live, I will not overlook this affair."

"Well, you see, Marse Jonas, I is one of dem as goes in for prudems—for keepin out of de fight as long as I can keep out of de fight; but when de fight does come, I's dar—I is—during dis life!"

"Hist!" whispered his master, as he carefully brought

his rifle forward. "I think I see one of the Indians peeping around yonder tree. Ah! I am too weak to raise the piece. Get down here, Tom, and let me rest it across your shoulder. There—that will do. Quiet now!"

"Do you see him, Marse Jonas?" whispered Tom, after keeping silent some half a minute.

Scarcely were the words spoken, when crack went both the rifles of the white man and the Indian at the same moment; and then the latter, uttering a wild yell, was seen to run staggeringly from tree to tree on his retreat; while his companion, taking advantage of the opportunity, bounded forward, and secured his person behind a large oak near at hand, keeping his rifle ready to fire upon his foe.

"Drop down, Marse Jonas," whispered Tom, "and let dis chile fix him."

Taking his master's hat as he spoke, Tom placed it on the end of a gun, and pushed it with some noise through the edge of the bushes, a few feet distant from where he lay. Scarcely was it visible to the savage, when, believing it to contain the head of his enemy, he brought his piece to his eye, and sent a ball whizzing through it.

Fairly chuckling at the success of his ruse, Tom instantly dropped the hat, and made a thrashing among the bushes, uttered a few groans, and then kept perfectly quiet; and Mr. Parker, comprehending his design, kept perfectly quiet also, though managing meanwhile to reload and prime his piece.

But though he believed his shot had proved effective, the wary warrior was resolved upon prudence and caution. First, reloading his rifle, he next carefully reconnoitered the thicket; and then, finding all still, he suddenly darted from his tree to another, and from that to another, and so by a sort of semi-circular movement came up as it were in the rear of his enemies.

Still finding all quiet, he at length advanced cautiously to the bushes, and began to part them gently. In this direction the thicket extended some twenty yards from the place where our friends were concealed; and with the assistance of Tom, Mr. Parker now noiselessly got himself into a position to cover the approach of the savage. Then waiting in breathless silence, till the latter had so far advanced as to make his aim sure, he fired again. A sharp yell of pain, and a floundering among the bushes followed; and Tom, seizing his axe, at once bounded forward toward his adversary.

The Indian was badly wounded, though not sufficiently so to prevent him making use of his rifle; but fortunately for the negro, it only flashed in the pan, with the muzzle fairly pointed at his heart; and the next moment the axe of Tom descended with Herculean force, and ended the work

With a shout of triumph, Tom now rushed from the thicket,

and, without heeding the call of his master, set off in pursuit of the only remaining savage, whom he could easily follow by his trail of blood. About a hundred yards from where he had been shot, he found him concealed behind a log, and in a dying condition. Too weak to make a defence, the Indian looked up at his enemy, and, extending his hand, said:

"How de do, brudder?"

"Jus dis way!" cried Tom: "dis is just how I does to all sich rascals as you!" and with the last words the bloody axe descended, and was buried in the brain of the Indian.

Tom now went back to his master, and proudly recounted his exploits.

"Thank God, we are saved!" said Mr. Parker, warmly grasping the hand of his faithful servant; "and I owe my life to you, Tom."

"'Spect de Lord fit on our side, wid dis yere choppin'-axe," muttered Tom, as he coolly wiped the blood from his formidable weapon.

He then carefully raised his wounded master, and, getting him upon his back, carried him safely to the house, where both were received with tears of joy by the terrified family.

Mr. Parker's wounds proved not so serious as was at first supposed; and the night following he and his family were removed to the nearest station by a small party of scouts, who had been sent out to warn and protect the more exposed settlers against the expected incursions of the Indians, who, as we have shown, had already begun their bloody work of laying waste the border.

Mr. Parker finally recovered, though not in time to take part in the sanguinary strife which followed; and Tom, for his gallantry was given his freedom, and lived many years to boast of what he had done " during dis life, merely jus wid a choppin'-axe."

The Guerrilla Queen.

"Before I tell you my story, gentlemen," said Captain Sheldon, as a small party of us sat around the festive board, "I will give you a toast. Fill up your glasses, and let it be drank in silence."

And as we all complied, the captain rose and said, with much solemnity—

"To the memory of the brave heroes who fell at Monterey."

An impressive silence of some moments followed, during which we all drank and the speaker resumed his seat.

"I believed I promised you a somewhat romantic story, in which I happened to play a rather important part," proceeded Captain Sheldon, as one collecting his thoughts for a direct, straightforward narration "Well, here you have it, then; and I am inclined to think the facts will interest you, even if my manner of telling them does not.

"It is needless," pursued the captain, "to enter into any description of the storming of Monterey, for with the general facts you are all familiar; and it is also needless to tell you that, as one of that glorious band of heroes known as the Texas Rangers—or, as General Worth was pleased to style us, the Texas Dragoons—I saw some pretty hard fighting during that memorable siege.

"We had taken Fort Teneria, the Bishop's Palace, and some other strong positions, and had concentrated our forces upon the town, and were forcing our way as best we could to the Cathedral Plaza, where the main body of the enemy was then stationed. The conflict was terrible and at its height, and the roar of cannon, the sharp rattle of musketry, the thunder of dashing artillery, the battering in of doors, the pecking through thick walls, the loud commands of officers, the shouts of the assailants, the groans of the wounded, and the shrieks of terrified women and children—all together made a most horrid din, such as I never wish to hear again.

"The streets being barricaded, and each building turned into a sort of fortified castle—from the flat roofs of which, behind breastworks of sandbags, the enemy continually poured down a most destructive fire—it became necessary for a portion of the troops to enter these buildings, force a passage through from one to the other, dislodge the garrison of each, and use them as safe coverts from which to annoy the foe in turn.

"In this hazardous occupation I had been engaged for several hours, and had witnessed some fearful scenes—as in cutting our way through from one house to the other, we had occasionally come in contact with men brave enough to bar our passage with their lives—when suddenly, just as I had thrown myself down on a seat, to get my breath and a few moments rest, I heard the wild shout that announced the successful passage of our little band into another adjoining building. Fairly mingled with this shout were the reports of fire-arms, the clash of steel and the shrieks of women. There was no time for me to be idle now; and starting up, I ran forward, with my sword in one hand and a revolver in the other. Making my way to the aperture which had been forced through the two walls, I entered an apartment dim with smoke, where all was excitement and confusion. Our party, still victorious, were mostly grouped around two wounded comrades; while near them lay two dead Mexicans, their companions having fled; and in one corner several women were huddled together, greatly terrified and shrieking for mercy, supposing us from all they had heard to be no better than so many savages.

"As I could speak Spanish so as to be readily understood, I stepped forward to the frightened females, and had just begun to utter a few words calculated to allay their fears, when I fancied I heard a heavy, jarring sound in an adjoining room, and a wild cry in Spanish of—

"'Spare him! spare him! he is my father!'

"Perceiving a door, which I thought might lead to the room in question, I sprung to it, tore it open, and, in the center of a small apartment, at once beheld three figures— an old man grappled with a young one—and a beautiful female, with her arms partly thrown around the elder, as if to draw him away and shield him, while a prayer for mercy was issuing from her lips.

"'Hold!' I shouted, in a tone that instantly arrested the action of all parties. 'Señor,' I quickly added in Spanish, addressing the old gentleman, 'you must at once yield yourself a prisoner of war, or I cannot be answerable for the consequences!'

"'He had already done so, Señor Caballero, when this fellow attempted to rob him, and he grappled with him to prevent himself from being plundered,' said the female, turning upon me a most beautiful face, and fixing upon me a pair of most bewitching black eyes.

"'What! have we a common highwayman and thief among us?' cried I, turning fiercely upon the Ranger whose now downcast and guilty look at once convinced me that the accusation was just.

"He began to stammer forth some excuse; but I interrupted and ordered him out of sight, with the threat of most severe punishment in the event of my hearing anything more to his disgrace.

"'Oh, thanks, noble sir! many, many thanks!' cried

the female, springing forward, seizing my hand, and impulsively carrying it to her lips. 'Oh, spare him!' she continued, fixing her large, soft, lustrous eyes upon me, in the most fascinating manner in the world; 'spare him! spare my father! and Heaven will bless you, and Paula will ever remember you with gratitude!'

"'Be assured, fair lady, he is only a prisoner of war and not a hair of his head shall be injured!' was my gallant reply, as I looked steadily into the dark, soul-speaking eyes so near to mine, and felt a strange, romantic fascination stealing over me.

"'Father, do you hear that?' said Paula, joyfully. 'See what it is to meet with a noble officer! Pray step into that closet there, and bring him some refreshments.'

"'Thanks, fair lady!' said I, as the old gentleman opened a side door and disappeared as directed. 'Hard fighting, and a long fast, are truly calculated to give a man an appetite, and I flatter myself I shall be able to do justice to your fare.'

"'Oh, this siege is terrible for all parties!' said Paula; and she continued talking on the subject for a minute or two, when she stopped suddenly, and saying, 'Pray excuse me till I can see what detains my father,' she hurried out through the same door, closing it after her.

"At this moment some of the men came in from the other room, when I informed them what had occurred, and that shortly we were to have something to break our long fast. But when some five minutes had passed away, without the re-appearance of either Paula or her father, we all began to grow impatient; and going to the door, I opened it, and discovered it was only a ruse of the girl to effect her own and her father's escape—for the door merely opened into a vestibule, which led into a garden—the house itself being built rather after the English than the Spanish style.

"Well, the escape was a trivial thing in itself, and, after a few playful comments from my comrades, the subject was dropped and the incident forgotten, we having enough before us of a more serious nature to occupy our minds.

"I pass over the siege—for that is a matter of history. The American army, as the world knows, was victorious; and after three or four days hard fighting on both sides, the Mexicans capitulated, and were allowed to march out of the city with the honors of war.

"A few days after this event, the Rangers were mustered out of service, and I found myself once more master of my time and person. I lingered about the town for a few days longer, and then set off with a train for Camargo, on my return to the United States.

"I pass over several little incidents, which might or might not interest you, but which have no bearing on the story it is my purpose to relate. About twelve or fifteen miles from Mier, the train halted late one hot afternoon; and being told that a small party of our men had ridden on to Mier, and might easily be overtaken, I resolved to push on alone for that purpose.

"The road, somewhat hilly, and passing over an almost barren waste of country, I knew to be dangerous, from the prowling bands of robbers and guerrillas that infested it; and had I not felt certain of overtaking the party in advance before nightfall, I should not have attempted it alone.

"But as fortune would have it, I got benighted without overtaking my comrades; and in one of the most gloomy and dismal places on the route—a deep, dark hollow, between two steep hills—I found myself suddenly jerked from my horse to the ground, by means of a lasso, which had been thrown over my head with unerring aim, and which, falling over my arms, so completely pinioned them to my body, as to prevent my drawing a single weapon in my defence.

"Scarcely had I struck the ground, when two men sprung upon me, and I could see the bright blades of their weapons gleam in the dim light.

"'For God's sake, gentlemen, do not murder me!' I cried in Spanish, though with little hope that my prayer would be heeded—for I had seen more than one cross on my route, to note the spot where some solitary traveler

"Hold, Guido—stay your hand!" said the same feminine voice.

See page 318.

had fallen a victim to these so-called knights of the road.

"'Who are you?' gruffly demanded one of the two, as he determinedly put his hand upon my throat and raised his knife, as I believed, for the fatal stoke.

"'Why don't you finish him, Guido?' said a voice at a short distance from me; and glancing my eyes in the direction of the speaker, I dimly perceived three or four figures grouped together, one of whom had my horse by the bit. 'Why don't you finish him, I say? what is it to you who or what he is?'

"'Why, if he's a gentleman,' returned Guido, as he deliberately brought the point of the sharp weapon down upon my naked throat, 'who knows but he might pay us a handsome ransom for his life!'

"I caught at the suggestion, and instantly replied:

"'I will—I will! I *am* a gentleman of means, and will pay you any ransom that we may agree upon, at any place convenient to both.'

"'Fools! why do you dally?—dead men tell no tales!' cried another voice behind me, which not only sounded like that of a woman, but which, strangely enough, I fancied was not altogether unfamiliar to me.

"'Can it be possible that one of the gentler sex decrees me to death?' said I; while the ruffian, whose hand and knife were upon my throat, seemed to wait for some reply before the completion of his bloody work.

"'Hold, Guido—stay your hand!' said the same feminine voice. 'Who are you, sir?' was next addressed to me.

"Instantly the truth flashed upon me I had heard that voice before—it was a woman's—and that woman had had reason to remember me gratefully.

"'If it is Paula who asks that question, I am the officer who saved her father at the storming of Monterey,' was my reply to the interrogation.

"'Ha! is it so indeed?' said the same voice. 'Back, there, Pablo and Guido! and as the ruffians released their hold of me, a woman's face was brought close to mine, and that face I could see was Paula's. 'It is true!' she proceeded after a close scrutiny of my features; 'this gentleman did save my father, and for that act is now free. Señor Cabellero,' she continued, addressing me, 'accept my regrets for the trouble we have given you, and my congratulations that nothing more serious has occurred! Arise, sir—you are free. Mount your horse and away with a God-speed and without question! and when you relate this adventure to your friends, tell them you found gratitude even in the breast of Paula Mendolez, the Guerrilla Queen.'

"'Thanks, fair lady—a thousand thanks for my life!' said I, as I started to my feet, though even then fearful of a treacherous stab from the sullen and disappointed bandits.

"'Away!' said Paula, sternly; 'and let us never meet again—for though we part as friends now, we should next meet as foes. We are quits now. You saved my father's life, and I have saved yours. Adios!'

"It needed no special urging to get me into the saddle; and finding myself clear of the robbers, and once more under way, I drove the spurs into my horse; and, in less than an hour, the foam-covered beast stood panting beside my comrades in the town of Mier.

"Such, gentlemen, is in brief the story I promised," concluded the captain, refilling his glass. "I see you all look as if you would ask for more facts—but I have none to give. Who Paula Mendolez really was, and what became of her, I know no more than you. I only know we met and parted in the manner I have stated, and that I still feel very grateful to her for having my head on my shoulders to-night, to tell you the story. Fill up, gentlemen, and here is to the very good health of the Guerrilla Queen."

The Last Stake.

"So you would like to know how I first became acquainted with my bride?" said an old friend of mine, by the name of George Carson, whom I met on his bridal tour. "Well, 'thereby hangs a tale;' and as the story is both romantic and tragic, and has a moral, you shall have it.

"Shortly after the 'gold fever' broke out in California," pursued my friend, "I was, as you know, among the first to venture into that then almost unknown region, with a view to amassing wealth, by what I at that time regarded as the very simple process of digging up gold by the bushel. I arrived out there, as you also know, with a select party of friends, and forthwith we set off for the mines. Having fixed upon a locality, we all went to work in high spirits, and continued together about a month; by which time we had made the not very agreeable discovery that 'all is not gold that glitters;' and that, even in the gold regions, there is an immense amount of earth which has nothing in it that can glitter.

"Up to the time named, though working industriously,

we had not cleared the expenses of living—to say nothing of the expenses of our outward voyage—and consequently we all began to grow querulous and argumentative. One said the gold was here, and another said it was there, and a third that it was nowhere—at least in a sufficient quantity to pay for the trouble of unearthing it. Gold was there, without question, for we had actually seen some—but not in such chunks as we had grappled in our dreams—and though we all felt satisfied that if we had the mines at home, and could get our board for a dollar a week, we might make a respectable living by digging and washing it, yet we were by no means satisfied we could do the same in California.

"But then, if we could believe the stories of strangers, who occasionally passed through our camp, there were solid veins of solid gold in every place except where we were; and as nearly every man of us had an idea that he knew best how to find solid veins, we divided our party into pairs, and set off 'prospecting' for these wonderful localities. My partner and I, not finding ours very readily, soon began to differ in opinion; and at length he went one way, and I another. After searching for a day or two longer, I fortunately fixed upon a spot which turned out the golden ore to some considerable profit; and I began and continued to work alone for a week—luckily shooting game enough in the vicinity to supply the most pressing wants of nature.

"My solitary camp was none of the pleasantest, however, especially at night; and though now doing well exceedingly, and flattering myself that I should some day be a gentleman of means, it was not with the same regret that Robinson Crusoe discovered the 'tracks in the sand,' that I one day found myself joined by a young and rather delicate-looking stranger, with black hair and eyes, and pale, classical, intellectual features.

"Henry Gordon—for such was his name—was a native of New England, who had come hither to get rich—simply, as he expressed it, that he might put himself on an equality with a young and beautiful heiress, whose mercenary parents were decidedly opposed to their only daughter throwing herself away upon one in indigent circumstances. He was about four-and-twenty years of age, had received a good education, and was refined in manner and sentiment; and the more I saw of him, the better I liked him, and consequently, the more I reflected upon the purse pride of human nature, which could not regard one man, while in the image of his Maker, as good as another, simply because he had not the same amount of this world's dross, or the yellow dust we were so industriously seeking.

"Henry Gordon and I continued together for several weeks—one or the other of us going below to obtain the necessary articles for subsistence, after the game had become so scarce as to require too much of our time in procuring it; and during this period I became greatly attached to him, and deeply sympathized with all his feelings.

"'Shall I ever become rich and get back to my native land?' he would frequently say, in a desponding mood; 'shall I ever look upon my dear Agnes as her equal in wealth? and shall I find her true to the lonely wanderer? She promised to be true—she promised to wait for me—wait years for me, if necessary. I believe she sincerely loved me, and had none of the selfish feelings of her parents; but oh! it is so long to wait! And I am so unhappy here! so miserable! This labor is not fitted to one of my delicate organization; and I sometimes think I shall find my grave in California, and breathe my last breath among strangers, afar from her for whose sake I came hither.'

"I encouraged him as well as I could, and bade him not despair. I told him we were doing well where we were; and though it might take a long time to get rich by digging gold, yet I thought that a sufficient capital might soon be realized, to enable him to start in some kind of business, by which he could make money faster, and easier, and more congenial to his feelings; and as wealth would suddenly be acquired by some, I saw no reason why he and I might not be among the fortunate few.

"The hard work of the mines, however, and exposure to the weather—to heats, and damps, and sudden changes, and the irregular fare of the mountains—did not agree with him. Somewhat sickly when he came, he grew paler and more sickly every day; and at last he fell quite ill, and was obliged to suspend his labors. I attended him as well as I could; and he recovered so as to be able to leave the mines, but not to resume his occupation there.

"All this time he was much mentally depressed, and continually talked of his Agnes, but in a tone of deeper despondency than ever, and sometimes praying that he might live to return, if only to see her again ere bidding adieu to earth.

"'If I cannot acquire wealth,' he would say—'If I cannot win her—if we cannot unitedly pass through the vale of life together—then the next happiness I pray for, is, that I may die in her native clime, and be buried where she may sometimes look upon my solitary grave!'

"At last, after thanking me, with tearful eyes, for all the kindness I had shown to him, he bade me farewell; and taking with him his hardly-earned gold, he set off for San Francisco.

"Months passed on, and I continued among the mountains, changing my locality from time to time, and on the whole, meeting with very fair success, till the rainy season set in; when, flattering myself that, with the capital I now had, I could do better in some more congenial pursuit, I set off for San Francisco also.

"Shortly after my arrival there, as I was passing down the principal street, which then consisted of mere shanties and booths, a familiar voice hailed me; and as I turned around, Henry Gordon bounded up and grasped me by the hand.

"'My dear fellow,' he said, 'I am so delighted to see you! for I had begun to fear that you had got sick and perished among the mines. But you are looking remarkably well, and I hope you have been prosperous according to your deserts!'

"I replied that I had no reason to complain, and that it gave me great pleasure to be able to congratulate him in return upon his healthy appearance.

"'Yes,' he rejoined, 'I am better than ever, in every way—mentally, physically, and pecuniarily. I have got my health, my energies, and my hopes, and am now on the fair road to fortune and happiness. I came down here with the little means I had, set quickly to work in a small way, buying and selling, and, being favored by fortune, am now worth my thousands. Do you see that large shanty yonder?' pointing down the street. 'Well, that and all it contains is mine. Come, my friend, you shall make your home with me; and if you wish to start in business I will put you in the way to make a fortune.'

"'And what of Agnes?' said I, as I accompanied him to his new business home, where I found a couple of clerks busy in disposing of goods at rates which I fancied might make any man wealthy in a very short time.

"'Ah! good news of her!' he said, with sparkling eyes, 'better news than I had hoped; for I have received a letter from her, in reply to mine, in which she states that her father has been unfortunate in business, and is now reduced to want. Carson, this is glorious news to me! and it will be the proudest and happiest day of my life, when I shall once more reach my native land, and take her hand, and assure her mercenary parents that now the poor outcast can give her riches beyond their wildest dreams of wealth! Oh, George, I must get rich—very rich! My ambition now aspires to the position of a millionare, that I may build a palace for my Agnes, and lord it over the purse-proud fools who despised me in my day of poverty, and thought me beneath them, merely because I had not the talisman I now possess! Oh, it will be a glorious triumph for Agnes and me!'

"'But have a care, Gordon,' returned I; 'do not seek too much! Remember the fable of the golden eggs!'

"'Oh, I will be cautious! and yet I will be bold!' he rejoined, with spirit and pride. 'Aladdin's lamp is in my ued! and I will grow rich—very rich! and yet a year from this shall see me homeward bound! Come, let us crack a bottle of wine together, and drink a toast to my glorious Agnes! After that we will talk over your prospects; for you must grow rich also, and go back with me, and enjoy my triumph! You were my first and only friend here,' he added, with faltering voice and tearful eyes; 'and, save Agnes, you shall be first in my heart there—for Henry Gordon is one who can never forget a friend.'

"I remained in San Francisco several months, making my home with Gordon, and entering into various speculations, some of which proved successful, and some otherwise; so that, at the end of the period named, I found, on summing up, I had come out about even—the only money I had really made being what I had dug from the earth.

"He, however, had been more prosperous—for, like the fabled Midas, every thing he touched seemed turned to gold. In consequence of this repeated good fortune, he grew more sanguine, and venturesome to a degree that startled me, for I was afraid some unlucky venture might ruin him. But whenever I warned him, he laughed at my fears, and frequently replied:

"'Have I not often told you that I hold the lamp of Aladdin?'

"Another thing gave me not a little uneasiness: the

more he acquired, the more he seemed to want; and though he now possessed far beyond what at first his most sanguine hopes had told him he could obtain, yet he seemed as far as ever from arriving at the ultimate of his desires; and eager to gain, by any and every means, he began to resort to the gambling hells, (which now loomed thickly up around us, with the blasting and desolating power of the deadly upas,) and there he staked largely and excitedly, and rode, as it seemed, a triumphant conqueror even over the very fates themselves.

"Finding I had not bettered my condition in the settlement, I finally resolved upon a return to the mines; and with many an earnest word of caution to my now sanguine friend, I took leave of him. As my story, however, relates more directly to him than myself, I pass over the interval of my absence, which was several months.

"On my return to town, I sought the quarters of Henry Gordon with no little anxiety. I found his place of business looking less thriving than usual; but he himself, as I had feared, was not there. On my inquiring for him, I was directed to a large and magnificent saloon—or golden-paved hell—which had of late become his constant resort.

"I did not seek him there immediately—for I had business which took me another way; but the following evening, observing the place in question brilliantly lighted up, I ventured in; and there, one among a large crowd which surrounded a faro bank, I discovered my friend, betting heavily, and all eyes turned upon him. He stood in such a position that the light shone clear and full upon his features; and it was with a start of surprise, and a pang of sorrow, that I now looked upon his pale, almost ghastly face, with its compressed lips, knitted brows, and eager, fiery eyes, which he kept fixed upon the cards in the hands of the dealer. His fortune had turned—I could see that plainly; and with the wild, maddened desperation of one conscious of the fact—and that, if he could not recover, by a bold stroke, what he had lost, he was a ruined man—he was now staking his all upon what proved literally to be the chance of life and death.

"Spell-bound by his singular appearance, I stood, for a few minutes, gazing sadly upon his altered countenance, and secretly cursing the vice which had become his bane. At length, just as I was about to push forward to him, to drag him away from his doom, he staggered back, and pressed his convulsively-working fingers to his forehead, while large beads of perspiration gathered upon his agonized features. The next moment I heard him exclaim in a voice of despair, whose tones seem yet to ring in my ears:

"'Oh, my God! I am a ruined man

"The crowd made way for him to pass—a few with looks of compassion, but more with smiles of derision—

28*

for these were the men who had sought his ruin, and could glory in their success.

"I pushed eagerly forward, and grasped his hand.

"'My dear fellow,' said I, 'come with me.'

"At first he did not recognize me, but threw me from him with violence, saying:

"'Begone, fiend! I am ruined already—what more would you have?'

"'Henry,' returned I, soothingly, "do you not know your friend, George Carson?'

"He swept his fingers quickly across his eyes, as if brushing away a mist, and replied, in a hollow, agonized voice:

"'George Carson, is this you! I thought it was another—I took you for the fiend in human shape, who first tempted me to my destruction! George,' he pursued, hurriedly, grasping my arm, and dragging me apart from the crowd—'George, I am a ruined man—ruined for this world and the next! I have lost all—*all*—every thing!—fortune—hope—happiness—my Agnes!'

"'But you can easily retrieve all, Henry, if you will but keep away from these dens of iniquity.'

"'No! no!' he somewhat wildly rejoined: 'it is too late! too late! too late! George, I am glad you are here. I wanted to see a friend, but never expected to again. Here—take this ring—and if you ever return to the States, seek out Agnes Waltham, and tell her it came from me, with my blessing!'

"'What means this strange language, Henry?' said I, beginning to grow alarmed: 'surely you will take it back yourself?'

"'I may not live,' he muttered, turning aside his face. 'Promise me, if I do not live, and you ever return, you will seek out Agnes, and give her that ring, with my blessing!—promise me, George Carson, in God's holy name!'

"'I do, Henry—I solemnly promise! But surely you have some covert meaning to these strange words! Come! you must come with me! I will not leave you for a single moment, till you are calmer and more like yourself.'

"'But you have promised me, George, have you not? sworn to me, if any thing *should* happen, that you will give that ring to Agnes, with my blessing?'

"'I have promised, Henry—I have sworn. So come! let us leave this scene of vice.'

"'One moment!' he said; and turning quickly on his heel, he pushed eagerly into the crowd, which had again closed around the faro bank.

"Almost the next moment I was startled by the report of a pistol, followed by exclamations of horror; and with a presentiment of the worst, I bounded forward, just in time to see them raising poor Henry Gordon from the table, upon which he had fallen—shot through the brain by his own hand—literally the gambler's victim—sacrificed on the very altar of unholy desires!

"I kept my promise," concluded my friend, "and gave the ring to Agnes Waltham—and another on her wedding day—for the first love of Henry Gordon is now the wife of him who rejoiced in his prosperity, grieved over his fatal vice, and bitterly mourned his untimely end."

Adventure of a Colporteur.

Accidentally meeting one day with an old school-mate, whom I had lost sight of for a number of years, I learned in the first few minutes of our conversation that he had been a traveling colporteur, but had lately married and settled in the West, turned storekeeper, and was now on a visit to some of his friends at the East.

To some very natural inquiries which I made, he replied by telling me the following thrilling and romantic incident:

"The life of a colporteur," he began, "is a very hard and trying one. Traveling from place to place, as he does, through the more thinly-peopled sections of the country; imitating his Great Master so far as to be with the poor always; selling his religious works where he can—giving them away where money is wanting and he sees a chance of their doing good; holding meetings in the wilderness, perhaps a hundred miles from any regular church or pastor; visiting the sick; officiating for the dead; endeavoring to console the mourner; exposed to heat and cold, sunshine and storm; sometimes riding the whole day without food, and often passing the night in the most unhealthy and wretched quarters; continually meeting with incidents and accidents of the most disagreeable nature; now receiving the blessings of the good, and anon the bitter curses of the bad: all this, my friend, is very trying to one poor human system, and there are few men so constituted as to be able to hold out in the good work for any great length of time.

"During the few years which I spent in this manner, in what I may call the wilderness of the West, many events occurred, which, could I now recall, and had I time to relate, I believe would deeply interest you; but I will only give you the most remarkable one of all, and the one most closely interwoven with my life and destiny.

"One dull, gloomy, drizzling day, during the spring of the last year I served in the capacity I have mentioned, I found myself, near the setting in of night, passing through a long, dreary wood, where for miles I had not seen any habitation. In fact, since noon of that day, I had passed but one dwelling—a poor, miserable log-hut—where for myself I had obtained rather a lunch than a meal, but had not been able to procure any thing for my weary horse. How far I had yet to go to reach a habitation where I could find shelter for the night, I could not say, and in consequence I began to feel quite uneasy. My horse was fatigued and hungry, and myself cold, wet, and uncomfortable.

"Spurring on my jaded beast, however, in the hope that I should yet find some comfortable lodging on the way, I rode on some two miles further, and descended into a steep, narrow valley, through which flowed a swift mountain stream, and across which led the narrow road I was pursuing

"It was now getting quite dark; and as I reached the stream and heard the gloomy murmur of its swollen waters, and knew not if it were safe to attempt the ford, I felt quite disheartened, and was half tempted to turn back and encamp as best I could upon the high ground of the hill above.

"But looking around me, as my poor horse pricked up his ears and uttered a pleading whinney, I espied a light a few rods below; and riding down to it, I was greatly relieved and rejoiced to find it proceeded from a neat and comfortable dwelling, which stood back some ten or fifteen yards from the stream, and probably as many feet above the level of its waters.

"On knocking at the door, it was opened by a very genteel looking woman, some forty-five or fifty years of age, who, from her dress and appearance, I judged to be in deep mourning To my statement of who and what I was, and my application for permission to pass the night beneath her roof, she replied, in a kind and gentle tone, that she would be very happy to entertain me, if I would accept of her humble fare.

"Procuring a lantern, and a small measure of corn for my horse, I led him by direction to the other side of the hill, where, after hobbling, I turned him out to graze in a partially cleared field.

"On returning to the house, I was agreeably surprised to find a bright and pleasant fire, a smoking supper well under way, and, gracing the apartment with her mother, a young lady some eighteen years of age, whom at a single glance I considered one of the most beautiful and fascinating beings I had ever seen. She was of the medium height, with light hair, blue eyes, and a pale, lovely face, upon which every noble virtue seemed to have set its seal. She was modest, retiring, and intelligent, and her voice was one of great sweetness and melody. From the very first I became deeply interested in her—to me she was a delicate flower blooming in a dreary wilderness—and consequently I became more than usually interested in the family history as related by her mother.

"The elder lady was a widow by the name of Arlington, who, some three years previous to the time I speak of, had, with her husband and two children, removed from the astward, and settled in the lonely place where I now I and them. Some half a mile above their dwelling, and some two miles below what was then a small, but rather flourishing village, Mr. Arlington had erected a sawmill and gristmill. He had just got them completed and in good working order, when, one dark, stormy night, going out to raise the flood-gate, he had fallen into the water, been swept down the torrent, and drowned; the body being discovered the next day, some two or three miles below. One of the two children mentioned, the eldest, a son, some twenty years of age, had taken the place of his father since his death, and was now away at the mills; and the other, the daughter, Julia Arlington, was the one I have already described.

"'It was on a night similar to this, Mr. Perry,' pursued the widow, addressing me in a sad tone of deep feeling, 'that we met with that great misfortune which time can never repair—for what can compensate for the loss of a beloved husband and kind father? Never do I hear the hoarse murmurs of yonder stream, amid the dark and dismal watches of the night, that my mind is not borne back to that night of all nights of suffering suspense, and that awful realization which followed when the remains of him we so devotedly loved were brought here and placed before us, as if only for one final farewell of his clay-cold form! Oh! the anxious hours I pass, thinking of my son! who, for aught I know, may come to the same untimely end!

and on nights like this, when he is compelled to be away from home, I spend a great portion of my time in prayerful anxiety; and even the presence of a stranger is most heartily welcome, as a slight relief to the painful gloom, though we are seldom called upon to entertain one.'

"Mrs. Arlington shed tears as she spoke, and the fair Julia wept almost convulsively. I offered what consolation I could; told them to put their trust in Providence; that all seeming evils were for our good; and after some further conversation of a similar nature, and a narration in part of my own history, I read an appropriate chapter from the Bible, offered prayers, and retired for the night.

"The house was a small frame, a story and a half in height, containing two or three rooms on the ground floor, and two above—one of which latter was assigned me for a lodging, the widow and her daughter remaining below. Being greatly wearied with my day's ride, I quickly turned in; and thinking of the fair Julia—her bereavement, loneliness, and consequent desolation—I soon fell asleep, to see her again in my dreams.

"I might have slept for a couple of hours—I cannot say; but on waking, as I did with something like a start, I heard the rain pouring down in torrents, and even fancied the hoarse murmurs of the mountain stream, as it dashed swiftly past over its rocky bed, were sounding in my ear.

"'Thank God for this comfortable shelter!' was my mental prayer, and again I fell asleep.

"From this second sleep, which was more sound than the first, I was aroused by several wild, appalling shrieks. Starting up in bed, I was horrified, almost paralyzed, at hearing the terrible roar and rush of heavy waters around me, and of feeling the whole building tremble and shake, as if it were about to be wrenched from its foundation, torn asunder, and scattered in fragments.

"For a few moments I knew not where I was, and could not comprehend what had happened; but the continuous shrieks for help, and a fancied recognition of the voice of Julia Arlington, brought back my recollection to the point of retiring to rest, and then the whole truth seemed suddenly to flash upon me.

"And, merciful God! what a truth! what a horrible reality! The mountain stream had burst its former boundaries—had ascended its banks in a wild, roaring, raging flood—had partially submerged the dwelling of my kind hostess, and was now surging past with that terrific power which no strength or art of man can check; and which, in its awful force and sublimity, seems to mock his weakness, and tell him how frail, how helpless, how insignificant he is before one single element, when guided by the Almighty hand of Omnipotence.

"As shriek on shriek still rose above the creaking and

groaning of the swaying timbers of the dwelling—above the moanings of the blast, the plashing of the rain, and the gurgling, rushing, surging murmurs of the angry flood—I sprung from my bed, threw on a part of my clothing, hurried to the stairs, and commenced descending them rapidly.

"When a little more than half way down, I found to my dismay and horror, that my feet were buried in water, and I knew that the parties below must be struggling in the liquid element to keep themselves from drowning. Laboring as I knew they must be under the most intense and terrible excitement, they might naturally want the presence of mind which would enable them to escape immediate destruction by gaining the second story; and shouting to to them that help was at hand, I plunged boldly downward into some four feet depth of water, and went knocking about in the deep darkness among the different articles of furniture, but struggling forward to the point whence came the continued shrieks of fear and distress.

"The flood was still rising rapidly; it appeared to me that I could feel it gaining upon us every moment; the groaning and trembling house seemed about to be borne away, or come crumbling down around us; and I felt, if there were indeed any salvation for us, our lives depended upon the action of the momentous seconds which were so rapidly bearing us to the verge of eternity.

"Happily I soon reached the widow and her daughter, whom I found clasped in each other's arms, nearly beside themselves with terror, but instinctively keeping their heads above the water in which their bodies floated; and speaking to them some soothing words of hope which I little felt myself, I dragged them forward, found the stairs, and assisted them to the story above.

"By this time poor Julia Arlington had fainted; but the mother, with a slight revival of hope, seemed to regain her presence of mind; and as we both bent over her daughter, chafing her limbs, and dashing water in her face, till she began to show signs of returning consciousness, she said to me, with a deep feeling of a fond and grateful parent:

"'May the Lord Almighty bless you for this! You must have been providentially sent to our rescue; for without your aid, I am certain we should have been drowned below!'

"'Alas!' said I somewhat gloomily, as the rising waters seemed to roar around us even more fearfully than ever; 'we are not yet saved! we are not yet saved! and the good God alone knows what fate is in reserve for us!'

"'God help us!' exclaimed the restored Julia, a few minutes later, as she stood trembling and clinging to her mother and myself, and endeavoring to peer around her in the awful darkness: 'I fear we shall yet be swept away by this terrible flood!'

"'I have my fears, too!' I replied; 'but we will rely upon God's mercy, and hope to the last!'

Almost as I spoke, there came a louder creaking and groaning—then a crashing as of some breaking timbers—then a rocking to and fro, like a boat upon the waves—and then a seeming whirling and plunging downward and forward.

"'God help us now indeed!' I exclaimed; 'for we are already afloat—already in the grasp of the angry flood—and should be prepared for the worst, as becometh those who put their hope and trust in a Higher Power and a better world!'

"I need not dwell upon that never-to-be-forgotten night I could not, if I would, describe our feelings of alternate hope and despair; our unspeakable anxieties, as we went whirling down with the rushing tide - rocking, rolling, plunging through the seething, bubbling waters; now striking some rock or tree with almost force enough to crush our frail tenement; now checked in our progress till some feeling of hope would revive; now torn from our moorings and sent onward again, a frail bubble upon the bosom of a maddened flood, till despair would awe us to silence in view of the impending death!

"All that dark and awful night was passed in a manner

which if you cannot imagine, I have no language to describe.

"Reaching at daylight a long, broad level, we floated out of the main current, and made a lodgment upon rising ground, as Noah's ark might have rested upon the summit of Mount Ararat.

"Here we remained through the day, in painful anxiety—watching the timbers, drift-wood, and wrecks of buildings which went floating past us—and humbly thanking God for our own wonderful preservation. Before noon the storm had begun to abate; and we saw the sun of that day set gloriously in the west, with the water subsiding around us.

"We passed another night beneath the same roof; but on the second day we were enabled to walk forth, and make our way to a settlement in the vicinity, where we were hospitably received, and where the anxious mother and sister were joined by the son and brother, whose escape from death had been almost as miraculous as our own.

"In conclusion I have only to add, that the acquaintance of two, begun amid such fearful and trying scenes, soon deepened into a friendship, which ripened into a pure and holy love; and Julia Arlington is now the wife of him who labored for her salvation through that long, dark, terrific night of tempest, flood, and staring death."

A Night with the Wolves.

"A NUMBER of years ago," said an old settler, whom I met on my western travels, "I took my family to Wisconsin, and located myself in the woods, about ten miles from the nearest settlement, and at least five from the nearest neighbor. The country round was mostly forest; and wild beasts and Indians were so numerous in that quarter, that my friends at the East, to whom I gave a description of my locality, expressed great fears for our safety, and said they should be less surprised to learn of our having all been cut off, than to hear of our still being alive out there at the end of a couple of years.

"However, I did not feel much alarmed on my own account—and my wife was as brave as a hunter; but then we had three children—the oldest only ten—and sometimes, when I was away from home, the sudden growl of a bear, the howl of a wolf, or the scream of a panther, would make me think of them, and feel quite uneasy.

"For a while, at first, the night-screeching and howling

of these wild animals alarmed the children a good deal—and sometimes my wife and me—especially when we mistook the cry of the panther for an Indian yell; but we soon got used to the different sounds, and then did not mind them so much; and after I had got a few acres cleared around the dwelling, they generally kept more distant at night—just as if they comprehended that the place, now in the possession of their enemies, was no longer to be an abode for them. Besides, I now and then shot one, which thinned them a little, and probably frightened the others, for they gradually became less bold and annoying.

"During the first year, I had two rather narrow escapes—once from a bear, and once from a panther; but the most remarkable adventure of all, was the one which happened during the second winter, and which I have always designated as a 'Night with the Wolves.'

"One bitter cold morning—the ground being deeply covered with snow, so crusted and frozen that no feet could sink into it—I brought out the horse for my wife to ride to C*****, the nearest settlement, where she had some purchases to make, which she wished to attend to herself. Besides being well muffled up in her own clothing, I wrapped a large buffalo robe around her; and admonishing her that the woods were full of danger after dark, I urged her to be sure and get back before sunset which she promised to do.

"All day long, after her departure, from some cause for which I could not account, I felt very much depressed and uneasy, as if something evil were going to happen; and when I saw the sun about half an hour high, and no signs of my wife returning, I got out my pistols, rifle, ammunition, and hunting-knife, saddled a young and rather skittish colt, and bidding the children keep within doors, and the house safely locked, I mounted and rode off to meet her, which I expected to do at every turn of the horse-path. But at every turn I was doomed to disappointment; and when I had put mile after mile behind me, without seeing any signs of her, I became more and more alarmed, and dashed on still faster.

"It was just about dark when I saw the lights of C***** gleaming in the distance; but before I reached the town I met my wife hastening homeward—she having been unexpectedly detained by meeting an old acquaintance, who had recently come on from the eastward, and with whom she had remained to gather the news and take supper—the time passing away so quickly as to render her belated before she was aware of it.

"I was greatly rejoiced to find her safe and unharmed—but not a little puzzled to account for my presentiment of evil, which it appeared to me had taken place without cause—though in this respect I was greatly mistaken, as the sequel will show.

"We now set off at a brisk trot homeward—through a dense, dark, gloomy wood, which lined our way on either side—and had safely proceeded about five miles, when we were somewhat startled by a series of long, plaintive howls, at a considerable distance, and in different directions, and which our experience told us were wolves, seemingly calling and answering each other through the great forest.

The wolves of this region were of the larger and fiercer species; and though ordinarily and singly they might not attack a human being, yet in numbers and pressed by hunger, as they generally were at this season of the year, I by no means felt certain that we should not be molested.

"Accordingly we quickened the pace of our horses; and as we hurried on, I grew every moment more uneasy and alarmed, as I noticed that many of the sounds gradually approached us. We had just entered a deep hollow, where a few large trees stretched their huge branches over a dense thicket, when suddenly there arose several loud, harsh, baying, and snarling sounds close at hand. The next moment there was a quick rustling and thrashing among the bushes; and then some six or eight large wolves—lean, gaunt, and maddened with hunger—sprung into the path close beside us.

"This happened so suddenly and unexpectedly, that my wife gave a slight scream and dropped her rein; and the horse, rearing and plunging at the same moment, unseated her; and she fell to the ground, right in the very midst of the savage beasts, whose glaring eyes shone in the darkness like so many coals of fire.

"Fortunately, her sudden fall startled the wild animals a little; and as they momentarily drew back, she, with rare presence of mind, at once gathered her buffalo robe, which she had dragged with her, in such a manner about her person as to protect herself from the first onset of their fangs. The next moment the ferocious animals, with the most savage growls, sprung at her, at me, and at the two horses simultaneously. Her's at once shook himself clear of his foes and fled; and mine began to rear and plunge in such a manner that I could not make use of a single weapon, and only by main strength keep him from running away with me.

It was a terrible moment of exciting agony; and the instant that I could release my feet from the stirrups, I leaped to the ground with a yell—my rifle slipping from my hands and discharging itself by the concussion, and my steed rushing like lightning after his flying companion over the frozen snow.

"Luckily, I had my loaded pistols and my knife convenient to my grasp; and scarcely conscious of what I was doing, but thinking only that the dear mother of my little ones lay fairly beneath some three or four of the furiously fighting and snarling wild beasts, I grasped the weapons, one in each hand, cocked them at the same instant, and, fairly jumping into the midst of my enemies, placed the muzzles against the heads of two that had turned to rend me, and fired them both together.

"Both shots, thank God! took effect—it could not be otherwise—and as the two wolves rolled howlingly back in their death agonies, their starving companions, smelling and getting a taste of their blood, and instinctively comprehending that they were now fairly in their power, fell upon them with the most ravenous fury, and literally tore them to pieces, and devoured them before my very eyes, almost over the body of my wife, and in less, I should say, than a minute of time.

"Ascertaining, by a few anxious inquiries, that my wife was still alive and unharmed, I bade her remain quiet; and picking up my rifle, I proceeded to load all my weapons with the greatest dispatch.

"As soon as I had rammed the first ball home, I felt tempted to shoot another of the animals; but at that moment I heard a distant howling; and fearing we should soon be beset my another pack, I reserved my fire for the next extreme danger, and hurriedly loaded the others.

"By the time I had fairly completed this operation, our first assailants, having nearly gorged themselves upon their more unfortunate companions, began to slink away; but the cries of the others at the same time growing nearer, warned me to be upon my guard.

"I had just succeeded in getting my wife more securely rolled in her protecting robe, as the safest thing I could do in that extremity—and myself, pistols in hand, in a defensive attitude over her prostrate body—when some eight or ten more of the savage and desperate creatures made their appearance upon the scene.

"There was a momentary pause as they came into view and discovered me—during which their eyes glared and shone like living coals—and then, with terrific growls and snarls they began to circle round me, each moment narrowing the space between us.

"Suddenly one, more daring or hungry than the others, bounded forward, and received a shot from one of my pistols directly between his eyes; and, as he rolled back upon the snow, a part of the others sprung upon him, as in the case of the first.

"But I had no time to congratulate myself that I had disposed of him; for almost at the same instant I felt the lacerating fangs of another in my thigh, which caused me to shriek with pain; and my poor wife, with an answering shriek, believing it was all over with me, was about to get up and face the worst; but shouting to her not to stir, that I was still safe, I placed my pistol against the head of my assailant, and stretched him quivering upon the snow also.

"I still had my rifle in reserve; and pointing that at the fighting pack, I poured its contents among them. How many were wounded I do not know; but almost immediately the space around us became once more cleared of our howling enemies—some limping as they fled, and appearing to be harassed by the others.

"Again it appeared to me we had met with a wonderful deliverance; and though the wound in my thigh was somewhat painful, a brief examination satisfied me that it would not prove serious; and I hastily proceeded to reload my weapons—my wife meantime getting upon her feet, embracing me tenderly, and earnestly thanking God for our preservation.

"'Oh, the dear children!' she exclaimed, with maternal tenderness; 'little do they know how near they have come to being made orphans, and left alone in this solitary wilderness! Let us hasten home to them! Oh, let us hasten home to them, while we have an opportunity!'

"'We have no opportunity,' I gloomily replied. 'Hark!' there are more of our foes in the distance—do you not hear them?'

"'And are they coming this way, too?' she tremblingly inquired.

"'I fear so.'

"'Oh, great God! what then will become of us!' she exclaimed; 'for I am almost certain that we shall not both survive a third attack.'

"'I see but one way of escape,' said I, anxiously. 'We must climb a tree, and remain in the branches till morning.'

"'We shall surely freeze to death there!' she replied.

"'I trust not; but at all events, as our horses are gone, we have no alternative. I think your buffalo robe, well wrapped around, will protect you from the cold, as it has done from the wolves; and as for myself, I will endeavor to keep warm by climbing up and down, and stamping upon the limbs.'

"'But why not kindle a fire?' she quickly rejoined, her voice suddenly animated with a hope that I was obliged to disappoint.

"'For two reasons,' I replied. 'First, because we have not time—do you not hear another hungry pack howling?—and secondly, because we have not the materials—the loose brush and sticks being buried under the snow.'

"'God help us, then!' groaned my wife; 'there seems nothing for us but death! Oh, my poor, dear children! May the good God grant that they be not made orphans this night!'

"I bade her take heart and not despair; and then selecting a large tree, whose lower limbs were broad and thick, but above the reach of our enemies, I hastily assisted her to a good foothold, and immediately climbed up after her.

"We were not there a moment too soon; for scarcely had we got ourselves settled in a comparatively comfortable position, when another hungry pack of our enemies appeared below us—howling, snarling, and fighting—their up-turned eyes occasionally glowing fearfully in the darkness.

"But we were safe from their reach; and all that long, dismal night we remained there, listening to their discordant tones, and thinking of the dear ones at home.

"The night was intensely cold; and in spite of all my efforts to keep my sluggish blood in circulation, I became so benumbed before morning, that I believe I should have given up and perished, except for the pleading voice of my wife, who begged me, for God's sake, to hold out, and not leave her a widow and my children fatherless.

"Daylight came at last; and never was morning hailed with greater joy. Our foes now slunk away, one by one, and left us to ourselves; and a few minutes after their disappearance, I got down and exercised myself violently; and having thus brought back a little warmth to my system, I assisted my wife to alight, and we at once started homeward.

"I scarcely need add that we arrived there in due time, to find our poor, night-long terrified children almost frantic with joy at our safe return."

Colonel Bowie of Arkansas.

MANY years ago, shortly after the triumphant conclusion of the revolt of Texas against Mexico, all eyes seemed turned in the direction of the newly acquired country. The South, in particular, regarded the wonderful triumph of a handful of hardy, free-born citizens, over the sordid and slavish hosts of the tyrannical Mexican Government, as an ordination of Providence that they should go in and possess the land. Accordingly several of the States—Alabama, Georgia, Tennessee, and Western Virginia in particular—sent company after company of stern, resolute men, with their families and wagon-trains of household goods and chattels, far into the interior of their new, rich, and blooming heritage.

Most generally the emigrating party consisted of three or four families, who designed settling in contiguity with each other, for purposes of self-protection, and with a view to the locating of villages and townships; but occasionally a solitary traveler, one possessing the extreme spirit of adventure, well mounted and well equipped, might be seen quietly pursuing his way over the rich, rolling lands to the westward of Nacogdoches. It is with one of the latter our story has to do, but at a period slightly anterior to the fall of the Alamo.

It was one of those soft, quiet days so peculiar to the central regions of Texas, when the very atmosphere, loaded with its balmy perfume, seems to incline all animated nature to repose, that a solitary traveler was slowly wending his way over the famous rolling red lands which stretch for hundreds of miles beyond the river Sabine. That he had ridden fast and far was evident from the appearance of his horse, whose foaming flanks and drooping head evinced an unusual degree of fatigue. It was a day, as we have said, calculated to call forth a dreamy, reflective mood; the surrounding country was rich in all the beauties of that delightful clime; the glorious magnolia, the snowy cottonwood, the sweet-scented china, mingling with a thousand other perfumes from the blossoming trees and draping vines, threw their aromatic odors upon the slumbering air; and both horse and rider for the time seemed to relapse into a quiescent state corresponding to the scene.

He was a man of apparently small stature, dressed in the style peculiar to the hardy adventurers of that region. A felt hat, with its long, broad, slouching brim, threw a quiet shadow over his bronzed, but somewhat youthful face. His features, though effeminate to a degree, were likewise stern and decisive; and a glance at his small, keen, blue eye, would have assured any one acquainted with human nature that he was not an individual to be molested with impunity. He wore the usual hunting-frock of the borderers; and in a belt beneath were thrust a couple of brace of silver-mounted pistols, and a long, heavy, peculiarly-shaped knife, to which he was the first to give a name that has perpetuated his own. Trowsers of coarse stuff, with ornamented buckskin leggings covering the tops of a pair of heavy boots, completed his attire.

The day was far advanced; and looming up in the West were a few black clouds, which betokened the approach of one of those terrific storms which sometimes sweep over that country with a desolating power. For some half an hour the horseman quietly pursued his way, his eyes bent upon the ground, and his mind evidently far away upon other scenes, though still feeling the soothing influence of the one which surrounded him. At length he reached the bank of a small stream, where the bushes grew thick upon either side of the road he was pursuing; when, just as his thirsty animal had bent his head to the water, he was suddenly startled by the report of a rifle; and a tingling sensation on his forehead, as the ball whizzed past assured him how near that moment had been to his last.

Reining up his mettlesome beast, and drawing a pistol from his belt, he glanced quickly and nervously about him, as if to guard himself from the attack of numbers, and then settled his gaze for a few moments upon the point whence the ball had been fired. He saw nothing except a thin wreath of smoke curling among the clustered leaves, at a distance of perhaps some twenty paces; and not caring longer to remain a quiet target for his invisible foe, who might even at that moment be taking a more certain aim, he plunged his rowels deep into the flank of his noble horse, and, dashing through the stream and up the opposite slope, soon cleared the thicket, and went speeding onward like the wind.

It was now, for the first time, that he perceived the advancing storm; and aware from its appearance, and the sullen, heavy booming of its still distant thunders, that it would be one of no ordinary power, he began to experience no little anxiety about finding a place of shelter for himself and beast. He had ridden for hours without seeing any sign of habitation; and the prospect before him gave no promise of finding one ere reaching his destination for the day, which was still many a long league distant.

Half an hour's further hard riding, however, brought him to an old, dilapidated building, which, from its appearance, had served some early Spanish settler; and as night and the storm were now close upon him, he decided it should serve him in turn, at least during the continuance of the tempest. Riding in through what had once been the main entrance of the building, he found himself partially sheltered under a roof constructed by some passing traveler, who had thrown a few saplings along the ruins, and interlaced them with a thatch of brush and grass. It was not yet dark; but the night was fast setting in, assisted by the advancing clouds. which had rolled far up toward the zenith, and long since veiled the sinking sun. Almost incessant flashes of lightning, which descended in crinkling chains, lit up the deepening gloom; and each was followed by its own peal of thunder; which, with a few exceptional crashes, became one almost even, continuous roar.

By this light, and what still remained of day, the traveler could see about his place of refuge, which presented no very cheerful aspect. A few broken stones and other rubbish were piled up here and there; but in one corner lay a litter of straw, which, should the night prove too inclement for his further progress, he flattered himself would serve as a comfortable resting-place for his own weary limbs. Dismounting from his horse, he tied him to one of the saplings overhead; and then removing the fragments from around his feet, to guard against injury, and looking carefully to his weapons, he deliberately sat himself down to await the issue.

The storm broke fiercely, the wind shrieked dismally, the lightnings flashed incessantly, the thunders crashed continuously, and the rain, pouring down in torrents, soon wetted our traveler to the skin. One, two, three, long dreary hours passed, and still the storm raged so furiously, that at last, reluctantly, our hero relinquished all hopes of pursuing his journey further for the night—for even should the tempest clear away, it was already late, and he knew that the different streams on his route would be so swollen as to make the fords dangerous. He therefore prepared to encamp where he was; and pushing a portion of the straw together, he threw himself down upon it; and wet though it was—and weary, wet and hungry though he was himself—he felt some little satisfaction in finding that his long uncertainty and indecision had at last come to an end; and with a lingering sigh for his poor beast, which could fare no better than its master, he soon fell into a dreamless sleep—the thought of his late narrow escape not tending to a deeper impression upon his mind than a kind of inward gratitude that his good fortune or a kind Providence had saved him.

The storm passed on, the rain ceased, the thunders died away in the distance, and still the traveler slept. At length, just as the first faint streak of day had begun to tinge the east, he roused with a kind of start, and, raising himself on his elbow, looked curiously about him, with the air of one who is trying to recall events immediately preceding his state of unconsciousness. As he peered about the old ruin, by the dim gray light—feeling cold, wet and hungry—his eye fell upon his horse, which seemed to be asleep; and remembering how long both had fasted, and that their fast must continue until they should reach a settlement, he resolved to resume his journey forthwith.

As he changed his position, however, to spring to his feet, his eye suddenly encountered the body of a man, lying in the straw, not three feet distant. The back of the stranger was toward our hero, and his face he could not see; but thinking it some one, who, like himself, had been driven in by the storm for a night's lodging, he first looked carefully to his weapons, and then, moving over to the other, quietly laid his hand upon his shoulder, and said.

"Well, stranger, so we are bed-fellows, it seems!"

The man moved not, and spoke not a word.

"I say, stranger," pursued the first, giving him a hearty shake, "I think you must be even a sounder sleeper than myself."

Still no movement—no answer.

"What ails the fellow?" mentally queried our traveler, as he turned his quiet companion over in the straw; and at the same moment the horse, aroused by his master's voice, started to his feet, with a loud whinny. "Good Heavens!" continued the speaker, as by the faint but increasing light he looked upon the ghastly face of the human form beneath him—"there is something wrong here—the man is dead! Ha, *murdered*, as I live!" he quickly added, with a visible shudder, as, bending more closely over him, he discovered traces of blood upon his garments.

There was a small hole through his vest; and hastily baring his breast, our traveler discovered that he had been shot through the heart, and had probably died almost instantly. But who had done the deed? and for what purpose? He felt in his pockets, which were empty, and reasoned that the man had been murdered for his money. Such murders were too common in Texas at that day to excite any great surprise; our hero had been accustomed to just such scenes through his whole eventful career; but he felt highly indignant at what he considered the barbarity of murdering and robbing a man, and leaving him to decompose above ground, in a place where it was not unlikely he would prove an annoyance to respectable travelers. In connection with this murder, he thought of his own narrow escape of the preceding day, and argued that his stopping-place might be the temporary quarters of a gang of desperadoes; in which case prudence would seem to advise him to be upon the road as quick as possible.

Accordingly, he turned away from the murdered stranger, after pushing the straw somewhat over the body, and made a step toward his horse; but just as he did so, his eye, glancing through a fissure in the old ruin, fell upon two men coming up the road, whose appearance gave no token that they would prove any very agreeable companions. Both carried rifles, and it was reasonable to suppose they were otherwise armed; and the first thought of our hero was to mount his horse and dash away. But he was no coward; he had been through many a desperate struggle, with heavy odds against him; and there was a kind of bitter satisfaction in thinking that one of these men might be his amiable friend of the ambush. With the rapid decision for which he was remarkable, he resolved to remain, and conceal himself behind a portion of the wall, from whence he could have a view of whatever might occur within, should the ruffians, as he believed them to be, see proper to enter. To locate himself in the desired position was but the work of a moment; and from there he found he could both see the road and the interior of the building, and yet not himself be exposed to a casual glance.

As his horse continued at intervals to whinny, he knew he must soon be heard by the approaching party, and he was anxious to see what effect this would produce upon them. He had not long to wait; for the men were advancing with rapid strides, and a louder whinny than usual seemed to reach their ears; when, stopping suddenly, and looking hastily around them, one of the two, after an apparently brief consultation with the other, pointed his finger toward the building. With this they turned at once from the road, and, gliding among some bushes, approached the place at a quick, stealthy pace. From the change in their position, the stranger was now in some danger of being discovered; but as it was not yet light enough to distinguish objects at any considerable distance, he threw himself flat upon the ground, to await the result; and this rather as a man inclined to act boldly, than as one actuated by any feeling of fear.

It was perhaps a couple of minutes from this time, ere the two men, issuing from a near cluster of bushes, glided up to the main entrance and looked cautiously in.

"I say, Bill," whispered one, but loud enough for the listener to hear, "I knows all about it now; that thar's the hoss of a feller as I tuk a shot at yesterday; and ef he's got any rocks, they're our'n."

"Hush, Joe!" returned the second, in the same cautious whisper; "he's sleeping thar, and there's no use o' our waking him for nothing. Let's go in and do for him, and talk arter we git his pile."

"Halves, you know!" said the other.

"Of course—honor bright—you know that's me, Joe; but I don't see no use o' our calling in the rest to share."

"Nary once, Bill—this here's my game. I had the first shot, and I've a right to it; and ef the other hounds wants ary persimmons, let 'em find the tree and climb for 'em."

It was apparent to our hero, from their remarks, that

these ruffians had had nothing to do individually with the killing of the man within; but as it was evidently their intention to murder him, he felt none the less hostile to them on that account.

With the last remark of the one addressed as Joe, the two men, leaning their rifles against the wall, and drawing their knives, glided up to what they supposed to be the sleeper. Owing to the light being yet dim, and the body mostly concealed in the straw, they were unable to discern that the man was dead; and determining to make their work sure, and their share equal, they sprung upon him simultaneously, and both plunged their knives up to their hilts in his body.

"Why, hello, Joe," cried Bill, with an oath, "this here's a dead man!"

"Why, so it is!" exclaimed the other, adding a tremendous oath, which we will not repeat. "This must be the feller as Tom shot—you know he was bragging as he had done for one on 'em—but I didn't think as how the ugly hound had left him here to trap us with. But whar's the man as owns the hoss?"

"Here!" said the traveler, in a tone that seemed to freeze the blood of his hearers; and as the two ruffians started up and looked around, they beheld him standing in the doorway, with one of their rifles brought to a deadly aim.

He had seen them put aside their rifles, for the purpose of deliberate butchery; and with a stealthy pace he had glided around and seized them, and now had the villains at his mercy.

"See here, stranger, don't fire! We cave—we owns up beat at our own game—and ef you'll jest let us off, you ken take what tin we has about us."

"Fools!" returned the traveler; "do you take me for a common thief and robber like yourselves? Which of you fired at me yesterday? Speak! quick! or, by the living God! I will shoot you both where you stand!"

It is impossible to convey to the reader the peculiar sound of the voice of the speaker. It cannot be described as either loud, fierce, or harsh, but rather as something cold and freezing, expressive of an inflexible will, an unalterable determination. His eye, too—that naturally small, quiet, almost calm blue eye—now seemed to gleam with a latent fire; while his thin lips compressed, and his whole face expressed a calm but unalterable and deadly resolution.

"That was Joe, here," replied one of the startled ruffians; "but he didn't mean to shoot at you!"

"No," chimed in Joe, "I was jest firing at a bird, as you rid along."

"Liar!" hissed the other—"and that lie shall be your last!"

Scarcely were the words spoken, when crack went the rifle, and Joe fell back upon the dead man, shot through the brain. Throwing down the piece, the stranger caught up the other, and quietly saying, "You will please follow your companion," he had already brought it to an aim, and his finger was just pressing the trigger, when, with a "For God's sake, spare me! I have a wife and children!" the other threw himself down upon his knees, and held up his hands imploringly.

"And would you have spared *me*?" demanded the traveler. "No! justice claims her due—your hour has come—you must die! Your wife and children, if you have any, will be better off without you. Too many such sneaking, cowardly villains encumber the soil of Texas! Had you the courage of a man, I would give you a chance for your life; but a paltry coward, above all things, I despise!"

"I'm no coward!" cried the other, leaping to his feet; "and the man lies as says I is! So fire away and be —— to you!"

"Who are you?" inquired our hero, touched with some little feeling of admiration for the villain, for courage always inspired him with a certain degree of respect.

"I'm Bill Harvey, of Arkansas."

"Enough!" was the answer: "I know you now, though you do not remember me. You shall have a chance for your life—but you can only live through my death What arms have you about you?"

"I've got nothing now 'cept this knife, or else I'd not stood here doing nothing while you was taking sight. But ef you knows me, as you say, I'd like to know what you knows about me! and ef it's all the same to you, I'd like to know who *you* ar'."

"Your foe!" returned the other, in the same cold, indescribable tone. "Do you ask what I know of you? I know you to be a liar, a gambler, a thief, a robber, and a murderer, with the courage of a bull-dog, which is your only redeeming trait. Nay, sir, no words! I have no time to waste—I have been delayed too long already. This is your chance for life: I will discharge this rifle in the air (suiting the action to the word,) and with this knife, (drawing the singular weapon we have before described, I will meet you in single combat—now—here—and may God have mercy on your miserable soul!"

"S'pose, then, we fight outside, whar we can see better?" said the other.

"Do you want a chance to run?" sneered the stranger.

"Ef you knows Bill Harvey, you knows he never runs whar thar's a fair fight. I did knuckle down a minute ago, and that was the meanest thing I ever done in my life; but I was tuk kinder by surprise like; and ef ever I does it agin, to white man or nigger, may I never see the inside of heaven!"

"Quick, then, take your position!" said the other; and he turned and walked back a few paces, in front of the old ruin.

Harvey came out, with his knife firmly clenched in his hand, and a look of fierce determination upon his rough, bronzed features. He was a large, powerfully built fellow, with black eyes, black hair, and bushy whiskers; and as he stood facing his small, slender, almost effeminate antagonist, a spectator would have argued that the latter could have no chance to cope with him by mere physical force The two took their positions about ten paces apart, and each fixed his eyes with stern, wily caution upon the other, like two beasts of the forest preparing for an encounter.

"Are you ready?" asked the traveler.

"Yes, ready to cut your little heart out!" rejoined Bill; and added, with a tremendous oath: "I'll do it too, ef you don't get skeered and use your barkers."

Scarcely were the words uttered, when our hero darted toward his adversary, with a sort of running bound, not unlike that of a panther when about to leap upon its prey. As he neared his foe, he made a feint as if to strike him; when the latter, throwing out a quick guard, returned a blow, which, if it had reached its mark, wou'd have ended the contest in his favor

But it did not reach its mark. With a suppleness and agility rarely seen even among the border fighters, our hero sprung aside, and, fairly turning the flank of his enemy, buried his own knife to the hilt in his back. Harvey staggered, and tried to recover himself; but quick as lightning the knife was withdrawn and buried in his breast; and he fell bleeding to the ground, exclaiming:

"My God! I'm done for!"

Here the stranger coolly wiped the blood from his knife, and, bending over his wounded foe, said, in that same cold, freezing tone:

"Harvey, you asked my name—I now see proper to give it."

And as the wounded man fixed his eyes upon him, with an expression of mingled pain and curiosity, while the blood, streaming from his wounds, assured the other that his life was fast ebbing away, he added:

"*I am Colonel James Bowie of Arkansas!*"

"Rather say the devil!" groaned Harvey; and with a sudden gleam of baffled malice, he added: "Ef I'd a know'd your name before, I'd been better prepared for the fight. You've kill'd me, and may my curse go with you!" and shutting his teeth hard, and fetching a long, gasping breath, he turned his head aside and soon lay still in death.

Colonel Bowie walked quietly back for his horse,

mounted the animal, and rode away as if nothing remarkable had occurred, leaving the different bodies where they had fallen.

This was his last duel. He was then on his way to join that band of gallant spirits who so desperately fought for the liberties of Texas; and at the Alamo he fell, covered with wounds, and with what the world calls glory.

The Backwoodsman's First Love.

It was during the early settlement of the northern counties of Virginia, a few years anterior to the American Revolution, that a young man—perhaps we should rather say boy, for his age was scarcely turned of sixteen—stood leaning against a large, oil tree, in front of a dwelling of better exterior than was common at that day in that section of country.

It was a clear, cold, but pleasant autumnal night; and the fair moon, riding high in the heavens, poured down her silvery light through the clear, frosty air, casting deep shadows here and there, and giving to the bold scenery around a picturesque variation. The youth was not warmly clad, but he seemed not to feel the cold, as he stood, with folded arms, leaning against the tree, his eye riveted upon a lighted window of the dwelling before him, whence a low sound of voices, occasionally mingled with a merry, ringing laugh, reached his eager ear. Could his face at that moment have been clearly seen, it would have shown a contracted brow, compressed lips, and a somewhat wild and fiery fierceness of the eye, which would seem to bode no good to whatever object had roused his vindictive hate.

The evening wore away, the hour grew late, but still the youth stood in the self-same attitude, having for hours scarcely changed his position, or moved a single muscle of his stern features. At length the outer door of the dwelling opened, and two figures appeared—a youth and a maiden—both dimly perceived by the light behind. For a few moments they stood conversing in low tones; when the clear, musical voice of the maiden was heard to say:

"Good night, Henry, and let it not be long ere I see you again."

"Good night, my dear Rose," was the rejoinder, "and happy dreams to you."

There was another low, "good night," from the one addressed as Rose; and then the speaker retired, the door closed, and the young man walked leisurely away, in an apparently meditative mood.

As he was about to disappear among the surrounding trees, the youth, who had been so long upon the watch, suddenly started from his listless attitude, and, clinching his hands nervously, as if he had some hated object already within his grasp, took two or three hasty strides toward the retreating figure, apparently with the intention of overtaking and calling him to a strict account; but suddenly, as if actuated by another thought, he stopped, turned quickly on his heel, and the next moment reached the door of the dwelling, upon which he rapped with a kind of nervous impatience. His summons was answered by a colored domestic, who, on seeing him, exclaimed:

"Why, Marse Simon, dat you?"

"I want to see Rose Walton," said the young man sternly. The black seemed to hesitate for a moment, and the other added: "Go and tell her so! and be quick about it, if you don't want to get yourself into trouble!"

As the black was turning away to communicate her message, the person inquired for made her appearance. She was a fine, comely lass of seventeen, with fair face and bright eyes, and a general appearance exceedingly captivating.

"Why. Simon," she said, in a tone of surprise, "methinks your visit is rather late!"

"I'm aware," replied the youth, in a tone of bitterness, "that Rose Walton would rather I'd stay away altogether."

"Then why do you come at all?" was the quiet rejoinder.

"That's my business," answered Simon, in a gruff, surly tone.

"Certainly," returned the maiden, rather haughtily, "that is your business, unquestionably; and as it don't concern me, I will leave you to transact it with yourself."

She was about to turn back, and make her words good,

when the youth suddenly, and somewhat fiercely, grasped her by the arm, and rejoined:

"Not so fast, my beauty! I've got a word to say to you!"

"Unhand me, sir!" cried Rose, indignantly—"or I will call for help!"

"You'd better call on your new love," sneered Simon.

"I will call on some one that will chastise your insolence!" she retorted.

"No threats, Rose!" returned the youth; "I'm not just in the mood to bear 'em. I feel, just now, as if the devil was in me; and if anybody was to interfere now between us, I don't know what mought come on't. Rose," he pursued, in a low, hurried, passionate tone, "I know I'm a big, ugly, awkward, uneducated youth; but I've got feeling as well as others—I've got passions as well as others—and (interjecting a wicked oath) I'll tell you what it is, Rose, whoever trifles with 'em had better take care! Rose, you know I love you—love you to madness; you know you encouraged me in it; you know you gin me to expect that some day you'd be my wife; but lately, from some cause, you've treated me coldly—you've hardly spoke to me civil—you haven't met me as you used to do—you've seemed as if my company wasn't pleasant to you."

"I think you must be mistaken, Simon," returned the other, in a softened tone.

"No, I'm not mistaken, Rose!" he vehemently replied; "I *know*—I've seen for myself. I'll tell you what the cause is of this change in you. You've got your fancy fixed upon another that you like better. You always had a liking for Harry Leitchman; and now that you think you've got him safe, you're ready to drop me. But it won't do, Rose—I tell you it won't do. The man that dares to step between me and you has got to answer for't! Yes, Rose, (with another wicked oath,) afore he shall get you away from me, I'll have his heart's blood!"

"Why, Simon, don't speak in such a manner!" said the girl, in considerable alarm—"you terrify me!"

"Can't help it, Rose—you'll find it just as I say. Boy if I am, I've got the strength and passions of a man; and if I find the last is trifled with, the other shall serve me for a revenge that shall ring along the borders when you and me are dead and gone!"

"Why, Simon, what do you mean?" cried Rose Walton, growing more and more terrified at the wild passions of the other; which she, for mere pastime—to gratify a foolish vanity—had carelessly and thoughtlessly fanned into a flame that might now destroy her. "I never heard you talk so strangely before."

"Because I was never so certain I had cause," replied he. "For some time back I've suspicioned that something was wrong; I've kind o' thought that Henry

Leitchman was taking my place in your favor; and only yesterday I overheard him say as much to one of his friends. To-night I met him, and suspicioning that he was coming here, I drew back out of sight and followed him. Rose, for many a long hour I've been standing by that there old sycamore, watching the room where I knew you and Harry was. I could hear you talk, but I couldn't hear what you said; and I could hear you laugh, and that said plain enough that you was happy. I saw you both come to the door, and heard your tender 'good night;' and, Rose, some dreadful wicked thoughts came over me then, and I started after Harry. If I had a followed him, I don't know what mought have came on't—but I thought I'd come back and hear what you had to say first. Now tell me, Rose, and tell me the truth—Do you prefer Leitchman to me?"

"Why, how can you ask such a question, Simon?" answered the girl, evasively, and slightly changing color.

"But I do ask it, Rose, and I want you to answer me!"

"Well, come in, then, a few minutes, and let us talk the matter over."

"No, Rose, I'll not come in to-night—you can answer that question where you are."

"Why, do you want me to flatter you to your face, and tell you that I like you the best?"

"No, I don't want any flattery—I've had enough of that

32*

—I've had too much of that. I just want you to be sincere, for once in your life—you've trifled with me enough, Rose. You either like me best, or you don't— you either prefer me to Harry, or you don't—and I want to know which?"

"And can you for a moment suppose," said the girl, in a soft, insinuating tone, "that I prefer him to you?"

"I judge more by your actions than your words, Rose."

"What! do you accuse me of prevarication?" she replied, with some spirit.

"And if I did, I reckon I'd hit pretty near the truth," he rejoined. "Now answer me, straightforward—are you ready to dismiss Leitchman, and have no more to say to him?"

"Sir!" cried Rose, with a flush of indignation—"I think you forget that you are talking to the daughter of Colonel Walton. I will allow no one to question me as to whom I like or dislike! If my manners are displeasing to you, you certainly have the privilege of remaining away."

"But I can't remain away, Rose—you know that."

"Then take me as you find me, Simon, and be contented. Do not forget that I am something older than you—that I have a spirit which will not be dictated to by any one—and, least of all, by one younger than myself."

For some ten minutes longer, the conversation was continued in much the same strain—the girl, with the cunning and skill of an accomplished coquette—the quick perceptions of one master of the human heart—alternately exciting and tranquilizing the spirit of her rough, impetuous, but ardent admirer; playing upon his feelings as one plays upon the strings of an instrument of music; now with soft blandishments taming down his rough, fiery jealousies to gentle words; now rousing him from a too tender strain to expressions harsh, wild, threatening and fearful.

At length the interview closed, and the youth retired from the unequal combat scarcely wiser than he came. He was not satisfied, but he scarcely knew with what he had to find fault. That the girl was intellectually his superior, he secretly admitted, and the conviction was not a pleasing one; that she was a coquette, he was convinced; that she had been playing upon his feelings, he half believed; that she she was worthy of a true and honest affection, he seriously doubted; but that he loved her—ardently, wildly madly—he was too certain for his own peace of mind.

With a thousand strange fancies crowding upon his brain, not one of which he then felt himself competent to analyze, he hastened his steps down a winding walk, and soon entered a rough, narrow road, which at that day ran through a thinly populated country from one settlement to another. Mechanically he turned to the right, and in a thoughtful, abstracted mood, for some quarter of an hour, pursued his way through a thick, dark wood, barely able to see his course by the light of the moon, which here and there seemed to struggle through the interlacing branches of the gigantic trees that lined his pathway on either side.

At length he entered a hollow, where an opening, made by a broad but shallow stream, let in the light of the moon more clearly; and there, seated upon a stone, he espied a human figure. A single glance assured him that it was his rival, and the sight roused into activity all his jealous and vindictive passions. The same wicked intentions which he had experienced when first setting out to follow Leitchman, after his interview with Rose, now came over the youth with redoubled force, and he felt that the earth was too small to contain them both.

Henry seemed not to hear the approach of Simon, but sat buried in a reverie, evidently induced by the soothing murmurs of the purling stream, and the sentiment awakened by the fascinating witchery of the fair girl with whom he had so recently parted.

For a few moments the youth seemed to hesitate; and then advancing straight to the other, he said, in a surly tone:

"What are you doing here?"

The young man started, looked around, and ascertaining who was his interrogator, replied—

"What is that to you, Simon? You are not my keeper"

"It's a good deal to me, Leitchman, as I'm able to make you understand, keeper or no keeper."

"Why, how now, Simon! You appear to be getting rather insolent for a boy!"

Henry was two years the senior of Simon, and, though not so tall, was more gracefully built, and more comely in person.

"Don't call me boy, Henry Leitchman!" cried Simon, in a furious tone, striding up to the other with clinched hands, his whole sinewy frame fairly trembling with passion. "Don't call me boy ag'in, or, by heavens! I'll strike you as you sit!"

"Nay," said Henry, rising, "if that is your game, you'll find there are two that can play at it."

"Yes, much better than at t'other game," sneered Simon; "for two can't play at that, and me be one of 'em!"

"What do you mean?" demanded Leitchman.

"Well, s'pose you try to guess," replied the youth; "and if you can't guess—if you haven't got wit enough to guess, and it's my opinion you haven't—you'd better go back to Rose Walton, where you've wasted too much of your time already, and ask her."

"Aha!" said the other; "I begin to understand you now. If I am not mistaken, you are getting somewhat jealous."

"Have your stupid brains been able to get all that there into 'em?" returned Simon. "Well, then, let me tell you, I'd be very sorry to get jealous of *you!* but I don't want you to waste any more time in that there quarter. Rose don't like it, and I don't like it, and that settles the matter."

"See here, Simon," said the young man, slowly and deliberately, "you had better go your way, and let me attend to my own business. This looks as if you had followed me to fix a quarrel upon me; but it strikes me you are making a fool of yourself."

"Well, its my opinion," retorted Simon, "you'll find something else strike you harder than that;" and suiting the action to the word, he drew back his arm, and planted a heavy, almost stunning blow, full upon the face of him he now considered his deadly foe.

Leitchman staggered, but quickly recovered himself, and sprung at his antagonist with the fury of a wild beast. The next moment the two combatants were locked in a fierce embrace; and both came heavily to the ground, and rolled over and over in the struggle of life and death. But the iron, muscular strength of Simon soon proved more than a match for that of his older opponent, who found to his dismay that he was rapidly yielding to the grasp which the youth had obtained upon his throat. Determined not to ask quarter from one he had always regarded as his inferior, he made a last, despairing effort, and, drawing a small clasp-knife from his pocket, and forcing open the blade, struck the youth in his side—though, being weak from the contest, he inflicted a light, rather than a dangerous, wound. Simon, roused to fiendish fury by the pain, and what he considered an underhand attempt upon his life, suddenly released his hold upon the throat of his adversary, and, wrenching the knife from his hand, plunged it furiously several times into the breast of the latter, exclaiming, with with an oath:

"Take that! and that! and that!"

"You've kill'd me!" said Henry, in a low, feeble tone.

"Oh, my God! you've killed me!"

Simon started to his feet, and felt a strange, indescribable sensation of awe and terror creep through his iron frame. Had he done a murder?—had he committed that great deed which would make him amenable to the highest penalty of the law? It was a terrible thought—a thought that seemed to freeze his before heated blood, and send it coldly and shiveringly to his very heart. Was he indeed a murderer?—a being to be branded with that awful crime? —a being to be hunted down by his fellows as some wild beast? He was himself a poor and almost friendless boy; but he who lay before him—who had fallen by his hand—

had rich and powerful connections; and he knew enough of the world to be certain that justice, in his case, would not be stayed in her course by any influence which he or his indigent family could bring to bear.

"Harry, are you dead?" he said, in a voice of agony, as he bent over the insensible form of his late rival, whom he would now have given the world to restore to life. "Speak to me, Harry—one word, just one single word—and tell me you're going to live; and I'll give up all—I'll give up Rose, who's more to me than all the rest—and I'll go far away, and never trouble you nor her any more!"

But there was no answer; the wounded man lay still, weltering in his blood; and after looking at him a moment or two longer, as he lay there, pale and ghastly, in the soft, silvery light of the watching moon, Simon turned and fled, muttering as he ran:

"He's dead! he's dead! I've killed him! and now I've got to fly where none can reach me. Good-bye, Rose. If it hadn't been for you, I'd never have done this deed; but now it's done, I've got to fly where I shall never look upon your face again."

With the speed of a murderer running from justice, he flew to his humble cabin in the woods, and, waking his parents, told them, with rapid utterance, and wild tears in his eyes—the last tears he ever shed through tender emotion—

what he had done, and all for his passionate love of the beautiful Rose Walton.

Then seizing his rifle, and such few necessary articles as he could conveniently carry, he took a hurried farewell of his afflicted friends; and alone, in the very bloom of youth, set out for the untrodden wilds of the then far distant West, never to return.

The wounded man recovered, and subsequently married the object of his choice; but for many long years the wandering youth was harrowed with the thought that the brand of the murderer was upon him.

Years still rolled on, and the name of that boy grew famous upon the borders, and became a terror to the red men of the forest, who found in him their most bitter, vindictive, relentless and invincible foe. His career, begun in blood, was traced in blood through a long period of time; and only ceased when the foes of his race had retreated from before the conquering march of their white invaders, or had found their final rest in the happy hunting-grounds of the Great Spirit.

Who that is familiar with the history of the early settlements of the Great West, is now ignorant of the heroic deeds, the daring exploits, and hair-breadth escapes of the great border hero, General Simon Kenton? And yet how few have ever known the cause which first led him to the wilderness, and made him so reckless of an unhappy life? For he was the man of the youth whose first wild passion and its almost tragical consequences we have here recorded

A Wolf in Sheep's Clothing.

A DISCUSSION having sprung up between some gentlemen who had met in a social circle, as to whether it was most proper to consider every man honest till he proved himself to be a rogue, or to consider every one a rogue till he proved himself to be an honest man, one of the party, who had aforetime been a traveling bank agent, said he would narrate an incident of his own experience, which, if it amounted to nothing more, he thought would at least prove pretty conclusively that it is never safe to judge of a stranger by his appearance.

"The Spring of 18—," he began, "found me a traveler through a certain portion of the West, on business connected with the bank of which I was at that time the agent, and for the transaction of which business I carried with me a considerable sum of money. At the town of L****, in the State of Kentucky, where I chanced to remain some three or four days, putting up at one of the principal hotels, I became acquainted with a gentleman who arrived in the place the day after myself, and whom, from his appearance and representations, I believed to be a clergyman from the eastward, traveling partly for his health and partly on a visit to some distant friends.

"We became acquainted somewhat incidentally, and from the very first I was much taken by his appearance. He was some thirty years of age, of a slight, genteel figure, had pale and somewhat ascetic features, was dressed in a plain suit of black, and wore a white neckcloth and gold spectacles.

"In the course of conversation he gave me considerable information concerning himself; and in return I acquainted him with my business, and informed him that I should shortly set out *en route* for the city of N****** in the adjoining State of Tennessee.

"'Why, then, sir,' he said, 'if it be agreeable to you, we will become fellow-travelers, for that is also one of the places I wish to visit myself.'

"'I should be most happy of your company,' I replied; 'but, unfortunately, my business will require me to lay over at some two or three different towns on the way.'

"'It will not make any material difference to me,' he rejoined; 'and merely for the sake of your company, I will suit my time to yours. Traveling as I am for health and pleasure, and not business, I am in no haste—a long stage is always irksome and fatiguing—and I am satisfied I shall enjoy the trip much better by keeping myself with so congenial a companion.'

"This arrangement having finally been agreed upon, the Rev. Mr. Kinney stated that he had a friend somewhere in the vicinity whom he wished to visit; but though this would require his absence for the present, he would return punctually at the time appointed for my departure.

"Shortly after this he left the hotel, and I saw nothing more of him till near the hour agreed upon; but he returned according to promise, and we both set off together—the stage, which conveyed us from the town of L****, being crowded with passengers.

"At the village of S*****, where I made my first halt, Mr. Kinney also made his, and we both, as before, put up at the principal public house. I proceeded to transact the business which called me thither, and he to amuse himself by sauntering through the place, and admiring the rather romantic scenery in the vicinity. Three hours sufficed to arrange all my affairs for a fresh start; but as the stage only passed through the village once in twenty-four hours, I supposed I should have to remain over till the following day.

"In this respect I was agreeably disappointed; for shortly after returning to the hotel, my clerical friend appeared, and inquired what time I should be ready to set forward.

"'I am ready now, for that matter,' I replied, 'but there is no stage till to morrow.'

"'Fortunately, my friend,' he rejoined, 'I have just met with an old acquaintance, who, with a team of his own, is on his way from a village a few miles back of here to the town of P******, where I believe you mentioned it was your intention to make another halt; and if agreeable to you, we can gain one stage by going through with him; so that when the next regular conveyance comes along, you will probably be ready to take it and save at least one day's delay.'

"'The idea,' I replied, 'is a very agreeable one to me— for in these small places, after business is over, time always hangs heavily upon my hands; but I do not wish to be intrusive, and your friend may not care to be encumbered with a stranger.'

"'Oh, I will settle that!' he rejoined; 'in fact I have already done so; for thinking that you, like myself, would like to resume your journey at the earliest practical moment, I have spoken to Mr. Worrell to that effect, and he has expressed himself as being highly pleased at having us for companions.'

"Not to prolong my story with needless detail, I will merely state that the matter was soon arranged to the satisfaction of all parties— my reverend companion seeking his friend, and the latter bringing him back to our hotel in a covered, one-horse vehicle, to which was speedily transferred myself and baggage.

"When we set out from S*****, it wanted about an hour and a half of sunset; and it was calculated that, by good driving, we could reach P**** a little past midnight, which would give me the whole of the morning in advance of the regular stage, and enable me to be ready to take it when it should pass that way.

"For some three or four hours every thing went on very pleasantly—the road being a good one, and leading through a fine but rather sparsely settled country, and Mr. Kinney relieving the tedium of travel by congenial conversation.

"During our intercourse I had become much attached to him. He was a man of no little intellectual capacity, of manners the most pleasing, and apparently possessed a rare refinement of thought and speech. He had studied much, read much, traveled much, and had been at all times a deep and practical thinker—at least such seemed evident from his conversation. There was scarcely a subject that he did not seem familiar with, and he could at all times express his ideas clearly and concisely. Though contending for the highest morality, he was not, so far as I could judge, wanting in that true benevolence which excludes bigotry, and affirms a conviction that there are good men among all classes and denominations. In short, by one means and another, he made himself so agreeable, that I more than once thanked fortune for our acquaintance, and secretly regretted that our arrival in the city of N****** would probably bring about a final separation.

"Night having set in as we journeyed onward—and our route, owing to the deep darkness of the heavy wood through which the road mostly lay, being too uncertain for any thing like speed—and Mr. Worrell also becoming deeply interested in the remarks of his clerical friend, who just at this time had become more than usually entertaining—our horse was allowed to pick his way forward at a gait most pleasing to himself.

"When it was, therefore, that we left the main road, I do not know; but at length my attention was called off from the absorbing narration of the Rev. Mr. Kinney, by discovering, from the motion of our vehicle, that we were actually plunging into deep ruts or gullies, and jolting over stumps or stones, in a manner inconsistent with the idea of being upon a regularly traveled stage-route.

"'Excuse me for interrupting you,' said I to my clerical friend, 'but have we not got off the main road?'

"'Upon my faith, it would seem so!' he replied. 'Eh! friend Worrell—how about this? Surely no stage passes over ground like this?'

"'There must have been a heavy rain here, and gullie

the road,' answered Worrell; 'for my horse has been along here too often to mistake the way.'

"'I think it will all come right presently, Mr. Withers,' said the clergyman, addressing me. 'The road is somewhat rough, it is true; but I believe it is the main road, nevertheless. Let me see! where was I? Oh, yes—I remember!' and forthwith he resumed his story, and went on to its conclusion, occupying some fifteen minutes more, and we all this time jolting, rocking, and pitching as badly as ever.

"'Well, upon my word, friend Worrell,' he said, as soon as he had finished his narration, 'I am seriously inclined to believe you have got out of the main road indeed!'

"'I do not see how that can be,' replied the other; 'for certainly the instinct of my horse would not permit him to turn aside from a route which he must know leads to good quarters.'

"'Still,' said I, 'there is a possibility of our having turned off from the main route; and I think, before we go any further, a careful examination should be made.'

"'So think I,' coincided the Rev. Mr. Kinney.

"'Well, gentlemen,' rejoined Worrell, 'I will wager half-a-dozen bottles of wine that we are right; but to satisfy you, I will agree to make an examination in five minutes, if we do not come to smooth traveling before that time.'

"We rode on, slowly but roughly, our way being very dark and running through a heavy wood; but after a lapse of more than the time specified, finding our road had not improved, I insisted upon a halt and a careful examination of the locality.

"'Certainly,' said Mr. Kinney, 'an examination must be made here, for I think myself there is some mistake. Do not disturb yourself, however, Mr. Withers,' he added, as he left the vehicle with his friend, 'but remain quietly where you are, and we will soon have the matter set right.'

"After leaving the carriage, my two companions walked away together a few paces, as if to make an examination of the surrounding scene, and I heard them conversing together in low, cautious tones.

"And then it was, I scarcely know how nor why, that a strange feeling of distrust and suspicion began to creep over me. Who were these men? Pshaw! one of them was a clergyman—and could I suspect a man of his sacred calling? and the other was his friend. Ha! but did I know him to be a minister of the gospel? Might he not be a wolf in sheep's clothing? I then remembered having heard of noted desperadoes and robbers assuming a clerical appearance for the purpose of carrying out some sinister design; and my suspicions being now fully aroused, I thought rapidly and even painfully, and recalled a hundred little incidents, nothing as it were in themselves, but now seeming to form a chain of evidence that should be duly weighed and considered.

"Who was this Mr. Kinney? I had met him as a stranger in a strange place; he had in a manner pressed himself upon my acquaintance; he had proposed accompanying me, and had done so, notwithstanding such obstacles as would have deterred most travelers from a like proceeding; he had absented himself, perhaps to find a confederate; he had unexpectedly, and somewhat mysteriously, found a friend on the route, and persuaded me to accept of a private conveyance instead of the regular coach; and we had apparently got lost on a plain road, or else turned into some by-path in a manner that seemed to prove some design rather than accident!

"What could all this mean? It might mean much, or it might mean nothing. But I was not a poor traveler; I had a large sum of money in my possession; a large sum of money might be a temptation to men of reputed integrity, to say nothing of its effect upon professional robbers or highwaymen; and under the circumstances, was it not best for me to look out for myself? I thought so. Could there be any harm in my being upon my guard? Certainly not. If they were honest men, I should do them no wrong; if they were dishonest men, I should but do justice to them and myself.

"All these thoughts flashed through my brain, seemingly

in a moment of time; and the first thing I did was to feel for my pistols, a loaded pair of which I always carried concealed about my person. I drew them forth, and examined them with my ram-rod. To my utter amazement and alarm, I found they were capped, *but empty!*

"Then it was that my suspicions became confirmed; and I remembered of once having left them in my room, to which my clerical friend had access. Instantly I felt the hot blood rush to my temples, and beads of cold perspiration seemed to start from every pore.

"Gracious heavens! perhaps I was on the point of being murdered!

"Quickly, but quietly, I reloaded my weapons, and capped them anew. Then stealing softly and silently from the covered vehicle, I found myself in a deep hollow, with a heavy wood on either side of the narrow by-road. My companions were still conversing in low tones at a short distance. Stealthily I crept up to within a few feet of them, just in time to hear the voice of the reverend gentleman say:

"'Yes, Charley, I tell you it can be done in that way. We will announce that we have made a mistake; and then, in our apparent endeavor to turn the carriage, we will manage to cramp and upset it. Then, as you pretend to assist Withers to get out, you can seize him in such a manner as to pitch him forward upon the ground, so that we can both spring upon him at the same time, drag him into the bushes, and put an end to him where his blood will not show upon the path.'

"I heard this, and, without waiting for a reply, stole round to the back of the carriage, to await the result. I could have escaped, but a large portion of my money was contained in my traveling trunk, and I was resolved that that should not fall into the hands of the villains, even if they escaped themselves.

"I had scarcely got myself into the position intended, when Mr. Worrell came up to the carriage; and addressing me, whom he supposed to be still inside, he said, with a laugh, that he believed he had lost the wine, for by some means or other we had got upon a by-road, but himself and friend would soon turn the carriage about and regain the main route. He then advised me to keep perfectly quiet, that he would manage the matter in a moment or two, and so forth and so on: to which I replied—speaking through the back portion of the vehicle, so that my voice sounded within—that, having an easy seat, I was not disposed to leave it unless he required more help.

"The two then commenced turning the vehicle, and so managed matters as to upset it as they intended. I still carried out my part and uttered a groan as if from within.

"'Good Lord, sir, are you much hurt?' exclaimed Worrell, in a sympathetic and anxious tone.

"I groaned again.

"'Ah! sir, what a blundering accident!—let me assist you!'

"And as he began to feel carefully forward for that purpose, I slipped quietly round to the side where he stood, and, seizing him from behind, fiercely hurled him to the ground, where his head, fortunately for me, struck against rock and deprived him of consciousness.

"'Villain!' cried I, cocking my pistols and turning upon Kinney, whom in the faint light I discovered in the act of springing forward, 'you are caught in your own vile snare, and shall not escape. Take that, thou doubly-damned monster, and return to thy master!'

"I pulled one trigger as I spoke, but the cap only exploded and the pistol remained undischarged. The next moment, along with a bitter curse, there came a flash, a report, and a seeming blow upon my forehead; and by a strange feeling of dizziness which immediately followed, I comprehended that I was shot myself, and believed that my hour had come. Staggering backward, I fell to the ground; but did not lose my consciousness, nor my presence of mind; and as the ruffian sprung forward to finish his work, I raised my other pistol, just as he was in the act of bending over me, and providentially sent its contents so directly through his heart that he fell back dead, almost without a groan.

"Gentlemen, I need not prolong my story. I was wounded by Kinney's shot, but not seriously—the ball having glanced from the frontal bone without fracturing it, —producing dizziness and confusion without depriving me at any moment of consciousness. I therefore was enabled to get up in time to bind Worrell before he recovered from the effects of his fall; and righting the vehicle, and placing him and his dead companion within it, I led the horse back to the main road, and drove on to the nearest village, some two or three miles distant, where I roused the inn-keeper and several of the inhabitants, told my story, and placed both the living and the dead in the hands of the proper authorities.

"Subsequently I appeared at the trial of Worrell, and had the satisfaction of seeing him convicted and sentenced to a long period of imprisonment. During that trial it came out that both he and Kinney were well known robbers, belonging to an organized band of desperadoes; and that even before the appearance of the pseudo clergyman at L****, there had been concocted a design to waylay and murder me for my money. Unsuspecting myself, I had fallen into their easiest trap, and by a kind Providence had barely been saved from a fearful doom.

"But I assure you, gentlemen, the lesson was one which I have never forgotten, and shall ever remember; and I think no one can blame me for henceforth insisting upon every man proving himself worthy of confidence before I put faith in him."

On the Scout.

Horse-stealing, during the early settling of the **Great West**, was one of the means, if not of border warfare, at least of border annoyance, to both the whites and Indians. The Indians stole from the whites whenever they could, and in retaliation the whites frequently formed themselves into small parties and penetrated through the dense forests to the Indian towns for a like purpose. Sometimes these predatory parties were successful, and got off with their booty without molestation; but it frequently happened that they were pursued by the party wronged; and when overtaken, a fierce and bloody conflict was generally the result.

About the year 1791, or 1792, the settlers along the Ohio river being sufferers in a great degree from the incursions of their forest neighbors, a small, intrepid band of hunters, or scouts, resolved to act upon the aggressive; and as their numbers were too few for venturing an attack upon the savages at their towns, they decided upon the next best thing—the stealing and running off of as many horses as they could manage.

This party was composed of the best men that could be got together for such a daring, lawless purpose, but numbered only seven all told. And yet these seven were all experienced hunters, trained from their very youth to a perfect familiarity with all the mysteries and perils of the forest—from the finding of their way to a given quarter, for a hundred miles, by signs only known to the practiced woodsman, to the rousing and killing of all the wild animals, and even more savage men—and regarded themselves as a company sufficiently strong for the purpose they had in view.

In fine spirits, therefore, they set out on their latest-planned expedition; and crossing the Ohio from the Virginia shore, they proceeded, with strong determination and due caution, to push their way through the almost unexplored forest, which stretched away for many a goodly league from the right bank of the river named.

Always keeping a subdued fire, if any, in their camp at night, and at least two of their number watching by turns, they penetrated far into the Indian country without meeting with any mishap, and at last found themselves in the vicinity of an Indian town, somewhere near the dividing ridge between the head-waters of the Muskingum and Sandusky rivers.

The Indians, being so far inland from the settlements of the whites, were not of course expecting such visitors, and were in consequence entirely off their guard; and t... ...ight following their arrival in the vicinity, our little band of adventurers stole cautiously around the outskirts of the town, and, getting in among the horses, succeeded in securing fourteen of the best, each man bridling and mounting one and leading another. These they managed to get away with little or no noise, and without attracting the notice of their enemies; and when they found themselves a couple of miles from the village, with neither sign of pursuit nor of their proximity having been discovered, it required all the caution and prudence which they had acquired in their long years of stern experience, to prevent them from congratulating themselves on their success by a series of hilarious shouts and yells. They did not ride fast through the night, for their present safety would not admit of it, however much a goodly distance from their enemies might have increased their security; but they kept their horses steadily in motion, in a southern direction, and anxiously watched for the coming dawn. Just before the break of day they halted, and hastily prepared their morning's meal; and then, with the return of light, they remounted and dashed away, believing that the Indians would now discover their loss, and probably set off in hot pursuit.

All through that anxious day they urged their animals through the thick, dark wood, at the utmost speed that could be accomplished, and only halted for their camp at night when they found, from the jaded condition of their horses, it would not be judicious to take them further without food and rest. Selecting a pleasant little dingle, through which flowed a tiny stream of pure water, and where luxuricus grass and wild flowers proclaimed the fertility of the soil, they hoppled their horses and picketed them; and then, starting a fire, they cooked their own supper, and ate it with the relish of hardy and hungry men

Knowing that a goodly stretch of country now lay between them and the village where they had committed their depredations, our borderers had little fear of molestation; but they were not disposed to neglect all proper precautions, and two of their number remained on guard through the night, which passed off without disturbance.

At an early hour the next morning, they again set forward, in fine spirits, and rode hard all day, reaching about nightfall an excellent camping-ground on the right of Will's Creek, in the present county of Guernsey, Ohio, and near the site of the present town of Cambridge. Here one of the most active of the party, one William Linn, complained of violent pains and cramps in his stomach, and declared himself unable to ride another mile. A halt for the night was accordingly decided on; but for some cause, which not a man of the company could rationally explain, all regarded this camp as more dangerous than the one of the night preceding; and the extra precautions were taken of placing three sentinels at different intervals on the back trail, to keep a sharp look-out for pursuers; while the other three, who were well, were to prepare their evening meal and minister to the sick man as best lay in their power.

Such simple remedies as they chanced to have with them were given to Mr. Linn, but without producing any favorable result; in fact, he gradually grew worse instead of better; and his pains at times became so excrutiating as to compel him to screech out in tones that could be heard afar through the dreary solitude of the gloomy forest. Rough, hardened, and unrefined; as were the companions of the sick man, they were men of heart, and not devoid of sympathy for a suffering fellow-being, and they did what they could to aid, cheer, and console him, cautioning him at the same time to suppress if possible his cries of agony, lest the sounds should reach pursuing or out-lying foes and bring destruction upon all.

The three at the camp having refreshed themselves by a frugal but hearty meal, they immediately relieved the three sentinels, who proceeded to do the same; after which, towards midnight, the whole party collected together, and held a consultation upon the supposed danger. As they had seen no Indians since quitting their village, some forty-eight hours previously, and no signs of any during their present watch, and as it was now waxing late into the night, and no trail could be easily followed after dark, it was thought that no apprehension of an attack need be felt; and that with one man to stand guard and wait upon the suffering Mr. Linn, the rest might camp down in safety and get a few hours of needful rest. The party to act as sentinel was decided by lot, and fell upon one William McCollough—a cool, brave, intrepid Indian hunter, who subsequently rose to the command of a company in the war of 1812, and fell at the battle of Brownstown in Hull's campaign.

The immediate camp of our adventurers was on a small branch of Will's creek; and around the cheerful fire there kindled, five weary men lay down to snatch a few hours of repose, and were soon fast asleep—Linn and McCollough only remaining awake—the former wrapped in his blanket and stretched on the ground between the fire and water, rolling and groaning with pain—and the latter stationed on the edge of a thicket, just beyond the reach of the fire-light, where he could best see about him, and be ready to give instant alarm at the first approach of danger.

In this position of affairs some three or four hours passed away; the only sounds that broke the solemn stillness being the slight movement of some of the horses picketed near, the dismal hooting of an owl, the distant howling of a wolf, and the occasional groaning of the sufferer, with perhaps the exchange of a few words between him and the sentinel—the fire, meantime, burning gradually down, and, in its dying flickers, throwing strange, fantastic shadows over the quiet scene.

At length, Mr. Linn, with a louder groan than usual, and a sharp cry of pain, raised himself upon his elbow, and exclaimed:

"Oh, my God! my God! I can't stand this no longer—every breath I draw is killing me. Here, Bill—quick! let me try one thing more—some hot salt and water—and if that thar don't help me, may Heaven have mercy on my poor, sinful soul! Take my cup here," he added, somewhat gaspingly, as McCollough stepped hastily forward, "and heat me some water, with a handful of salt in't, and let me try that. Quick! quick! for God's sake! for I'm in the agonies of death!"

McCollough seized the cup alluded to, and running to the water, only a few feet distant, filled it, and hastened back to the dying fire; but as he stooped down and raked some coals together, for the purpose of heating it, he suddenly discovered, with a feeling of considerable uneasiness, if not alarm, that the water in the vessel was unusually muddy.

"Excuse me, Linn!" he said, starting hastily to his feet, and glancing quickly and suspiciously around him; "but I'm afeard all the rest o' us is in danger as well as you."

"Ha! what's the matter?" asked Linn

"So'thing's muddied this water, by gitting into it; and that so'thing, I'm afeard, is Injuns!"

"Better call up the boys, and git their opinions, and, if thar's danger, have 'em ready for it!" returned Linn, with a groan of blended fear and pain.

Linn had not ceased speaking, ere McCollough was actively carrying out his suggestion; and the five heavy sleepers were suddenly roused, each with a vigorous shake and the single word "*danger*," which was communicated in a low but ominous tone to the sense of hearing. As one after another they started up, with expressions of alarm, and instinctively grasped their weapons, McCollough exclaimed, with a warning gesture:

"Hist! boys—keep quiet—don't make a noise! It's eyther nothing, or thar's trouble about; but don't let's draw it on to us by child's play."

He then went on to state what he had discovered, and what were his suspicions; and as soon as he had finished, the opinion of his comrades was quickly and unanimously given, that the "sign" justified a belief in danger, and that he had done right in waking and putting them on their guard, and that prudence demanded a careful search, which they forthwith proceeded to make.

Separating themselves, and quickly gliding away beyond the fire-light, they stealthily approached the bank of the little stream, and passed up and down it for several rods, listening to the faintest sound, and peering cautiously into the darkness; but, unfortunately for them, as the sequel will show, neither hearing nor perceiving aught to justify a belief in the proximity of savage foes. When they had all again collected together, one of the party said, addressing McCollough:

"Bill, you're ginerally purty sure on Injun sign, but I'll lay one of my captur'd hosses agin yourn, that you've made a mistake this time."

"Bill did right in waking us, though," said another, "for there mought have been Injuns about, and we lost all our top-knots."

"And thar may be yit, for what you know, Tom," rejoined McCollough; "for so'thing above has riled the water, and it's jest as like to be Injuns as any thing else; and the fact that we hain't found 'em, don't prove they arn't thar even now; eh! Joe Hedges, what say you?"

"Well, it's my opine, Bill, that the water's eyther been riled from raccoons, ducks, or some other animal, and that we mought as well turn down agin and sleep till daylight. I'll guarantee the camp for a quart of whiskey."

This reply was greeted by a laugh from all save McCollough and Linn; and after a few words with the latter, expressive of a kind of rude sympathy for his sufferings, the five men, who had been so suddenly roused by the guard, again stretched themselves around the fire—McCollough, meantime, proceeding to heat the salt and water and administer it to the sufferer—who, immediately after drinking it, said he felt a little easier, and thought he should be able to get some rest at last.

An hour later, as McCullough stood at his former post, somewhat abstractedly gazing at the few red embers, which were all that now remained of the smouldering fire, a slight, a very slight noise, on the bank of the little stream, attracted his attention. He looked up suddenly and with a start; but before he had time for action, there flashed upon his astonished vision a line of fire, followed instantly by a dozen sharp reports, by groans and cries of pain from his companions, and by loud, fierce whoops and yells from a large body of savages, who had silently stolen down the bed of the stream and now came bounding forward to the destruction of their enemies.

McCollough was himself untouched by the fire of the Indians; but he saw that some of his companions, including poor Linn, were badly wounded; and knowing that his own life would solely depend upon his successful flight into and through the forest, he instantly turned and bounded away with all his might, several of the savages perceiving and bounding after him with wild and fearful yells.

Now it so happened that the party who gave chase to

McCollough had not yet discharged their pieces; and finding he was likely to escape them in the darkness, they suddenly drew up in a line and poured a close volley after him. But at the very instant they fired, his foot struck the bog of a quagmire, and he pitched headlong upon the soft morass; whereupon his enemies, seeing him suddenly disappear, and believing him dead or mortally wounded, gave a few whoops of triumph, and turned off in pursuit of the others, three of whom were also making good their flight.

As soon as his enemies were out of hearing, McCollough cautiously worked his way out of the treacherous morass, and then set off, afoot and alone, to make his way through the dreary wilderness to the nearest station, thankful that even his life was spared. In his first flight he had thrown away his gun, and had now only his hunting-knife; and being without provisions and the means of procuring any, he foresaw much suffering for himself, even if he escaped with life. But suffering through privation was seldom a matter to be treated seriously by the bold borderer; and McCullough, even when compelled to hunt for roots and berries, to keep himself from perishing by starvation, did so with a light heart, thinking only how happy he was at his wonderful escape from his savage foes.

The next day, to his great surprise, for he believed all

the others killed, he fell in with John Hough, one of his companions, and the two continued their journey together, and reached Wheeling in safety, where they reported their misfortunes and the loss of their companions. But even yet they were destined to an agreeable surprise: for the day following their own arrival, two more of their comrades, Kinzie Dickerson and John Whetzel, made their appearance, naked and nearly famished. These two had also met on their retreat, and had struggled through the fearful journey together.

The unexpected meeting of these four, for a time led them to hope that, in some almost miraculous manner, some of the others might have escaped also—but they hoped in vain. William Linn, Thomas Biggs, and Joseph Hedges, were all killed in and near the fatal camp; and here their horribly mutilated bodies were found and decently buried, by a party from Wheeling who went out in search of them.

The four who escaped lived many years to tell the tale we have recorded, and take an active part in other wild border scenes and tragedies; but all are now dead—all went long since through the Dark Valley to the so-called Land of Shadows.

THE END.

www.ingramcontent.com/pod-product-compliance
Lightning Source LLC
Chambersburg PA
CBHW022110290426
44112CB00008B/625